# TIMELESS

### ETERNAL TRUTHS FOR
### EVERYDAY LIFE

## PHILIPP A. BALLMAIER

# TABLE OF CONTENTS

# PREFACE

Before the dawning of time, God has purposed to save a people who are innumerable. Not out of any merit of their own, but out of the goodness of His free and sovereign love. It was for His good pleasure that He created us.* God is the Creator of all things* and He has put eternity into the hearts of men.* God has not left us to our own devices, but He has made Himself known to us.

My purpose is not to make myself known, but rather to make God known. Man will go to great heights to make himself known, but my God will not share His glory with another. He is the Great Sovereign Lord, Who has spoken in times past through many, mighty acts, but now has revealed Himself in His Son Jesus Christ.*

I am just a voice crying out in the wilderness*—a mere mortal who serves a great God. Let my tongue be the pen of a ready writer* who proclaims to you the goodness of God.

To Those of the Household of Faith,*
- Just a Voice


*Philippians 2:13, Colossians 1:6, Ecclesiastes 3:11, John 1:18, John 1:23, Psalm 45:1, Galatians 6:10

# INTRODUCTION

All of humanity exists on a moving clock. You and I were created in time. We dwell in time. And one day, our time will come to an end. Time is an inescapable reality. The only way a being could exist outside of time is if they were not bound by it.

Our God is not bound by time. He transcends it. He is the efficient first cause of everything. This timeless God has revealed His eternal truths to us. The same truth that was evident to Adam is the same truth which holds true today. Since God exists outside of time, He is the only One Who has the answer to life's everyday problems.

Will you trust in the changing philosophies of time or will you hold fast to the God Who is timeless?

# JANUARY
## WHO IS GOD?

Have you ever paused to think about the character and nature of God? I know I should. Christians ought to cultivate a daily practice of reflecting on His attributes. An artisan does. His eyes capture God's glorious attributes revealed in nature. On the other hand, an intellect won't even let his eyes look at the pages of the Bible until he discovers God. Eventually, only the very wise will open God's Word in order to gain a deeper understanding of who God is.

As you read through these first 31 devotionals, please reflect not only on the character of Yahweh, but also on the practical implications His truths have for your every day. Ultimately, our knowledge of God should not only be an ordinary, academic study, but rather a life-changing experience.

I pray you will be truly enriched to know who God is.

# YAHWEH
## THE SELF-EXISTENT GOD

"I AM who I AM."
Exodus 3:14

### WHO IS GOD?

Every person has asked this question. It was a question Moses wrestled with when he asked for God's name. Yet the Divine response to him was: "I AM Who I AM."

This same self-existent God Who made promises to Abraham, Isaac, and Jacob is the same God Who saw His people afflicted in Egypt. But our great Jehovah brought titanic deliverance to them. The children of Israel would always remember His name, because Jehovah, their God, miraculously delivered them from the hands of the Egyptians.

God has always been unmoved in the heavens, and He remains faithful to His people. He remains faithful to you. In all of life's uncertainties, rest in Yahweh's covenant promises that He has purposefully and specifically for you.

*Father, You have been a shelter to us in every generation.* [1] *Help us to hold fast to Your covenant faithfulness when we are tempted to take our eyes off of You.*

*I pray these things in Jesus' name. Amen.*

# EL OLAM
## OUR ETERNAL GOD

Have you not known? Have you not heard? The Lord is the everlasting
God, the Creator of the ends of the earth. He does not faint
or grow weary; His understanding is unsearchable.
Isaiah 40:28

## WHO CAN FATHOM ETERNITY?

All of us are born in time and we are subject to it. We live and move
under a clock that is winding down. Not so with God. He is not bound
by time nor is He dependent on it.

The Israelites had forsaken the worship of their everlasting Creator in
exchange for the worship of idols. In doing so, they had abandoned
God's everlasting and inexhaustible source of strength—on their behalf!

Here we read Isaiah pleading—begging for God's people to turn back
to worship the One True everlasting God Who has set the clock of
human history in motion. It is in His strength that God's people will
find the deliverance that they need.

Who is renewing your strength? Wisdom teaches us not to look to
any other source for salvation, but only to look to our great
Jehovah. He is our everlasting God, our El Olam! Turn to God.
Allow Him to be your strength.

*Father, so often I place my confidence in my own strength, but You alone
are my everlasting God. Help me to place all confidence and trust in Your
heav-enly provision for me.*

*I pray these things in Jesus' name. Amen.*

# EL ELYON

## OUR SOVEREIGN GOD

I cry out to God Most High, to God who
fulfills His purpose for me.
Psalm 57:2

### DO YOU REMAIN AT REST IN GOD'S HANDS?

During one of the most difficult times in his life, David wrote Psalm 57. He was fleeing from the hands of Saul and frequently hiding in diverse places. Yet he does not waver in unbelief, * but places his trust in the Most High God.

The same God, Who purposed that David would be king, will not allow His plans to be frustrated. He is sovereign over all, and He does what He pleases. * Even though Saul sought to thwart the Lord's plans, David rested assured in God's eternal purposes.

Dear friend, do you find yourself in the midst of various trials? If so, then do not fret, but rather place your trust in the Lord. He is our El Elyon who is not caught off-guard by our trials.

＊━━━━━◆━━━━━＊

*Father, I thank You that there are no unpleasant surprises that move You. Help me to rest in Your sovereignty when life seems to be getting out of control.*

*I pray these things in Jesus' name. Amen.*

*Romans 4:20, Daniel 4:35

# EL SHADDAI
## OUR ALL POWERFUL GOD

When Abram was ninety-nine years old the Lord appeared
to Abram and said to him, "I am God Almighty,
walk before me, and be blameless."

Genesis 17:1

## WHO KEEPS HIS PROMISES AND CALLS ALL THINGS INTO EXISTENCE? *

Is it not our all-powerful God? Surely there is nothing that is too hard for Him. *

It was no small thing for Abram to expect a child when he was ninety-nine years old. But this is exactly what God had promised. The promised seed would not come through Ishmael, but through Isaac. God would work the miraculous through Issac.

Christian, do you find yourself in a seemingly impossible predicament? If so, then take comfort. Know that your El Shaddai has ordained all your circumstances according to His perfect counsel. * He, Who has led you here, will show Himself mighty through your sufferings.

In light of this truth, place all of your burdens into His loving hands.

———————————◆———————————

*Father, I thank You and praise You for Your marvelous works. There is surely nothing that is too hard for you. When I am tempted to doubt, give me eyes of faith like Abraham, who contrary to hope, in hope believed. **

*I pray these things in Jesus' name. Amen.*

*Romans 4:17, Jeremiah 32:27, Ephesians 1:11, Romans 4:18

# ELOHIM

## GOD, OUR CREATOR

Then God said, "Let us make man in our image after our likeness. And let them have dominion over the fish of the sea and over the birds of the heavens and over the livestock and over all the earth and over every creeping thing that creeps on the earth."

Genesis 1:26

### WHO IS THE CREATOR OF ALL THINGS?

The Scriptures ascribe creation to God alone. Thus, it is through the Godhead that we are endowed with reason and understanding.

This same God Who created us also sustains us. He has ordained man to rule over the lesser things, but God provides our daily necessities. All of our sustenance is given to us through His loving providence; therefore, it is wise to acknowledge my proper place before Him. He is the Creator, and I am His creature.

Have we come to grips with that truth? Dearly beloved, let us ascribe all honor and glory to Him Who made all things.

———————◆———————

*Father, I thank You for the many blessings You have bestowed upon me. There are so many things in life that I take for granted. Help me to be thankful to You, my Creator, for all of life's blessings.*

*I pray these things in Jesus' name. Amen.*

13

# QANNA

## OUR JEALOUS GOD

For you shall worship no other god, for the Lord, whose
name is Jealous, is a jealous God.
Exodus 34:14

### IS JEALOUSY A BAD THING?

Society has certainly painted the concept of jealousy in a negative light, but the Scriptures teach that not all jealousy is sin. The word for "jealous" in Hebrew is the word *Qanna*. It also appears in Exodus 20:5, as the Second Commandment: You shall not bow down to them or serve them, for I the Lord your God am a jealous God.

In both passages, "jealous" is linked with the idea of worship.

The children of Israel were not to make any carved or molten images of God. They were commanded to set their affections on Him alone. God, in His goodness, has established a covenant with His people. He is zealous for us that our affections should wholly be devoted to Him.

When we give our affections to idols, we are not faithful to God. In light of this truth, we must be a people who engage our hearts fully in our devotion to God alone.

---

*Father, You have made an eternal covenant with Your people. You will share Your glory with no one. Help us to be a people who abstain from idols so that we can remain wholly devoted to You.*

*I pray these things in Jesus' name. Amen.*

# ADONAI
## THE LORD OUR GOD

Abraham answered and said, "Behold, I have undertaken to speak to
the Lord, I who am but dust and ashes."
Genesis 18:27

## WHAT IS GOD'S TITLE?

When interceding for the people of Sodom and Gomorrah consider how
Abraham addresses God.

He first acknowledges Yahweh's authority over him. The father of faith
addresses God as "Adonai" which means "Lord." Then Abraham acknowledges his place before God: I am but dust and ashes.* In doing so, the
intercessor acknowledges God's preeminence over him.

Let wisdom teach us that while God is our loving Father, He still has
claim over every area of our lives. We can approach Him boldly, but it
must be in reverence. Let us therefore imitate Abraham's reverence when
approaching the Lord in prayer.

God is Lord over all creation.

———————◆———————

*Father, I thank You that Your Son has procured direct access for me to approach
You. Help me to enjoy the privilege of prayer with boldness in reverence.*

*I pray these things in Jesus' name. Amen.*

*Genesis 27:18

15

# JEHOVAH-NISSI
## GOD, OUR BANNER

And Moses built an altar and called its name,
The-Lord-Is-My-Banner.
Exodus 17:15

### IN WHOSE NAME DO I TRUST?

Certainly, Moses understood that God was the banner over His people. When the Amalekites came to attack their camp, Jehovah instructed Moses to hold up his rod. When Moses held up his rod, the Israelites prevailed.

When looking to the Lord, Israel became victorious over their enemies.

Let wisdom teach us not to raise our battle ax unless it is in the strength of our Banner. The forces of darkness relentlessly attack the church, but we conquer in the name of our Lord Jesus Christ. In light of this truth let us rest in our great Jehovah-Nissi, Who has already made us victorious over Satan. The Lord is my Banner.

---

*Father, though the forces of darkness attack us, they shall not prevail. I thank you that I have a victory that overcomes the world which is my faith.\* Help me to take up no other banner, but the name of our Lord Jesus Christ.*

*I pray these things in Jesus' name. Amen.*

\*1 John 5:4

# JEHOVAH-RAAH

## GOD, OUR SHEPHERD

"The Lord is my shepherd; I shall not want."
Psalm 23:1

### WHAT TYPE OF SHEPHERD DOES THE CHURCH POSSESS?

We serve a Shepherd Who laid down His life for the sheep.* He satisfies us with the good things that are from above.* The sweet psalmist of Israel experienced this type of goodness firsthand.

It was through all seasons, but especially difficult ones, where David, the shepherd, experienced the faithfulness of God. In times of despair He found rest and encouragement through the Lord. His steadfast hope and trust in Yahweh kept him rooted in all types of storms.

Dear friend, do you find yourself in a season of weariness? If so, then take heart. Though you drink from the bitter cup of affliction our great Jehovah-Raah has made with you an everlasting covenant ordered in all things and secure.* In light of this truth, do not doubt His goodness, but rather keep your eyes fixed on Him.

————◦————

*Father, it is so hard to see the big picture in our trials. The billows of life crash up against us in a relentless fury. Give us eyes of faith to see Your goodness in every circumstance.*

*I pray these things in Jesus' name. Amen.*

*John 10:15, Psalm 103:5, 2 Samuel 23:5

# JEHOVAH-RAPHA
## GOD OUR HEALER

For I am the Lord who heals you.

Exodus 15:26

## WHO IS IT WHO HEALS US FROM OUR INFIRMITIES?

The Israelites were brought miraculously through the Red Sea, and now they had come to Marah. It was a three-day journey through the wilderness of Shur, and the people had grown thirsty. Finally, they found water, but to their dismay it was unsuitable to drink. In faith Moses looked to the Lord, and the bitter waters of Marah were healed.

In the same manner, God has healed His people from their sins. He has supplied us with innumerous blessings from above. Yet often times we are a people who suffer great pain and sadness. Dear friend, if you find yourself in a place of deep despair, then look to the Lord Who has healed you from the power and curse of sin. If He can restore us back into fellowship with Himself, then He can certainly bind up our wounds. Who can heal you?

Is it not our great Healer Who is called Jehovah-Rapha?

———————◇———————

*Father, You have delivered me from the power of sin. You have taken Your Law, and have written it on my heart.\* There are times when I am subject to great pain and sadness. In these dire seasons, please help me to look to You as my Healer.*

*I pray these things in Jesus' name. Amen.*

\*Jeremiah 31:33

18

# JEHOVAH-SHAMMAH

## OUR EVER PRESENT GOD

All the way around shall be eighteen thousand cubits; and the name of
the city from that day shall be: 'THE LORD IS THERE.'

Ezekiel 48:35

### IS THE PRESENCE OF GOD CONFINED TO ONE PLACE?

It must have been a strange vision for Ezekiel to see the glory of the Lord
departing from the Temple. The Israelites were familiar to the glory
of God dwelling in a physical temple. Yet, how can the heaven of
heavens contain Him?*

In this final vision, the prophet Ezekiel sees a temple and city called
Jehovah-Shammah. This name signified that wherever the people of God
worshiped Him, He would be in their midst. The physical has given way
to the spiritual reality. We no longer need to go to the physical Jerusalem
to worship, because God is present wherever His people are.

The Apostle Peter calls us living stones* which are being built up a spiritual house.* Thus, God's people are not afar off from Him, but rather
enjoy His communion daily.

In light of this truth, let us take joy in the fact that the Lord's presence is
with us in all seasons of life.

_Father, what a joy it is to have fellowship with You. Your glory is not
confined to one central location, but rather You are our great Jehovah-
Shammah. Help me to experience the joy of Your presence on a daily basis._

_I pray these things in Jesus' name. Amen._

*1 Kings 8:27, 2 Chronicles 6:18, 1 Peter 2:5

# JEHOVAH-TSIDKENU
## GOD, OUR RIGHTEOUSNESS

In His days Judah will be saved, and Israel will dwell safely;
Now this is His name by which He will be called:
THE LORD OUR RIGHTEOUSNESS.
Jeremiah 23:6

## WHAT DOES GOD REQUIRE OF HIS PEOPLE?

God's holiness demands that we be righteous in His sight.

The shepherds of Jeremiah's day were not adequately caring for God's people. They were proclaiming "Peace, peace," when there was no peace. The reality was that Judah was not right with God. Therefore, He promised them a true Shepherd Who would fulfill His righteous requirements and be for them what they could not be for themselves.

Our great Jehovah-Tsidkenu has fulfilled the righteous requirements of the Law on behalf of His people. We, who are united to Christ by faith, are now dressed in new garments of purity. Let us therefore not look to our own righteousness, but rather place all our hope in our great Jehovah-Tsidkenu.

---

*Father, I thank You that You no longer see me in filthy garments of sin, but that I am now adorned in rich robes of righteousness. Grant me the grace to rest safely in the righteousness that I now have in Christ.*

*I pray these things in Jesus' name. Amen.*

# JEHOVAH-MEKODDISHKEM
## GOD, OUR SANCTIFIER

And you shall keep My statutes, and perform them:
"I am the Lord who sanctifies you."
Leviticus 20:8

## WHAT DOES IT MEAN TO BE SET APART FOR THE LORD?

In the Old Testament Law, the Israelites were to keep themselves purified from various forms of defilement. They were to observe the Sabbaths and keep God's commandments. Yet after the command is given in our text above, a declaration is made. "I am the Lord who sanctifies you."

The Hebrew name noted here is *Jehovah-Mekoddishkem*. God sanctifies. It was God Who set them apart and established His covenant with them. This was not due to any merit in themselves, but due to God's unconditional love for them.

Our great Jehovah-Mekoddishkem has set us apart for His name's sake. He has chosen us and made us a royal priesthood.* In light of this truth, let us, who have been set apart, walk worthy of our calling before God and observe and keep all of His commandments.

---

*Father, You have called us, You have chosen us, and You have set us apart. We are a holy people who are set apart for Your purposes. Let our conduct be worthy of the Gospel.\**

*I pray these things in Jesus' name. Amen.*

*1 Peter 2:9, Philippians 1:27

# JEHOVAH-SHALOM
## GOD, OUR PEACE

So Gideon built an altar there to the Lord,
and called it "The-Lord-Is-Peace."
Judges 6:24

## WHAT CONSTITUTES TRUE PEACE?

The Israelites were under heavy oppression from the Midianites. Because God's people would not obey His commands, He had delivered His people into the hands of their enemies. Yet in the midst of their suffering, God appointed a deliverer for them.

Gideon was an unlikely hero, but a man whom God would use nonetheless. Instead of God's righteous anger, Gideon found favor with Jehovah. And because of God's favor, the Israelites would soon experience freedom from their oppression, and their peace with God would be restored.

Is this not the same promise which the Lord has made to us? We, who were once His enemies, are now friends of the Most High God. In Christ, we have found favor with God and have been reconciled back into a relationship with Him. Today, we have peace with God. In light of this truth, let us rejoice in the fact that Jesus is our Jehovah-Shalom.

———◆———◆———◆———

*Father, I thank You that I am no longer Your enemy. I am invited to draw near to You through the redemption that is in Christ Jesus.\* Help me to meditate on the fact that Jesus is my Peace.*

*I pray these things in Jesus' name. Amen.*

\*Romans 3:24

# JEHOVAH-JIREH

## GOD, OUR PROVIDER

And Abraham called the name of the place, "The-Lord-Will-Provide";
as it is said to this day, "In the Mount of the Lord it shall be provided."
Genesis 22:14

## WHAT DOES FAITH LOOK LIKE IN ACTION?

Certainly we can look to Abraham who offered up his son Isaac to the Lord. When Isaac asked where they would get the sacrifice, Abraham's response to his son was: My son, God will provide Himself the lamb for a burnt offering.* Thus it was that the great Jehovah-Jireh provided for them a ram caught in the thicket by its horns. *

We understand that God had put Abraham through a test of faith, but this man of God had a deep-seated understanding of the Lord's faithfulness. He never wavered at the promises of God through unbelief, * but contrary to hope in hope believed. *

Dear tired soul, do you doubt the faithfulness of God? If so, then do not fear! The same God Who has made the ultimate provision for your soul will be your Jehovah-Jireh throughout all the seasons of your life. God will provide!

*Father, thank You for providing to us a sacrifice for our souls. Grant us the grace to trust You daily for the provisions that we need.*

*I pray these things in Jesus' name. Amen.*

*Genesis 22:8, Genesis 22:13, Romans 4:18

# JEHOVAH-SABAOTH
## GOD, OUR CONQUEROR

"And I will shake all nations, and they shall come to the Desire of All Nations, and I will fill this temple with glory," says the Lord of hosts.
Haggai 2:7

## WHO GIVES VICTORY TO THE PEOPLE OF GOD?

In Haggai's day, the people were given the task of rebuilding the Temple. We read, though, that they became discouraged along the way. In light of this fact, God appointed Haggai to both encourage and exhort the people to finish the building of the Temple. The prophet reminds them that the Lord is with them, and that He will fill this new temple with His glory.

Our great Jehovah-Sabaoth will go before His people to make them victorious.

Dear friend, do you find yourself going through a season of discouragement? If so then take heart! The Lord of hosts goes before you with an accompaniment of many angels. Press on in the might of Jehovah, and you will find strength in time of need. God will give you the victory!

---

*Father, You have not left me to the battle alone. You have surrounded me with an innumerable number of hosts. They are Your ministers to me, but I have also been given Your Holy Spirit. Give me eyes of faith to see Your loving care all around me.*

*I pray these things in Jesus' name. Amen.*

# GOD'S OMNISCIENCE

Do you know how the clouds are balanced, those wondrous
works of Him who is perfect in knowledge?
Job 37:16

## CAN GOD LEARN ANYTHING?

God is absolutely perfect in knowledge. He knows everything. There is
nothing that the Lord needs to learn. There was never a time when He
learned, nor can any knowledge be added to Him. Our great Jehovah is
the source of all wisdom and knowledge.

Yet the knowledge of God can be mysterious to us.

Job, in the midst of sufferings, did not understand the ways of the Lord.
He was unable to comprehend the darkness of his calamities; yet, his
suffering gave him a greater vision of God.

It takes an act of faith to trust that God's ways are perfect, even when
we are faced with various trials. However, true faith speaks in this way:
But He knows the way that I take; When He has tested me I shall come
forth as gold.* When we find ourselves in the midst of deep valleys, let
us trust that our All-Knowing God knows the ways which we take.

---

*Father, it is not in man to direct his steps.\* In Your perfect knowledge, all You
ordain is right and good. Help me in trials to have the faith of Job which says:
Though He slay me yet I will trust Him.\**

*I pray these things in Jesus' name. Amen.*

*Job 23:10, Job 10:23, Job 13:15

# GOD'S TRANSCENDENCE

To whom will you liken Me, and make Me equal and
compare Me, that we should be alike?

Isaiah 46:5

## WHAT IS THE DISTANCE BETWEEN GOD AND MAN?

A.W. Tozer points out that we should not think of a spatial distance
between God and man, but rather a "quality of being." [2]

Here in the text, the prophet distinguishes the true God from idols. His
point is to show the people of Israel that there is no comparison between
Yahweh and their false gods. The Lord is our infinitely, glorious Creator
Who transcends His creation. Therefore, man sins when he seeks to bring
God down to his level.

Dear friend, do you have an accurate understanding of your place before
the Most High? Let wisdom teach us not to draw any comparisons, but
rather to bow down in worship and reverence to Yahweh.

———————◆———————

*Father, there is no one like You. All creatures great and small owe their
exis-tence to You. Forgive me for having an idolatrous imagination and
grant me the grace to bow down in humble reverence to Your great majesty.*

*I pray these things in Jesus' name. Amen.*

# GOD'S INFINITUDE

But will God indeed dwell on the earth? Behold, heaven
and the heaven of heavens cannot contain You.
How much less this temple which I have built!
1 Kings 8:27

## CAN YOU IMAGINE A LIFE WITHOUT LIMITS?

Solomon understood that a temple made with hands could not contain
His infinite majesty, and yet He mysteriously dwells amongst His people.
He lavishes on us an endless treasure trove of blessing.

The concept of infinity is unfathomable for us who are finite beings. We
are creatures who have limited abilities, and we are contained in space
and time. Yet not so with God. He is an infinite Being Who cannot be
confined or contained.

Dear friend, have you come to the end of your strength? If so, then
draw water from the wells of His grace. Though we operate with finite
resources, we shall find in Him an inexhaustible resource of blessing.

―――――◆―――――

*Father, I praise You that You are not limited like me. I could never exhaust
Your resources. Help me to be filled with admiration and awe of Your infinite
greatness.*

*I pray these things in Jesus' name. Amen.*

# GOD'S IMMUTABILITY

"For I am the Lord, I do not change; Therefore, you are
not consumed, O Sons of Jacob."
Malachi 3:6

## WHAT DETERMINES TRUTH?

Is it the changing norms of our culture or is it the unchanging Word of
God? We serve a God Who never changes. God remains forever fixed in
the heavens.

Here in the text, Israel was oppressing the weak and withholding the
tithes, which all belonged to the Lord. He remains forever as a God Who
stands up for the poor, the widow, and the fatherless. Malachi exhorted
the people to repentance, and he does so by appealing to God's
unchanging character. Thus, if the people will not honor the Lord with
theirpossessions, then they cannot expect to receive blessings from God.

What about you friend? Have you honored the Lord with your
possessions? Let us be God's people who put the Lord first in
everything that we do.

---

*Father, can a man rob You? Even the cattle on a thousand hills are
Yours.\* You have always remained unchanging in Your desire for mercy.
Give me the grace to honor You through my generosity to the poor.*

*I pray these things in Jesus' name. Amen.*


\*Psalm 50:10

# GOD'S UNITY

And this is eternal life, that they know You the only true God,
and Jesus Christ Whom You have sent.

John 17:3

## WHAT IS ETERNAL LIFE?

Our Lord provides the answer to this question here in the third verse.
The ancient world was very polytheistic. Christ is not only making a
declaration against idolatry, but He is also proclaiming that He shares in
the glory of the Father.

All of deity, all of the divine attributes, and all of the glory that is perfectly in the Father is also perfectly in the Son. I cannot possess eternal
life through any other means, but by the knowledge of the one True God.

Oh, the mysteries of the incarnation that all of God could be clothed in
flesh! Within the Persons of the Trinity we find complete oneness and
perfection of divinity. In light of this truth, let us give thanks and praise
to the Triune God for our salvation.

---

*Father, it was in Your good pleasure that You ordained the death of Your Son
for us. You chose us, Christ redeemed us, and the Holy Spirit sealed us.
Help me to meditate more fully on the perfect unity of the Godhead.*

*I pray these things in Jesus' name. Amen.*

# GOD'S ETERNALITY

Before the mountains were brought forth, or ever You had formed the earth and the world, from everlasting to everlasting You are God.

Psalm 90:2

## WHAT ARE THE IMPLICATIONS OF GOD'S ETERNALITY?

Our finite minds cannot comprehend the eternal nature of God's character. All of life is under complete subjection to the cruel taskmaster of time. Yet God is not bound by the inevitable forces of entropy, but rather remains forever seated on His throne.

In light of God's eternal nature, the psalmist is inspired to reflect on the frailty of man. The years of our lives pale in comparison with eternity. However, this is often a truth that eludes us. It is easy to get bogged down in the mundane details of life, but we must pause for a moment to reflect on our frailty.

One day, all of us are going to stand before God, and give an account to Him. Dearly beloved, let us consider our lives in light of eternity.

———————◇———————

*Father, so often I am weighed down with the various cares of life. Teach me to number my days \* so that I will be prepared for the eternal state.*

*I pray these things in Jesus' name. Amen.*

*Psalm 90:12

# GOD'S HOLINESS

For thus says the One who is high and lifted up, who inhabits eternity, whose name is Holy: I dwell in the high and holy place, and also with him who is of a contrite and lowly spirit, to revive the spirit of the lowly and to revive the heart of the contrite.

Isaiah 57:15

## WHO CAN APPROACH GOD?

When He gave the Law to Israel, God covered Mount Sinai in a cloud of dread. So terrible was the sight that the people asked for God to remove Himself from their midst. There is a mysterious awe about the holiness of God, but His holiness reveals His righteous character.

Here in the text, Isaiah reminds us that the Transcendent One is still near to those who humble themselves. If the Israelites would forsake their idols and repent, then the Lord would surely restore them. Let wisdom teach us that the highway of holiness* is marked by the path of contrition. In light of this truth, let us humble ourselves before a Holy God.

---

*Father, how often do I forget that You are holy? I thank You that You have made me holy through the sacrifice of Your Son. Help me to remain humble in Your sight.*

*I pray these things in Jesus' name. Amen.*

* Isaiah 35:8

# GOD'S WRATH

Thus the Lord, the God of Israel, said to me:
"Take from my hand this cup of the wine of the wrath,
and make all the nations to whom I send you drink it."
Jeremiah 25:15

## DO YOU MEDITATE ON THE WRATH OF GOD?

The illustration provided in this verse is one of a drunkard who is reeling to and fro. Apart from Christ, the sinner is drunk with the wrath of God.

Today, people focus primarily on the love of God. But this is a grave error. In order for us to have a better understanding of God's love, we must also understand the wrath of God. The Lord is of purer eyes than to behold evil.* His righteous anger is directed toward those who have broken His Law.

Once a sinner understands that he or she is under God's wrath, only then will the Gospel paint a more glorious portrait of grace. In light of this truth, let us seek to have a fuller picture of God's Divine attributes.

---

*Father, so often I do not think about Your wrath. Help me to meditate on Your whole counsel so that I can have a better understanding of what Christ has done for me.*

*I pray these things in Jesus' name. Amen.*

*Habakkuk 1:13

# GOD'S FAITHFULNESS

The steadfast love of the Lord never ceases; His mercies never come to an end; they are new every morning; great is your faithfulness.

Lamentations 3:22-23

## HOW MUCH VALUE DO YOU PLACE ON FAITHFULNESS?

Our society is largely unfaithful. Commitment to marriage is sorely lacking today. Our culture has even forgotten our commitment to children. Even more so, is a lack of commitment to God's eternal truth. Yet God is faithful to us. He keeps His covenant promises to His children.

Jeremiah prophesied during a very grim point in Judah's history. He witnessed the Babylonian conquest of his land, which left his home in utter desolation. All of this was a direct judgment of God, but in spite of the devastation that surrounded him, he remained hopeful. His understanding of God's faithfulness anchored his soul in difficult times.

Dear Christian, do you find yourself in a low place? If so, then do not focus only on what your eyes can see, but remember that God is faithful in keeping His covenant promises to you.

---

*Father, I thank You that You remain faithful. You have promised never to leave me nor forsake me.\* Therefore, I hope not as the world hopes, but as one who serves a risen Savior. Let Your faithfulness be a constant reminder of hope to me in all seasons of life.*

*I pray these things in Jesus' name. Amen.*

\*Hebrews 14:5

# GOD'S GOODNESS

Good and upright is the Lord; therefore He instructs sinners in the way.
Psalm 25:8

## WHAT MAKES A PERSON GOOD?

The average person on the street will tell you that his good works make him good. Now ask that same person, "What is your standard of goodness?" You're likely to get several different answers.

Scripture teaches, however, that God is the true standard by which goodness is measured. Everything that is good proceeds from Him Who dwells between the cherubim in heaven.* In His moral excellence, He instructs sinners in the way.* He doesn't just leave us without any instruction, but willingly teaches us what He requires.

His goodness also extends to the provisions of our daily needs. Even the unconverted are often showered with blessings of food, blessings of family, and blessings of comfort. Most importantly, God is patient, giving every sinner a time to repent of their sins and to believe in the Gospel.

In light of this truth, let us count all the ways that the Lord has been good to us. His blessings to us are more innumerable than all the sands of the seashore.

———————◆———————

*Father, You are good in Your very being. All your ways are good and upright, and You are gracious to undeserving sinners. Help me to treasure Your instruction more than gold.*

*I pray these things in Jesus' name. Amen.*

*Isaiah 37:16, Psalm 25:8

# GOD'S JUSTICE

Of a truth, God will not do wickedly,
and the Almighty will not pervert justice.
Job 34:12

## WHY DOES GOD'S JUSTICE REMAIN NEGLECTED IN OUR MIDST?

It is easier to meditate on the love of God, but the truth of the matter is that all of His attributes are good.

Here in the text we are taught that the Lord will not pervert justice. His justice demands that He judge righteously in accordance with His perfect and holy character. Therefore, all of mankind finds himself or herself in a dire position: we have all broken the Law of God.

Fortunately for us, the Lord Jesus Christ fulfilled the Law and suffered the punishment due to us. It is, because of His selfless act, that God can be Just and the Justifier of the one who puts faith in Jesus. * In light of this truth, let our hearts be filled with gratitude because He has clothed us with new robes of righteousness.

———◆———◈———◆———

*Father, You are completely just. You must deal with sin, and You will make straight all which is crooked in this world. In a world where justice is constantly perverted, help me not to lose heart, but rather place my hope in Your eternal truth.*

*I pray these things in Jesus' name. Amen.*

*Romans 3:26

# GOD'S GRACE

And David said to him, "Do not fear, for I will show you kindness for the sake of your father Jonathan, and I will restore to you all the land of Saul your father, and you shall eat at my table always."

2 Samuel 9:7

## DO YOU EXTEND KINDNESS TO OTHERS?

I am not talking about a random act of kindness, but a completely, unmerited favor.

It was a customary practice for kings of conquest to wipe out the descendants of their predecessors. Yet King David showed Jonathan's son, Mephibosheth, unmerited favor and kindness instead of judgment. He is not only kind, but he grants favor to Saul's son.

In what ways has God shown kindness to us? All of us have rebelled against His laws, but instead of anger God shows us grace. He is perfectly gracious in His benevolence to mankind, as well as in the salvation of sinners.

Let us therefore take comfort in knowing that the God Who is perfect is also completely gracious.

---

*Father, I thank You that You are a gracious God. Your unmerited kindness to me is beyond comprehension. Help me to demonstrate this type of grace toward others in my life.*

*I pray these things in Jesus' name. Amen.*

# GOD'S MERCY

The Lord is merciful and gracious, slow to anger and
abounding in steadfast love.

Psalm 103:8

## WHAT IF GOD GAVE US WHAT WE DESERVED?

There is a cry among many that God is unfair, but if He really gave us
what was fair then we would be in hell.

Here in the text, the Psalmist declares that the Lord is merciful. The
mercy of God is characterized by compassion. In spite of our rebellion
against Him He does not deal with us according to our sins, nor repay us
according to our iniquities.* He knows our frame; He remembers that
we are dust.*

The perfectly holy and just God is also a perfectly merciful God.

Dear friend, have you considered how the Lord has been merciful to you?
Let us recount the ways in which God has shown us compassion, and
may our hearts be stirred with thanksgiving.

---

*Father, You have not dealt with me according to what my sins deserve, but
You have remembered my frame. Thank You for having compassion on me,
and sparing me from the wrath to come. Give me the grace to extend Your
mercy to others in my life.*

*I pray these things in Jesus' name. Amen.*

*Psalm 103:10, Psalm 103:14

# GOD'S LOVE

The Lord appeared to him from far away. I have loved you with an everlasting love; therefore I have continued my faithfulness to you.
Jeremiah 31:3

## WHAT MAKES THE LOVE OF GOD UNIQUE?

Humans may grow in their love for others, but God's love cannot be improved. God's love is a steadfast love, which never grows cold or wears out. It is a love that is not based on human merit, but is seated in the very nature of God. God's love has always been and will always remain. It is both perfect and complete.

Certainly, Jeremiah remembered the covenant of God with Israel. They were an undeserving people whom Divine Providence set His love upon. Though God's chastisement was on Judah, He promised not to utterly forsake them. He, Who established His covenant with Abraham, would always love His people.

In like manner, the Lord has made an everlasting covenant with His church. We, who have been saved from the power of sin, will be completely conformed into the image of Christ. Therefore, we can find solace in the fact that His love for us will never grow cold.

In light of this truth, let us not doubt the Lord's kindness, but rather rejoice in His unwavering love for us.

*Father, who can measure the greatness of Your love? You have loved Your people with an everlasting love.\* Grant me the grace to love others as You have loved me.*

*I pray these things in Jesus' name. Amen.*

\*Jeremiah 31:3

# GOD'S WISDOM

But the wisdom from above is first pure, then peaceable, gentle, open to reason, full of mercy and good fruits, impartial and sincere.

James 1:17

## WHAT IS WISDOM?

Wisdom is the ability to navigate the difficulties of life through the skillful application of God's Word. The scriptures teach us that there is worldly wisdom which leads to death, and godly wisdom which leads to life. * While we are able to grow in wisdom, God is perfect in wisdom. He is a willing Giver of wisdom to those who are in need.

James is writing to a congregation where there had been divisions and arguments. Many desired to be teachers, but the Apostle warns them against selfish ambition and jealousy. True wisdom is demonstrated through Christ-like behavior. We must always navigate through the trenches with godly skill. Let us walk, therefore, in the wisdom which yields the peaceable fruit of righteousness. *

---

*Father, so often I am tempted to be selfish. I envy and I covet for my own sinful desires. Please help me to put on the Lord Jesus Christ * so that I may navigate my relationships with godly skill.*

*I pray these things in Jesus' name. Amen.*

*Proverbs 14:12, Hebrews 12:11, Romans 13:14

# FEBRUARY
## WHO IS JESUS?

Jesus asked His disciples a very important question: "Who do men say that I am?" The answer they gave Him was very telling.

"Some say you are a teacher or a prophet."

Then our Lord asked them straight away. "Who do you say that I am?"*

This is a question that holds a lot of gravity. Centuries have been removed since the day when our Lord was crucified, but the question remains the same.

Who is Jesus?

Many still hold that He is a great teacher or philosopher. There are others who think that His life is just a good example for us to imitate. Yet there are very few who actually believe that He is the Son of God.

As you read these reflections, I want you to think about what you would say to an unbeliever if they told you that Jesus was not the Son of God. If a Jehovah's Witness came to your door, what would you say? What do you say when two elders from the LDS Church approach you? How would you respond to them?

My prayer is that you will not only see Jesus as Peter did, when he said, "You are the Christ, the Son of the living God,"* but that you will have an answer for the hope that lies within you.

*Mark 8:27-29, Matthew 16:16

# JESUS IS THE LOGOS

In the beginning was the Word, and the Word was with God,
and the Word was God.

John 1:1

## HOW CAN MAN EVER WRAP HIS MIND AROUND THE WORDS OF THE APOSTLE JOHN?

All the volumes in the world could never attain to their depths—that God became a man. In His wisdom, God has orchestrated our salvation through His only begotten Son, Jesus. Thus, the writer is extoling the glorious deity of Christ.

John does not mean to say that our Lord had a beginning, but rather that Jesus was present during the creation of the worlds.* In the beginning, He was there establishing the light, and separating it from the darkness.* Yet more specifically, in the scope and context of this passage, the author is referring to Jesus as the living Word. Jesus is the living testimony of God Who gives light to every man coming into the world.

Have you come to believe that Jesus is the Son of God? Let us not doubt the testimony of scripture concerning Him, but rather worship Him in humble adoration.

*Father, thank You for not leaving man to his own devices. In Your infinite and unfathomable love, You made a way of salvation for all who believe. Your Son Jesus is not just a mere mortal, but One Who is equal and co-eternal with You. Please make the glory of Jesus Christ more precious to me as I grow in grace.*

*I pray these things in Jesus' name. Amen.*

*Hebrews 11:3, Genesis 1:4, John 1:9

# JESUS IS PRE-EMINENT

He is the image of the invisible God, the firstborn of all creation.

Colossians 1:15

## WHAT DOES THE APOSTLE MEAN WHEN HE USES THE WORD "FIRSTBORN"?

The Greek word for "firstborn" denotes the idea of pre-eminence. Jesus is not merely a man born in time, but rather the eternal Son of God.

Here in the text, the Apostle Paul is working to show the Colossians that the same Lord, Who is over all creation, is also head of the body, the church, and who is the beginning, the firstborn from the dead, and that in all things He may have the preeminence.* Therefore, God's people are warned not to be cheated through worldly philosophies and wisdom, but rather to hold fast to the doctrines of Christ. It is only as the church abides in Christ that they will find power over their indwelling sin.

In like manner, the saints have a responsibility to remain steadfast in the doctrine in which they were called. This eternal truth is the only remedy for false teaching, and thus it is profitable for us to learn from the words of Christ.

Dear friend, can you discern the truth from the lie? Let us be those who have our senses trained to discern good from evil.*

———————◆———————

*Father, the church needs discernment in her hour of trial. Help me to abide in the love and the teachings of Your Son Jesus Christ.*

*I pray these things in Jesus' name. Amen.*

*Colossians 1:18, 2:8, Hebrews 5:14

# JESUS IS EVERLASTING

And now, Father, glorify me in Your own presence with the glory that I had with You before the world existed.

John 17:5

## WHO IS JESUS?

The question of Christ's divinity is an important question in our day. There were many in the first century who would not believe His claims to be the Son of God. Yet Scripture clearly teaches that all glory and all of eternity is ascribed to Him. He was present in the beginning of time, and He remains forevermore. He is the ageless One Who possesses infinite wisdom and power.

Thus, His prayer and desire for His sheep is that we would be unified together in love. All that the Father has given to the Son is ours by faith. Let us therefore remain united together in Him for the furtherance of the Gospel.

———————◦———————

*Father, let not the body of Christ suffer schisms. Help the Church to be a testimony of love for one another to an unbelieving world.*

*I pray these things in Jesus' name. Amen.*

# JESUS IS THE CREATOR OF ALL THINGS

All things were made through Him, and without
Him was not anything made that was made.

John 1:3

## WHAT THINGS WERE MADE THROUGH THE SON?

The Scriptures teach that all things were made through Him. Here in the text we see the extent of His creation. He was not a created being, but rather the Creator of everything.

There are no principalities, nor powers, nor any other thing* which does not owe its existence to Christ. We, therefore, have great reason for hope because we have an infinitely reliable Savior.

He, Who created the worlds, is more than able to save our souls from the grave. In light of this truth let us give all praise and honor to Christ Who has power over all of creation.

◆————◆————◆

*Father, give me eyes of faith to behold the majesty of Your Son. Help me to never cease from the praise and worship of His holy name.*

*I pray these things in Jesus' name. Amen.*

*Romans 8:38

# JESUS IS SUPERIOR

Having become as much superior to angels as the name He has
inherited is more excellent than theirs.

Hebrews 1:4

## HOW WOULD YOU DEFINE EXCELLENCE?

Modern day definitions are inadequate when referring to Christ. His
excellence transcends all of creation. The writer refers to Jesus as the radi-
ance of the glory of God.*

In Christ we see deity displayed.

When thinking of angels they are beings of great splendor, and yet their
glory pales in comparison to the Son of God. Therefore, since the testimony of Scripture declares Jesus to be superior to angels, we are warned
to take heed, according to His words. For if God did not spare angels
when they sinned, but cast them into hell and committed them to chains
of gloomy darkness to be kept until the judgment* then how much
greater will be the judgment against those who disobey the Son of God?

In light of this truth, let us not grow indifferent to the warnings of
Scripture, but rather listen to the teachings of Christ with obedient ears.

———————◆———————

*Father, if the testimony of angels demanded obedience, then how much greater
are the consequences of disregarding Your Son? I pray that I would not merely
know the Word, but also that I would be transformed by it.*

*I pray these things in Jesus' name. Amen.*

*Hebrews 1:3, 2 Peter 2:4

# JESUS IS THE SON OF GOD

Simon Peter replied, "You are the Christ, the Son of the living God."
Matthew 16:16

## HOW CAN A MAN BE BORN AGAIN?

The kingdom of heaven cannot be entered by way of flesh and blood. A Divine revelation must first enter into the heart of man.

Jesus Christ is the Son of God Who came down from heaven in order that He might reveal Himself to us. Apart from the incarnation there can be no Gospel. Therefore, true spiritual discernment cannot come by means of flesh and blood. I must be born again.

When I realize that salvation is impossible without God, my witness for Him will be much more effective. It is not up to us to save the souls of men. We are simply a conduit for others to believe on the Son of God. Let us therefore remain fully reliant upon the Lord as we minister to others.

———————————◆———————————

*Father, who has believed Your report?\* Your testimony concerning man is true. In this dark age, we need men and women who are led by Your Spirit. Help us not to fight the devil with an arm of the flesh, but rather through the power of the Holy Spirit.*

*I pray these things in Jesus' name. Amen.*

*Isaiah 53:1

# JESUS IS OUR PROPHET

I will raise up for them a Prophet like you from among
their brothers. And I will put my words in His mouth,
and He shall speak to them all that I command Him.
Deuteronomy 18:18

## WHAT COMES TO MIND WHEN YOU THINK OF A PROPHET?

Our culture thinks a prophet is someone who foretells future events.
While many of the Old Testament prophets foretold of future things,
their primary purpose was to declare the words of God.

In this text, Yahweh gives Moses the true test of a prophet. A prophet is a
person who speaks the truth of God to others. In a day when the people
were surrounded by sorcerers and false prophets, the Lord promised to
rise up a true Prophet. Ultimately, we see the fulfillment of this passage
in the Person of Jesus Christ.

The Apostle Peter refers to this promise in Acts* when speaking of the
Messiah. Every word that proceeds out of His mouth is true. Let us
therefore not turn to strange revelations, but rather saturate ourselves in
the words of Christ.

*Father, You have given us all things that pertain to life and godliness.* Your
Word is powerful and true. Help us to be faithful in delivering Your truth to
others.*

*I pray these things in Jesus' name. Amen.*

*Acts 2:30, 2 Peter 1:3

# JESUS IS OUR PRIEST

This becomes even more evident when another priest
arises in the likeness of Melchizedek.
Hebrews 7:15

## WHO IS MELCHIZEDEK?

Scripture tells us very little about him. We know that Melchizedek received a tenth of the spoils of war after he had blessed Abraham. He is first, by translation of his name, king of righteousness, and then he is also king of Salem, that is, king of peace. We are also told that he had no beginning of days nor end of life.*

Thus, the author of Hebrews compares the Priesthood of Christ, not to Aaron's priesthood, but to the priesthood of Melchizedek. While the priesthood of Aaron was never meant to last, it is Christ Who remains forever as our High Priest. We are no longer reminded of our sins every year, because we have an eternal High Priest Who has put them away once and for all.*

In light of this truth, let us approach God's throne in boldness knowing that our conscience has been made clean.

◆————————◆————————◆

*Father, thank You that I no longer have to approach You through another human being. I can freely offer up my prayers to You with a clean conscience. Grant me the grace to approach You in boldness knowing that Christ has permanently removed my sins from me.*

*I pray these things in Jesus' name. Amen.*

*Hebrews 7:1-3, Hebrews 9:12

# JESUS IS OUR KING

On His robe and on His thigh He has a name written,
"King of kings and Lord of lords."
Revelation 19:16

## WHO REIGNS ON HIGH?

The prophet Daniel was given a vision of four great beasts that came up out of the sea, different from one another. These four great beasts are four kings who shall arise out of the earth. While all of them conquered, their kingdoms were eventually brought to nothing. Only the Ancient of Days was given dominion over all kingdoms. His dominion is an everlasting dominion, which shall not pass away, and his kingdom shall not be destroyed.*

Thus the victory cry of the saints will forever be, "Worthy is the Lamb!"*

For Christ, our Passover Lamb, has been sacrificed.* Jesus is the sacrificial Lamb, Who put away the sins of His people. He has won the battle against Satan, and in Him we have been made more than conquerors.* He will have the final victory, and His Kingdom will reign forever and ever.*

Dear friend, are you growing weary in your present circumstances? If so, do not lose heart. God has already written your story and it has a happy ending.

❖

*Father, You have put all things under the feet of our risen Savior. There is no kingdom that will reign at His expense. Let not the present discouragements of this life impair my vision of the glory to come.*

*I pray these things in Jesus' name. Amen.*

*Daniel 7:3-17, Revelation 5:12, 1 Corinthians 5:7, Romans 8:37, Revelation 11:15

# JESUS IS THE APPOINTED ONE

Behold my Servant, whom I uphold, my chosen, in whom
my soul delights; I have put my Spirit upon Him;
He will bring forth justice to the nations.

Isaiah 42:1

## WHO STANDS IN THE GAP FOR GOD'S PEOPLE?

Isaiah prophesied to a people who turned a blind eye to justice. They had all together become corrupt, and they forsook the living God for the worship of idols. There was no one to stand in the gap. The prophet Ezekiel wrote, "So I sought for a man among them who would make a wall, and stand in the gap before Me on behalf of the land, that I should not destroy it; but I found no one."*

In a period of great spiritual darkness Yahweh promises to restore true justice.

Jesus Christ has been appointed to stand in the gap for us. He is the Lamb Who was slain from the foundations of the world.* He will fill the earth with glory, and His kingdom will usher in true peace.*

Beloved, come and take delight in the Lord Jesus Christ. He is the Appointed One Whom God has chosen to exact justice. His reign will usher in righteousness for all nations.

———————◆———————

*Father, we live in a day where man has perverted justice. No one stands in the gap. It is easy to be discouraged by the corruption of earthly governments. Yet, let my eyes be fixed on Your heavenly kingdom where true justice reigns.*

*I pray these things in Jesus' name. Amen.*

*Ezekiel 22:30, Revelation 13:8, Habakkuk 2:14

# JESUS IS THE LAMB OF GOD

The next day he saw Jesus coming toward him, and said,
"Behold, the Lamb of God, who takes away the sin of the world!"
John 1:29

## WHAT IS THE SIGNIFICANCE OF A LAMB?

In the Old Testament, lambs were offered up as daily sacrifices for the worship of God. They served as a temporary covering for sins, but they were not a permanent solution. Thus it was fitting for Christ to offer up Himself for our sins, because He is a perfect Lamb without spot nor blemish. While the Old Testament sacrifices were offered again and again for the sins of the people, it was Christ Who offered up Himself for our sins "once and for all."

Now we stand before God, not in our own righteousness, but in the righteousness of our spotless Lamb. Dear soul, do you find yourself dwelling on past sins? If so, then look no further than to the Lamb of God Who has permanently taken away your sin.

---

*Father, thank You that You have provided a Lamb Who has permanently removed my sins. Help me not to dwell on my sin, but rather to look to the Lord Jesus Christ.*

*I pray these things in Jesus' name. Amen.*

# JESUS IS LIFTED UP

And as Moses lifted up the serpent in the wilderness, so must the Son of Man be lifted up, that whoever believes in Him may have eternal life.

John 3:14-15

## WHERE IS SALVATION FOUND?

The children of Israel were setting out from Mount Hor. They were weary from travel, and began to complain against the Lord their God. As a result of their unbelief, the Lord sent fiery serpents to attack them. Many were struck and killed by the serpents, but in their distress they cried out to Yahweh for deliverance. He heard their prayers and instructed Moses to make a bronze serpent.

So Moses made a bronze serpent and set it on a pole. And if a serpent bit anyone, he would look at the bronze serpent and live.* Those who looked up at the serpent were miraculously healed, and delivered from God's judgment.

The miraculous account of the bronze serpent finds its way into the Gospel narrative. Jesus uses this story of Moses to teach us an important truth. His point is simply that there is no other source of salvation, but in Him alone.

Just as Moses lifted up the snake in the wilderness, so the Son of Man must be lifted up, that everyone who believes in Him may have eternal life.* Therefore, let us look to Jesus for the deliverance of our sins. In light of this eternal truth, let us place our trust in the Lord Who saves His people from their sins.

———————————◇———————————

*Father, there is no other name under heaven whereby man can be saved.\* I am in great danger when I lean on the arm of the flesh. Help me to look to no other than the Lord Jesus Christ for my salvation.*

*I pray these things in Jesus' name. Amen.*

*Numbers 21:9, John 3:14-15, Acts 4:12

# JESUS IS OUR SUFFERING SERVANT

Surely He has borne our griefs and carried our sorrows;
yet we esteemed Him stricken, smitten by God, and afflicted.
Isaiah 53:4

## HOW CAN THE HUMAN MIND FATHOM THE SUFFERINGS OF CHRIST?

No finite mind can comprehend the agonies of Calvary. He was crushed under the fierce wrath of God. The sins that we committed were placed upon His shoulders, and now instead of wrath we are given grace. It is no small thing that put our Savior on the Cross, but rather a world of iniquity that opened the floodgates of hell.

Thus, we err greatly when we trivialize our sin.

When temptation knocks on our door, let us be reminded of our Suffering Servant. The sinful acts we are about to commit nailed Jesus to the Cross.

Dear soul, do you deal lightly with sin? If so, then consider the great lengths to which Jesus suffered to pay for your sin. In doing so, you are living every day in light of the Gospel. Pause. Reflect and remember the sacrificial service of our Lord.

---

*Father, my sin is no small thing. You put Your Son on the Cross to suffer for it. Help me never to take my sin lightly, but please remind me to constantly put my sin to death.*

*I pray these things in Jesus' name. Amen.*

# JESUS IS OUR HUMBLE SERVANT

After that, He poured water into a basin, and began to wash the disciples' feet, and to wipe them with the towel with which He was girded.

John 13:5

## WHAT DOES HUMBLE SERVICE LOOK LIKE IN ACTION?

The hour was approaching, and Jesus' betrayer was at hand. Knowing that His time was imminent, He didn't do what we might expect Him to do. Jesus rose up from supper and laid aside His garments, took a towel and girded Himself.*

Jesus became the servant of all.*

In the moments leading up to His greatest test, Jesus washed His disciples' feet.

In a culture where we measure greatness through fame and self-aggrandizement, godly wisdom teaches us that true greatness only comes through humble service. As believers in Christ, have we lost the art of washing feet—especially our betrayers? In light of this truth, let us seek out Christ-like humility by putting the needs of others above our own.

———◆———

*Father, so often I forget that true greatness is putting others first. Let others say of me that I am a servant of all.*

*I pray these things in Jesus' name. Amen.*

*John 13:4, Mark 9:35

# JESUS IS THE BREAD OF LIFE

Jesus said to them, "I am the bread of life; whoever comes to me shall not hunger, and whoever believes in me shall never thirst.'"
John 6:35

## WHAT IS IT THAT YOU SEEK?

A day had been removed since Jesus miraculously fed the five thousand. Crowds had gathered in Capernaum to see Him again. Knowing what was in their hearts, our Lord called them to the mat.

"Truly, truly, I say to you, you are seeking Me, not because you saw signs, but because you ate your fill of the loaves."* In their hunger for physical food they neglected a more pressing consideration. It was their very souls, which were at stake.

Aware of their spiritual hunger and thirst, our Master re-directs the conversation.

Jesus said, "I am the bread of life. Your fathers ate the manna in the wilderness, and they died. This is the bread that comes down from heaven, so that one may eat of it and not die.* The manna their fathers ate in the wilderness paled in comparison to the true bread from heaven.

Dear reader, are you only laboring for food that perishes? Do not neglect your soul, but look to the One Who can sustain it with eternal life.

◆————————◎————————◆

*Father, You have given me true bread from heaven. I have all that I could ever want in Christ. Let not my soul exchange the glory of heaven for the perishable manna of earth.*

*I pray these things in Jesus' name. Amen.*

*John 6:26, John 6:48-50

# JESUS IS THE LIGHT OF THE WORLD

Again Jesus spoke to them, saying, "I am the light of the world. Whoever follows me will not walk in darkness, but will have the light of life."

John 8:12

## WHAT IS THE MARK OF A DISCIPLE?

Jesus was teaching in the Temple and the Pharisees sought to test Him. They boasted in keeping the Law of Moses and prided themselves in the outward observances of the Law. But they neglected the weightier matters of the law.*

The scribes and the Pharisees brought a woman who had been caught in adultery, and placed her in His midst. This they did to test Him.* While Jesus doesn't deny the condemnation of the woman, He masterfully flips this incident on its head. "Let him who is without sin among you be the first to throw a stone at her."* Then Jesus makes a bold declaration. "I am the light of the world. Whoever follows me will not walk in darkness, but will have the light of life."*

The test of a true disciple is not boasting in the letter, but rather being conformed by it. We are disciples of the Lord Jesus if we walk in the light of Christ. Let us not merely boast in our knowledge of Scripture, but be those who are transformed by its teaching.

*Father, deliver me from the snare of cold, dead orthodoxy. Purify my heart and help me to walk in Your ways.*

*I pray these things in Jesus' name. Amen.*

*Matthew 23:23, John 8:3-12

# JESUS IS THE DOOR OF THE SHEEPFOLD

"I am the door. If anyone enters by Me, he will be saved
and will go in and out and find pasture."
John 10:9

## HOW CAN A MAN OBTAIN ACCESS TO GOD?

Once again, the Pharisees prided themselves in being teachers of the Law, but Jesus calls them blind guides.* Our Lord had just healed a blind man, but they were in a rage. This miracle was done on the Sabbath and the Jews were not supposed to do any work on this day.

Jesus addresses their blindness by means of illustration.

The true Israel of God enters into the sheepfold*through Christ. He is the door through which man can have access to God. The Pharisees had made the Law of God to no effect through their traditions. Therefore, Jesus likens these men to thieves and robbers.* Religious zeal, if misguided, will blind a man. Oh that we would be guides that see, and who lead others to Christ. Let us show others the only Door through which they can access eternal life.

------◦------

*Father, keep me from the egregious sin of spiritual pride. Let not my love for the Law become a stumbling block to others. Help me to demonstrate my understanding of Your Word by pointing others to Jesus.*

*I pray these things in Jesus' name. Amen.*

*Matthew 23:24, John 10:1, John 10:1

# JESUS IS THE GOOD SHEPHERD

"I am the good shepherd. The good shepherd lays
down his life for the sheep."
John 10:11

## WHAT ARE THE MARKS OF A TRUE SHEPHERD?

A true shepherd is marked by a sacrificial love for God's people. He is a
protector of the sheepfold, watching out for wolves and other dangers;
whereas, a hireling leaves.

He who is a hired hand and not a shepherd, who does not own the sheep,
sees the wolf coming and leaves the sheep and flees, and the wolf snatches
them and scatters them. He flees because he is a hired hand and cares
nothing for the sheep.*

Here in the text, Jesus is drawing a contrast between a true shepherd and
a hireling. Jesus was the ultimate servant Who loved His sheep even unto
death. Yet this manner of sacrificial leadership was foreign to that of the
Pharisees. They did not love the sheep, but rather sought to extort them.
Therefore, Jesus showed His people a more excellent way.* If you are going
to be great in the Kingdom of God, then you will have to be a servant of all.*

Friend, what is your motivation for serving the people of God? Let your
service be fueled by a desire to see others know our Good Shepherd.

———————◆————◇————◆———————

*Father, You are a Great Shepherd. Thank You for giving us Your Son. He set
the ultimate example of humility and lowliness. Let it be said of me that I
gave myself sacrificially for the benefit of others.*

*I pray these things in Jesus' name. Amen.*

*John 10:12-13, 1 Corinthians 12:31, Mark 10:44

# JESUS IS THE RESURRECTION AND THE LIFE

"I am the resurrection and the life.
Whoever believes in me, though he die, yet he shall live."
John 11:25

## HAVE YOU EXPERIENCED THE POWER OF GOD?

It had been the fourth day since Lazarus had been placed in the tomb. By this time his dead body had begun to decay and rot. We read how that many of his loved ones gathered to mourn for him.

Word went out to Jesus that Lazarus had died, but He did a peculiar thing. When he heard that Lazarus was ill, he stayed two days longer in the place where he was. * But this raised the question, "Is this not the Son of God? Could He not have immediately raised him from the dead?"

Alas, the timing of God had not yet come, and therefore Lazarus remained where he lay. In a few days many would witness the resurrection power of Christ.

Our Savior, Who called Lazarus from the grave, possesses the same resurrection power to raise us to newness of life.* We are not left in despair, but we are now begotten again to a living hope.* Therefore, trust fully in the God Who has power to raise the dead.

---

*Father, You have not left my soul in the grave,* but You have raised me to new life. Help me not to live as one who has no hope, but rather as one who has a living hope.*

*I pray these things in Jesus' name. Amen.*

*John 11:6, 1 Peter 1:3, Romans 6:4, Psalm 16:10

# JESUS IS THE WAY, THE TRUTH, AND THE LIFE

Jesus said to him, "I am the way, and the truth, and the life.
No one comes to the Father except through me."
John 14:6

## HOW CAN A MAN TRULY KNOW GOD?

The ever present God remains an enigma to those who walk in darkness.

The Feast of Passover was approaching, and Jesus knew that His hour had come. As He foreshadows the passion of the Cross, Thomas asks a question. "Lord, we do not know where You are going. How can we know the way?" * All this time, Thomas had been with the Lord Jesus, and yet he had not believed. In all his doubting, it was Christ Himself Who was the way to the Father.

Isn't it interesting that the very answers to life's biggest questions are often right in front of us?

Let wisdom teach us that the pathway to God is a narrow way. If we are to truly know Jesus, then we must come on His exclusive terms. Our society has sought to broaden the way to eternal life. In response, we must be bold in preaching the narrow way of the Cross.

———————◇———————

*Father, You have marked out a single way for me to know You. I must choose life in Your Son if I am to be saved. Help me not to bow the knee to the god of this post-modern world, but rather submit myself to Your Word.*

*I pray these things in Jesus' name. Amen.*

*John 14:5

# JESUS IS THE TRUE VINE

"I am the true vine, and my Father is the vinedresser."

John 15:1

## WHERE DOES OUR TRUE STRENGTH LIE?

In the Old Testament, Yahweh had likened Israel to a vineyard. The nation flourished under His watchful eye, but when Israel decided to turn its back on God, rather than producing fruit, the nation produced thorns and thistles instead.

Though things looked bleak, Yahweh would offer hope to His people. He established a new covenant with the house of Israel. "After those days," says the Lord, "I will put My law in their minds, and write it on their hearts; and I will be their God, and they shall be My people." *

Jesus established a New Covenant with His people. This would not be written on tablets of stone, but rather on tablets of flesh.

The promise of this covenant has been received in these last days. All those, who have received this covenant, remain united to Him by faith. It is in Him that we are kept for the glory which awaits us. Therefore, let us not rely on the arm of the flesh, but be ever rooted and strengthened in Him.

Jesus said, "I am the vine; you are the branches. Whoever abides in Me and I in him, he it is that bears much fruit, for apart from Me you can do nothing."

◆———————◇———————◆

*Father, I am under Your constant care. Help me to abide daily in Christ so that my life would yield the fruit of the Spirit. *

*I pray these things in Jesus' name. Amen.*

*Jeremiah 31:33, John 15:5, Galatians 5:22

# JESUS IS MERCIFUL

"Father, forgive them, for they know not what they do."
Luke 23:34

## WHAT PERCEPTION DO YOU HAVE OF CHRIST?

Our society has turned the Cross into a noble thing, but what really happened to our Lord was anything but noble.

He went to the Cross, not as a hero, but as a perceived criminal. Isaiah tells us that He was numbered with the transgressors.* Yet Jesus did not revile His persecutors. In an hour of betrayal and injustice He interceded for them. His desire was for mercy instead of judgment.

In like manner, we also share in the disgrace of His betrayers. Our condemnation before God was just, but instead of justice Jesus met us with mercy. This is a timeless eternal truth. Let us, who have received mercy, also seek to be merciful to others.

---

*Father, we have committed the ultimate betrayal against You, but You have shown us kindness. I thank You that You don't deal with us according to our sins,\* but rather for being merciful. Help us to show the same kindness and compassion to others.*

*I pray these things in Jesus' name. Amen.*


*Isaiah 53:12, Psalm 103:10

# JESUS BORE OUR SIN

And about the ninth hour Jesus cried out with a loud voice saying,
"Eli, Eli, lama sabachthani!" that is,
'My God, my God, why have you forsaken me?
Matthew 27:46

## WHO BORE OUR SIN?

Jesus is quoting Psalm 22 when David cried out to Yahweh for deliverance. It is a most prophetic cry.

Could the Son of Man really not know why the Father had forsaken Him?

Oh, the agony of agonies! God turned away from His only begotten Son. His wrath towards us is gone, and now we enjoy His peace. This was the very culmination of David's prophecy. He became sin for us * and endured the wrath of God in our place. Jesus, our Sin-bearer, fulfilled both the Law and the Prophets.

In light of this truth, let us reflect upon the Gospel with a heart of gratitude for the great things which Jesus has done for us.

---

*Father, it humbles me to consider the great lengths to which Jesus suffered in my place. Thank You for making a way for me to delight in You. Help me to keep the Gospel close to my heart always.*

*I pray these things in Jesus' name. Amen.*

*2 Corinthians 5:21

FEBRUARY 24

# JESUS IS GRACIOUS

And He said to him, "Truly I say to you,
today you will be with me in paradise."
Matthew 23:46

## WHAT IS UNMERITED FAVOR?

Consider the thief on the Cross. He was a convicted criminal who had
nothing to offer Jesus. In desperation he called over to our faithful Master
with these words: "Lord, remember me when You come into Your kingdom." *

How ironic that two criminals were near to Jesus, but only one had been
truly convicted of their sins. This thief, however, had seen his sin for what
it really was, and in faith he looked just a few feet away to our Lord. In
this man's lowest hour, he had been met with the compassion and recep-
tion of Christ. Though he hung convicted of his crimes, he was no longer
condemned.

All of us are unworthy of the kindness of God, but He extends that same
favor to us. Look to Jesus and call to Him. Remember the grace Jesus has
shown us, and now, extend that same grace toward others.

---

*Father, I thank You for Your grace. You have uttered these words of kindness
to me: "Truly, I say to you, today you will be with me in paradise." * Help me
to extend that same grace toward others.*

*I pray these things in Jesus' name. Amen.*

*Luke 23:42, Matthew 23:46

# JESUS WAS OBEDIENT

Then Jesus, calling out with a loud voice, said, "Father, into Your hands I commit my spirit!" And having said this he breathed His last.
Luke 23:46

## WHAT IS THE PATHWAY TO TRUE FREEDOM?

Darkness had hovered over the land. Our Lord had been hanging on the Cross, where He would remain for the next three hours. In the ninth hour He utters these words: "Father, into Your hands I commit my spirit!" *

Though Jesus possessed all power in heaven and earth, He submitted Himself to the will of the Father. This He did not do begrudgingly, but willingly.

The true test of obedience comes in the moment of crisis. In spite of the anguish of my circumstances, can I commit all things to Him? There is freedom when I trust that God's ways are safest and best. In light of the Cross, let us submit all our ways into the loving hands of our Father.

---

*Father, I know not what life may bring, but I know that You are a loving God. In both good and adversity, I will commit my ways to You. I thank You for Your wise and loving direction in my life.*

*I pray these things in Jesus' name. Amen.*

*Luke 23:46

# JESUS IS COMPASSIONATE

Then He said to the disciple, "Behold, your mother!"
And from that hour the disciple took her to his own home.
John 19:27

## DOES GOD REALLY CARE?

We read about a most interesting exchange between Christ and His mother. "Woman, behold your son." * Even in His suffering He had not neglected the care of Mary. Our Lord committed her to John. Then He immediately gives charge to His disciple: "Behold, your mother!" *

These are words of great care.

Even in His darkest hour, Jesus did not neglect His compassion towards His mother. The Son of Man cares for others and loves not His soul unto death.

Dear reader, do you doubt the kindness of God? If so, then meditate on this faithful passage, because Jesus has great compassion and cares for you.

———————◇———————

*Father, You are a benevolent God Who cares for Your own. In all circumstances of life help me not to doubt Your great compassion for me.*

*I pray these things in Jesus' name. Amen.*

*John 19:26, John 19:27

# JESUS FULFILLED ALL PROPHECY

After this, Jesus, knowing that all was now finished,
said (to fulfill the Scriptures), "I thirst."
John 19:28

## WHY DOES JOHN ADD THIS DIALOGUE BETWEEN JESUS AND THE SOLDIERS?

We are told that it was "to fulfill the Scriptures." Our beloved King David had uttered a prophetic word in Psalm 69. "They gave me sour wine to drink." *

Is this not the Messiah of Whom the Old Testament prophets speak?

The sour wine from the sponge must have been a most bitter taste, but Christ was up to the task. Our Savior partook of the bitter cup of God's wrath, and procured salvation for His people. He has gone before us, and we are now secure in Him.

Let our understanding of prophecy help us gain a better understanding of Christ.

———————◆———————

*Father, what a marvel Your Word is to us! There are over 300 Old Testaments prophecies, and Your Son has fulfilled them all. Let not the root of unbelief take up residence in our hearts, but rather help us to believe on the Lord Jesus Christ.*

*I pray these things in Jesus' name. Amen.*

*Psalm 69:21

# JESUS IS FAITHFUL

When Jesus had received the sour wine, he said, "It is finished,"
and he bowed his head and gave up his spirit.

John 19:30

## WHAT DID CHRIST ACCOMPLISH THROUGH THE ATONEMENT?

In Jesus' last words, He finished the work of our salvation. His atonement has procured the redemption of an innumerable amount of sinners.

The requirements of the Law that were against us were satisfied through Him. Thus, the mission did not conclude in failure, but rather all which the Father had given to Jesus were saved.

Avoid any line of thought that makes the salvation of sinners only possible. Jesus is faithful.

Dear friend, do you doubt the totality of Christ's saving work for sinners? If so, then consider the very words of this text. Our salvation is not incomplete, but rather "It is finished!"

---

*Father, Your Son has not failed. Your righteous Servant has justified many. Thank You for securing my redemption through Your Son.*

*I pray these things in Jesus' name. Amen.*

# MARCH
## WHO IS THE HOLY SPIRIT?

There is a lot of controversy regarding the Person of the Holy Spirit.

We are a people who swing on the pendulum of extremes, but the church wouldn't be what it is today without this third Person of the Trinity.

J.I. Packer, in his book, *Knowing God*, [3] has some interesting things to say about the Holy Spirit. He says, "Why, were it not for the work of the Holy Spirit there would be no gospel, no faith, no church, no Christianity in the world at all." The Holy Spirit instructs us and empowers us for the advancement of the Kingdom.

The church relies heavily on the work of their Comforter.

As you read through these reflections, I want you to consider both the character and the works of the Holy Spirit. In the midst of all the noise regarding Him, my prayer is that you will allow Scripture to have the final word.

# THE SPIRIT'S VOICE

Therefore, as the Holy Spirit says, "Today, if you hear his voice."
Hebrews 3:7

## HOW DOES THE SPIRIT GUIDE US?

There are many different points of view on the guidance of the Holy
Spirit, but Scripture teaches that when the Spirit of truth comes, He will
guide us into all the truth, for He will not speak on His own authority,
but whatever He hears He will speak, and He will declare to you the
things that are to come. *

The writer to the Hebrews is admonishing us to obedience. We are
instructed by the Holy Spirit in the here and the now. The emphasis is
placed on "today." If we are to heed the words of Christ, then it must be
in the present moment.

Many neglect the Spirit's voice to the peril of their own soul. How many
souls, who seemed committed to the cause of Christ, have drifted away
from the faith? If we are to grow in godliness, then we must be quick to
receive the Spirit's instruction.

Let us put away all sloth and apathy, and keep a sensitive ear to the Holy
Spirit's instruction.

---

*Father, You have not left us as orphans. We have a Helper Who goes before us
and He teaches us all things. Deliver us from the dangers of spiritual apathy,
and empower us to walk in the wisdom of Your Word.*

*I pray these things in Jesus' name. Amen.*

*John 16:13

# THE SPIRIT IS ALWAYS WITH US

Where shall I go from your Spirit?
Or where shall I flee from your presence?
Psalm 139:7

## WHERE SHALL I GO FROM YOUR SPIRIT?

David asks a profound question. The same all-knowing Lord is also the ever-present One. I cannot flee from the presence of God.

Notice how David mentions the Spirit of God in this verse. How often do we pause and reflect on the Person of the Holy Spirit? This often-neglected Person shines a spotlight on the inward man, and brings to light the hidden things of darkness and will disclose the purposes of the heart.*

Can anyone hide himself in secret places, "So I shall not see him?" says the Lord; "Do I not fill heaven and earth?" says the Lord.

There are no deeds which sinful man can do in secret. He, Who is absolutely God, is the all- knowing and ever-present One. Let our hearts be so very tender and open to the conviction of the Holy Spirit.

———◆———

*Father, I often neglect to reflect on the Person and work of the Holy Spirit. Your Helper sees all things and remains with me always. Help me to remain open and sensitive to the conviction He brings to my heart.*

*I pray these things in Jesus' name. Amen.*

*Jeremiah 23:24, 1 Corinthians 4:5

# THE SPIRIT KNOWS ALL THINGS

These things God has revealed to us through the Spirit.
For the Spirit searches everything, even the depths of God.

1 Corinthians 2:10

## WHO HAS COMPREHENDED THE THINGS OF GOD?

This is a task which no mere mortal can accomplish. The wisdom of God is of a different quality all together. Man, in his learning, would have never conceived the wisdom of the Cross. It is a great mystery, which can only be comprehended by the Divine.

Paul tells the Corinthians that the Holy Spirit not only searches the depths, but also reveals these things to man. For who knows a person's thoughts except the spirit of that person, which is in him? So also no one comprehends the thoughts of God except the Spirit of God. *Accordingly, we are instructed not to trust in the wisdom man, but rather to look to the wisdom of God.

Dear friend, have you sought the Lord for the wisdom that you need? Let us rely on the Holy Spirit Who makes us wise unto salvation. *

---

*Father, the Cross is foolish to those who are perishing.* Let us not rely on man, but rather feed on Your Word. Help us to remain in the wisdom that the Holy Spirit has revealed to us.

*I pray these things in Jesus' name. Amen.*

*1 Corinthians 2:11, 2 Timothy 3:15, 1 Corinthians 1:18

# THE SPIRIT IS HOLY

Now when they heard this they were cut to the heart, and said to Peter
and the rest of the Apostles, "Brothers, what shall we do?"

Acts 2:37

## WHAT IS THE PRIMARY MINISTRY OF THE HOLY SPIRIT?

Peter, after being filled with the Holy Spirit, preached one of the most
powerful sermons recorded in Scripture. The book of Acts tells us that
many, after hearing this sermon, were cut to the heart.*

Pentecost had arrived, but this was no normal feast day. The Promise of
the Father had been poured out on the church.

It is from this point on that we see testimony after testimony of the
power of God in the disciples' ministries. What led to the radical trans-
formation in the lives of many? It was the work of the Holy Spirit that
convicted these men and women of their sins and brought them to Jesus.
Many centuries have come and gone, but it is still the Spirit Who works
real and lasting holiness in the saints.

In a day and age where many look to signs and wonders, we are reminded
that the Holy Spirit's primary work is to convict the world of sin, righteousness, and judgment. Let our hearts dwell more fully on the nature
and work of the Spirit's holiness.

———————◇———————

*Father, how often do I forget to dwell on the nature and work of the Holy
Spirit? He has been given to us so that Your church would bear the fruit of His
ministry. Help me to have a heart that remains sensitive to His primary work.*

*I pray these things in Jesus' name. Amen.*

*Acts 2:37

# THE SPIRIT IS ALL POWERFUL

All these (gifts) are empowered by one and the same Spirit,
who apportions to each one individually as He wills.
1 Corinthians 12:11

## WHO GIVES SPIRITUAL GIFTS TO THE CHURCH?

The Apostle Paul tells us that it is the Holy Spirit Who has provided these gifts to the saints. Notice how the Spirit "apportions" these gifts "as He wills."

There is no work of God that has ever been accomplished by the will of man.

The Holy Spirit possesses all power, both in heaven and on earth, to bring forth His sovereign purposes. We, as the bride of Christ, are the recipients of His good and perfect gifts. Therefore, we are to give all glory for the church's ministry to God alone. Let us not boast in our gifts, but remember that all our gifts are empowered to us by the Holy Spirit.

---

*Father, all that the church possesses is given to her from above. Your Spirit has sovereignly bestowed all gifts to the saints. Help us not to get puffed up through empty deceit, but rather ascribe all glory and honor to You.*

*I pray these things in Jesus' name. Amen.*

# THE SPIRIT IS ETERNAL

How much more will the blood of Christ, Who through the eternal Spirit offered Himself without blemish to God, purify our conscience from dead works to serve the living God.

Hebrews 9:14

## HOW CAN WE FATHOM ETERNITY?

The author of Hebrews admonishes his readers not to dwell in the types and shadows of the Old Covenant since the animal sacrifices offered up by Aaron served only as a temporal covering for sin. These ordinances possessed no remaining qualities. For this reason, we are instructed to dwell on the eternal nature of Christ's priesthood.

It was through the eternal Spirit that Christ offered Himself. His offering was not a temporal solution, but one which remains forevermore. Each Person of the Trinity plays a key role in our salvation. The Holy Spirit, Who is fully God, worked in perfect harmony with the Father and the Son.

We possess an eternal covenant based on the sure promises of Yahweh. Therefore, let us not remember our former sins, but rejoice in our complete salvation.

---

*Father, in Your eternal decrees, You have made a way for sinners to be reconciled to You. It was Christ, Who through the eternal Spirit, offered Himself for us. Let our hearts spring up with thanksgiving because our sins have been removed from us forevermore.*

*I pray these things in Jesus' name. Amen.*

# THE SPIRIT IS OUR CREATOR

The earth was without form and void, and darkness was over the face of the deep. And the Spirit of God was hovering over the face of the waters.

Genesis 1:2

## WHO HAS BREATHED LIFE INTO MAN?

In reflecting upon the creation of all things, it is the Spirit Who has breathed life into the nostrils of man. In the beginning of time, the Spirit was there "hovering over the face of the waters." This often-neglected Person of the Trinity, arrayed in all His glory, was present at the Creation of the worlds.

He Who brings about physical life has also given us spiritual life.

Every word spoken out of the mouth of God is inspired by Him. All Scripture is breathed out by God and profitable for teaching, for reproof, for correction, and for training in righteousness, that the man of God may be complete, equipped for every good work.*

It is through the God- breathed Scriptures that we find life-giving words. Let us pause for a moment and dwell on the Holy Spirit's work in both our creation and redemption.

---

*Father, Your Spirit has breathed life into my very soul. I thank You for my existence, and for Your life-giving Spirit. Help me to rely daily on the Spirit and Your Word.*

*I pray these things in Jesus' name. Amen.*

*2 Timothy 3:16-17

# THE SPIRIT WHO REGENERATES US

He saved us, not because of works done by us in righteousness,
but according to his own mercy, by the washing of regeneration
and renewal of the Holy Spirit.

Titus 3:5

## WHERE WOULD WE BE WITHOUT THE GOSPEL?

Paul is writing to believers who were under attack by false teachings. There were men who crept in amongst them that placed a strong emphasis on circumcision. This caused division and quarrels amongst the Cretan believers.

The Apostle reminds them of their identity in Christ.

Their sins have been washed away, and now they are renewed through the Holy Spirit. They are no longer those who walk around in anger or strife, but those who bear the marks of patience and love.

Many centuries have been removed, but nothing has changed. All of us used to walk in the passions of our lust, but now we have been regenerated through the Spirit of God. We are not to walk in darkness, but rather we are to walk in a manner worthy of our calling * and bear the fruit of the Holy Spirit.

---

*Father, it is Your Holy Spirit Who has applied the benefits of Christ's redemption to my soul. I am a new man in Christ. Help me not to walk in my former sins, but to walk in newness of life.\**

*I pray these things in Jesus' name. Amen.*

*Colossians 1:10, Romans 6:4

# THE SPIRIT WHO RESURRECTS US

If the Spirit of Him who raised Jesus from the dead will also give life to your mortal bodies through His Spirit who dwells in you.

Romans 8:11

## WHAT PURPOSE DOES THE LAW OF GOD SERVE?

Paul has been working tirelessly to show how hopeless our condition is before a Holy God. He has been building a case against a works-righteousness system. The Apostle's point is simply this: it is absolutely impossible to find salvation in the Law. The problem is not with the Law of Moses, but rather the problem lies within the heart of man.

Consequently, we need a Law that is written on the heart.

It is the Spirit of God Who gives life and renews our hearts. The Christian, who once hated the righteousness of God, now delights in it. All of this is made possible through the gracious gift of the Gospel.

This sets our minds at ease since we are no longer enemies of God. The Holy Spirit is now with us in all seasons of life. Dear soul, do you find yourself at war with God? If so, consider the benefits of the gospel of peace, and submit yourself under the instruction of the Holy Spirit.

*Father, I am no longer under the curse of the Law. Through faith, I have been raised by the Holy Spirit. Help me to continually rely on the Spirit in my battle against sin.*

*I pray these things in Jesus' name. Amen.*

# THE SPIRIT WHO DWELLS WITHIN US

Do you not know that you are God's temple
and that God's Spirit dwells in you?
1 Corinthians 3:16

## WHAT WAS THE SIGNIFICANCE OF THE TEMPLE?

It was God's dwelling place amongst the children of Israel.

Paul uses the temple as a means of illustration when addressing the church at Corinth. The Corinthian believers were a mess. Divisions over teachers caused arguments and contentions, so Paul reminds them that they are now the spiritual temple where the Holy Spirit dwells.*

In light of this truth, the Apostle warns them against philosophies that contradicted the wisdom of God. True wisdom brings unity amongst the saints.

Dear Christian, consider your manner of conduct before others. Are you striving to maintain the unity of peace? If not, then call to mind how you are the dwelling place of the Holy Spirit. Let us, as believers, pursue that pure and peaceable wisdom which is from above.*

---

*Father, my body is a temple of the Holy Spirit. Help me to fill it with the godly wisdom of Your Word.*

*I pray these things in Jesus' name. Amen.*

*1 Corinthians 6:19, James 3:17

# THE SPIRIT OF HONOR

Go therefore and make disciples of all the nations, baptizing them in the name of the Father, and of the Son, and of the Holy Spirit.

Matthew 28:19

## WHERE DOES THE CHURCH RECEIVE HER AUTHORITY?

The church is commissioned by the Lord Jesus Christ Himself.

In His last recorded words in Matthew's gospel, our Lord does three things. First He makes a declaration about Himself. "All authority in heaven and on earth has been given to me."* Next, He gives a command. "Go therefore and make disciples of all nations, baptizing them in the name of the Father, and of the Son, and of the Holy Spirit, teaching them to observe all things that I have commanded you."* Finally, He offers His disciples encouragement. "And behold, I am with you always, to the end of the age."*

The saints have been given the blessing of the Triune God. All honor and glory is ascribed not only to the Father, but also to the Son and to the Holy Spirit. We have been entrusted with the message of the Cross, and we are commanded to share it with all peoples. So don't be afraid to share the good news, but always remember that the Triune God is with you always.

———————◆———————

*Father, You have given us a wonderful message of hope. Help us to be faithful in preaching the Gospel to those who are in need.*

*I pray these things in Jesus' name. Amen.*

*Matthew 28:18, Matthew 28:19, Matthew 28:20

# THE SPIRIT OF UNITY

Now there are varieties of gifts, but the same Spirit.
1 Corinthians 12:4

## WHO GIVES THE CHURCH HER SPIRITUAL GIFTS?

There were disputes among the Corinthian believers over spiritual gifts. Paul reminded them that they are unified in the Spirit of these gifts. For by one Spirit we were all baptized into one body.*

The purpose of my gifting is not to be used for my selfish ambitions, but for the service of others. It is the glory of God which should fuel my motivation. The same Spirit, Who gives willingly, also loves the church. The Holy Spirit apportions various gifts to the church for the building up of the body of Christ.

Are you using your gifts for the benefit of others or do you harbor pride and selfish ambition? Let us be those who do not seek to use our gifts for our own benefit, but rather for the edification of others.

---

*Father, You have blessed many members of Your church with a variety of gifts. Help me to use my gifts for the building up of others.*

*I pray these things in Jesus' name. Amen.*

*1 Corinthians 12:13

# THE SPIRIT OF INSPIRATION

For no prophecy was ever produced by the will of man, but men spoke from God as they were carried along by the Holy Spirit.

2 Peter 1:21

## WHAT IS YOUR VIEW OF SCRIPTURE?

There has been much discussion over the idea of continuing revelation, but God has already spoken through the oracles of Scripture.

The words of life have been given to us through the inspiration of the Holy Spirit. Therefore, we must give earnest heed to the things that are written down for our instruction.* In the *1689 London Baptist Confession*, we read, "The Holy Scripture is the only sufficient, certain, and infallible rule of all saving knowledge."[4]

Do you prize the Scriptures as God's spoken word? It is a dangerous practice to veer away from what has already been revealed to us. In light of this eternal truth, let us open our Bibles with the expectation of hearing what the Spirit says, which has already been written down for our learning.

◆———————◆———————◆

*Father, You have provided me all things that pertain to life and godliness.* *
*Help me to live and feed off of Your Word.*

*I pray these things in Jesus' name. Amen.*

*Hebrews 2:1, 2 Peter 1:3

# THE SPIRIT OF INSTRUCTION

"But the Helper, the Holy Spirit, whom the Father will send in my name, He will teach you all things and bring to your remembrance all that I have said to you."

John 14:26

## WHO INSTRUCTS THE SAINTS?

The hour had drawn near for our Lord. Soon He would go to the Cross, but He still had many things that He wanted to teach His disciples.

Parting from loved ones is never a pleasant experience. It often brings pain and sorrow to the heart. Fortunately, our Lord brings good news to His friends. He would not leave them alone, but rather He would provide a Comforter Who would lead them into all truth.* It was imperative that the Son of Man go away, but this "goodbye" would not be for good. Soon they would be reunited with Him in glory, and there would be much reason to rejoice.

Dear soul, do not be weighed down with sorrow. Though you weep now, there will be much rejoicing in heaven.

---

*Father, You have not left us as orphans.\* You have given us a Helper Who leads us into all truth. One day we will be reunited with You and we will rejoice. Help us not to sorrow but to take comfort in the certainties of Your promises.*

*I pray these things in Jesus' name. Amen.*

*John 16:13, John 14:18

# THE SPIRIT'S WITNESS

"But when the Helper comes, whom I will send to you from the Father,
the Spirit of truth, who proceeds from the Father,
He will bear witness about Me."
John 15:26

## HOW CAN A CLAIM BE AUTHENTICATED?

The Pharisees had rejected the claims of Christ, and we read that they hated Jesus without a cause.* The Pharisees were not of God because they did not believe on the Son Who was sent.* Yet there was plenty of evidence to authenticate the claims of our Lord.

For there are three that bear witness in heaven: the Father, the Word, and the Holy Spirit; and these three are one.* The Holy Spirit, along with the other witnesses, substantiates the claims of Christ. The Spirit not only bears witness, but He empowers the church to bear witness to an unbelieving world. We, who are called, have His witness that we are children of God. Let us therefore proclaim, with boldness and power, the Gospel to all nations.

---

*Father, You have provided us with a powerful testimony. It is Your Spirit Who bears witness, not only to the unbelieving world, but also through the special calling of Your own. Help me to be a bold witness to an unbelieving world.*

*I pray these things in Jesus' name. Amen.*

*John 15:25, John 6:40, 1 John 5:7

# THE SPIRIT IS OUR HELPER

"And I will ask the Father, and He will give you another Helper,
to be with you forever,"
John 14:16

## WHO WILL HELP US?

The hour of trial had been rapidly approaching, and soon Jesus would go to the Cross. He had told His disciples that He would have to go away, but this left them puzzled. They had been with our Lord throughout His ministry. Where could Jesus be going? This naturally led to many questions, and it is through His dialogue with the disciples that He offers a wonderful promise.

Jesus would not leave the disciples unattended, but would rather give them a Helper. The Holy Spirit would be given to them, and He would be with them always. He would instruct and empower the church for the work of the ministry. This promise remains to this very day.

The church has been given a great Helper Who leads her into all truth. He is amongst us in the assembly and the Spirit indwells each and every one of us.

Dear soul, do you find yourself lacking wisdom? If so, then do not fear. You have a perfect Helper Who will lead you into all truth.

*Father, You are a good God Who is with your children always. Help us not to fret in times of perplexity or difficulty. Let us be reminded that we have a great Helper Who leads us into all truth.*

*I pray these things in Jesus' name. Amen.*

# THE SPIRIT'S WORK

"And when He comes He will convict the world concerning
sin and righteousness and judgment."
John 16:8

## HOW DOES THE HOLY SPIRIT TESTIFY OF CHRIST?

The Jews had rejected their Messiah, because they did not believe the testimony of the Law and the Prophets. They wanted an earthly kingdom to overthrow Rome, but Jesus came for a more pressing matter. There was a far more oppressive enemy that had to be overthrown.

Sin has separated us from fellowship with God, and a King is needed to liberate all people from its power. The Kingdom of God is spiritual. It cannot be entered into by flesh and blood. In order for a person to enter into that Kingdom, the Holy Spirit must reveal to him or her the righteousness of God. A person must see their sin for what it really is and acknowledge Christ as the Holy and Just One. It is Jesus Who will judge all mankind according to their deeds.

Dear friend, do you have loved ones who will not believe your report? Do not lose heart, but remember that it is the Holy Spirit Who needs to do a work in their heart.

———————◇———————

*Father, it can be discouraging to see our evangelism fall on deaf ears. Help us not to lose heart, but remember that it is the Holy Spirit's work to convict them of their sin.*

*I pray these things in Jesus' name. Amen.*

# THE SPIRIT OF TRUTH

"Even the Spirit of truth, Whom the world cannot receive, because it
neither sees Him nor knows Him. You know Him,
for He dwells with you and will be in you."
John 14:17

## HOW CAN WE COME TO KNOW THE TRUTH OF GOD?

We can only come to know the truth if we have the Spirit of God dwelling
within us. He is the Spirit of truth Who bears witness to the testimony
of Jesus. Apart from His witness we cannot know the way of eternal life.

The world has rejected the Gospel, because it has not known the One
Who was sent. If we are to be acquainted with Jesus then we must be
born again. It is the Spirit Who illuminates our darkened minds to the
things of God. Only through Him will my eyes be opened to see and
understand the way of eternal life. Daily, we need to rely on the Holy
Spirit for understanding as we open the Scriptures.

---

*Father, You have given us the Spirit of truth and He testifies to the
words of Christ. Help me to know Him daily as I seek to better understand
Your Word.*

*I pray these things in Jesus' name. Amen.*

# DO NOT GRIEVE THE HOLY SPIRIT

Do not quench the Spirit.
1 Thessalonians 5:19

## HOW CAN I, AS A BELIEVER, GROW IN GRACE?

In order for me to grow in grace I must yield moment by moment to the Holy Spirit. The working out of what God has worked in me happens in the practical living out of everyday life. In every circumstance, which God orchestrates, can I demonstrate the power of the Holy Spirit to an unbelieving world?

Here we are instructed not to quench or grieve the Holy Spirit. If I do not walk in a manner that pleases God then I will grieve Him. When that happens, I have deviated from the way of wisdom, and the voice of God is tuned out.

Dear friend, have you ignored the instruction of the Holy Spirit? If so, then submit yourself to Him as you open the pages of Scripture, and He will direct your steps.*

---

*Father, You have given us a Helper for our benefit. It is wise to receive His instruction. Let us not harden our hearts, but rather receive His godly counsel. I pray these things in Jesus' name. Amen.*

*Proverbs 3:6

# THE HOLY SPIRIT'S GUIDANCE

And they went through the region of Phrygia and Galatia, having been forbidden by the Holy Spirit to speak the word in Asia.

Acts 16:6

## WHAT IS THE PURPOSE OF A CLOSED DOOR?

Paul had a desire to minister in Asia, but the Holy Spirit had forbidden it. Instead, Paul is given a vision to go to Macedonia. It was there that the Spirit did an amazing work of God in the hearts of many.

The providence of God plays a key role in our everyday lives.

Often times we will be led down a seemingly strange path, but it is the Holy Spirit Who has orchestrated our steps. The purposes of God have not been thwarted. He is working out His perfect plan, and He asks us to trust Him. Will we remain flexible and open to His leading or will we harden our hearts in unbelief? In light of this truth, let us trust that God's ways are safest and best.

---

*Father, I thank You for Your all-wise guidance in my life. Help me to trust that, in all circumstances, Your ways are perfect.*

*I pray these things in Jesus' name. Amen.*

# THE HOLY SPIRIT'S JOY

But the fruit of the Spirit is love, joy, peace,
patience, kindness, goodness, faithfulness.
Galatians 5:22

## WHAT IS THE KEY TO HAVING JOY?

Paul mentions joy as a fruit of the Spirit. There is a well for the Christian, which is always full. Those, who are filled with the Holy Spirit, will find a continual supply of satisfaction. This joy does not exempt us from trials, but rather it is rooted in the very life of Christ. In spite of the circumstances that surround us, we can have fullness of joy in the Holy Spirit.

Dear friend, do you experience this kind of joy in your life? This joy can be yours if you seek after it with all your heart. In light of this truth, let our hearts yearn for the living waters which satisfy, not merely for a moment, but forevermore.

———————◆———————

*Father, You have given us life so that we can have it more abundantly. There is unyielding joy that is given to us in the Holy Spirit. Help us not to look for satisfaction in any other, but to draw waters from the wells of salvation.\**

*I pray these things in Jesus' name. Amen.*

*Isaiah 12:3

# THE HOLY SPIRIT'S BAPTISM

For in one Spirit we were all baptized into one body—Jews or Greeks, slaves or free——and all were made to drink of one Spirit.

1 Corinthians 12:13

## WHAT IS THE CHURCH?

While there are many layers to that question, the church is simply those who are redeemed by the blood of the Lamb. Yet we are not redeemed merely to remain isolated, but to dwell in community with one another.

The Corinthian Church had been given over to many controversies concerning spiritual gifts, but Paul reminds them that they were all baptized into one body.* As it was in Paul's day, so it is in ours. There are many differing opinions on the baptism of the Holy Spirit, but in reality, we are baptized into one body when we are united to Christ by faith. This union with Christ makes us brothers and sisters and we need to worship the Lord together in the unity of peace.

---

*Father, we are one in the Spirit and baptized into the same body. Let me dwell with others in unity as I use my gifts for the benefit of others.*

*I pray these things in Jesus' name. Amen.*

*1 Corinthians 12:13

# THE SWORD OF THE SPIRIT

And take the helmet of salvation, and the sword of the Spirit,
which is the word of God.

Ephesians 6:17

## WHAT IS THE CHRISTIAN'S WEAPON OF CHOICE?

In mentioning armor, Paul likens the Word of God to a sword. It is the weapon that we must wield if we are going to win the battle against the lies of the Devil. It is the Spirit Who operates through the Word of God to bring about the salvation of sinners.

Our warfare is won, not in the arm of the flesh, but in the power of the Holy Spirit.

Dear friend, do you prepare yourself for the lies of the Devil with the truth of God's Word? Be encouraged to fight against sin, the world, and the Devil by echoing these faithful words, "It is written...."*

---

*Father, our warfare is spiritual and it can only be fought in Your strength. Help me to leverage the Word of God in my fight against the Devil.*

*I pray these things in Jesus' name. Amen.*

*Luke 4:8

# THE SPIRIT OF WISDOM

That the God of our Lord Jesus Christ, the Father of glory, may give
you the Spirit of wisdom and of revelation in the knowledge of Him.
Ephesians 1:17

## WHO PUTS WISDOM INTO THE HEART OF MAN?

The mysteries of the Gospel are too deep for the natural man to comprehend. Only through the illumination of the Holy Spirit can I even begin
to marvel at the Cross.

Paul prayed that the eyes of our hearts will be enlightened.*

All of Divine wisdom, which is in the Father and the Son, is also in the
Holy Spirit. It is the Spirit Who opens our eyes to the wisdom of God.
Therefore, search out the deep things that God has concealed through the
power of Him Who calls us out of darkness and into marvelous light.*

———————————

*Father, the mysteries of Your will are a great deep. Thank You for giving us
Your Helper, Who is the Spirit of wisdom, to help us know You better. Help
me to pursue and prize godly wisdom above all else.*

*I pray these things in Jesus' name. Amen.*

*Ephesians 1:18; 1 Peter 2:9

# THE SPIRIT OF CHRIST

You, however, are not in the flesh but in the Spirit, if in fact the Spirit
of God dwells in you. Anyone who does not have the
Spirit of Christ does not belong to Him.

Romans 8:9

## WHO IS THE HOLY SPIRIT?

The Holy Spirit is the very Spirit of Christ Who proceeds from the Father.
If I have the Spirit dwelling inside of me, then I belong to God. Our very
spiritual life flows from the Holy Spirit.

Apart from Christ I was under condemnation. I had no power over
death, and I was under the curse of the Law. It was Jesus Who set me
free and then gave me a Helper. Through the power of the Holy Spirit, I
am able to crucify the flesh with all its sinful passions. Beloved, now that
you are free, you no longer walk in darkness, but rather walk as a child
of the light.

---

*Father, through Christ I have been set free. Your Spirit empowers me to walk
in obedience to Your Word. Help me to walk in the freedom that I now have
in Christ.*

*I pray these things in Jesus' name. Amen.*

# THE SPIRIT'S AID

Likewise the Spirit helps us in our weakness. For we do not know what
to pray for as we ought, but the Spirit Himself intercedes
for us with groanings too deep for words.

Romans 8:26

## WHAT COMFORT CAN I TAKE IN SUFFERINGS?

Paul writes to encourage believers to take heart in present trials. He does
this by appealing to two things: our future glory and the presence of
God. We, as believers, do not suffer as those who have no hope. The God
Who orchestrates all things is not only for us, but He is also with us.
The Holy Spirit gives aid in our weakness and He intercedes for us with
perfect wisdom.

Ultimately, we can rest assured that God will never leave us nor forsake
us.*

Dear Christian, are you weighed down with unimaginable grief? If
so, then take heart. You have a Helper Who is a mighty intercessor on
your behalf.

---

*Father, the trials of life tend to overwhelm me. Thank You for providing a
Comforter Who aids in my sorrows. Let me not despair, but rather take heart
in Your faithfulness.*

*I pray these things in Jesus' name. Amen.*

*Hebrews 13:5

# THE SPIRIT OF LOVE

And hope does not put us to shame, because God's love has been
poured into our hearts through the Holy Spirit
Who has been given to us.
Romans 5:5

## HOW CAN I KNOW THAT GOD LOVES ME?

Trials can cause us to question the character of God, but Paul reminds us that His love for us has been poured into our hearts, through the Holy Spirit. We have been given a Comforter Who illuminates our minds to the great love of God.

For while we were still weak, at the right time Christ died for the ungodly. For one will scarcely die for a righteous person—though perhaps for a good person one would dare even to die—but God shows His love for us in that while we were still sinners, Christ died for us.*

The Cross was the ultimate demonstration of the love of God, and therefore, we have a hope that is rooted in His infallible character. This eternal truth helps us to not lose heart in the disappointments of life, but rather hope in the certainty of His love for us.

———————◆———————

*Father, life can be saturated with various disappointments. Help me to remember that all circumstances are orchestrated by Your loving hand.*

*I pray these things in Jesus' name. Amen.*

*Romans 5:6-8

# THE SPIRIT'S DISCERNMENT

Now the Spirit expressly says that in later times some will depart from the faith by devoting themselves to deceitful spirits and teachings of demons.
1 Timothy 4:1

## HOW CAN WE BE DISCERNING IN THIS DAY AND AGE?

There were those in Timothy's day who twisted the doctrines of Christ by leading people into blind legalism. Paul's message to the saints is clear: Be on guard against false outward religion and enjoy the freedom that you now have in Christ.

The text tells us that the Holy Spirit expressly warns the church of false teaching. The instruction, that Timothy was given, holds true for us today. We must train ourselves up in the truths of Scripture so that we can guard against the false teachings of our day. God has not left us on our own, but has given us the Holy Spirit to help us discern truth.

Subsequently, those who have their senses trained for discernment will possess a deep understanding of the Word of God.

---

*Father, the Devil seeks to twist Your truth so that he can deceive even the elect. In an age of great deception, give me an ear to hear what the Spirit of truth says to me.*

*I pray these things in Jesus' name. Amen.*

# THE SPIRIT'S INTERCESSION

And He who searches hearts knows what is the mind of the Spirit,
because the Spirit intercedes for the saints according to the will of God."
Romans 8:27

## WHO KNOWS THE MIND OF GOD?

For what man knows the things of a man except the spirit of the man which is in him? Even so no one knows the things of God except the Spirit of God.*

The frame of man is limited and subjected to weakness. In the dark stretches of our journey we need wisdom and guidance. The Holy Spirit helps us in our weakness so that we know how to pray. Our all-wise Comforter intercedes for us with a perfect understanding of God's will. We, who are weak, possess the Holy Spirit who offers up perfect petitions on our behalf.

Beloved, do you lack understanding? If so then draw strength from the Holy Spirit who comprehends all things. He, who knows the mind of God, will be your perfect Intercessor.

———————◆———————

*Father, You have given me an all mighty Comforter. He proceeds from You, and He has been given for my instruction. Help me to rely on the Holy Spirit in prayer so that my requests would align with Your will.*

*I pray these things in Jesus' name. Amen.*

*1 Corinthians 2:11

# THE SPIRIT'S AUTHORITY

Pay careful attention to yourselves and to all the flock, in which the Holy Spirit has made you overseers, to care for the church of God, which he obtained with His own blood.

Acts 20:28

## WHO RAISES UP MEN FOR THE WORK OF THE MINISTRY?

In this text, the Apostle Paul ascribes this responsibility to the Holy Spirit. This same Spirit Who apportions various gifts also ordains the office of overseer. Paul warned the elders at Ephesus to watch their conduct, and to serve the church with the utmost care, serving the Lord with all humility.* Even as Paul did not account his life of any value, but only wanted to finish his course and the ministry that he received from the Lord Jesus, to testify to the gospel of the grace of God.*

This is the highest honor and task given to men since it is no small matter to oversee the very people of God.

Dear friend, pray for your elders and deacons. Be on your knees for them because they need wisdom to lead the flock with care. Let us, who are under the watchful care of our elders, submit to them as they submit to Christ.

---

*Father, it is no small task to oversee Your flock. Help us to honor and esteem those who watch over our very souls.*

*I pray these things in Jesus' name. Amen.*

*Acts 20:19, 24

# THE SPIRIT'S INVITATION

The Spirit and the Bride say, "Come." And let the one who hears say, "Come." And let the one who is thirsty come; let the one who desires take the water of life without price.
Revelation 22:17

## HAVE YOU ACCEPTED THE SPIRIT'S INVITATION?

The Holy Spirit invites us to come freely to the marriage supper of the Lamb. The ultimate price was paid, and our redemption is secured. We are no longer forbidden to come, but rather we are invited to come and be received with open arms.

Though there are many who sleep, the hour draws near. Our Lord Jesus Christ is returning with ten thousands of His saints.* He comes to judge, but His reward is also with Him.*

Have you accepted the invitation of the Gospel? If not, then hear what the Spirit says to you in this text. The time is drawing near, and the Master is coming at a time when you least expect.* Listen, therefore, to the Spirit's instruction so that you can be ready when the Lord returns.

---

*Father, the hour draws near, but the invitation still remains. Help me to be a voice of truth who invites others to Your banqueting table.*

*I pray these things in Jesus' name. Amen.*

*Jude 14, Romans 2:6, Matthew 24:44

# APRIL

## WHAT ARE THE WORKS OF GOD?

Do you ever pause and wonder at the marvelous display of creation all around you? All of nature testifies to the existence of God.* In fact He did more in one verse than all of humanity has ever accomplished: In the beginning, God created the heavens and the earth.*

Yet why did He create all these things? What is the purpose of our existence? Is He far removed from His creation or does He remain involved in its existence? These are questions which man has been trying to answer throughout his history.

Fortunately for us, God did give us answers to these questions. He wrote a book called the Bible, in which He reveals to us the redemptive narrative of human history. It is hard to imagine a broken world where God is still at work. Life is filled with sorrows and unimaginable grief, but the truth is, God is at work. He is working in the affairs and the lives of all people today.

As you consider these 30 reflections in the month of April, I want you to think about how God has worked in the lives of others. My prayer is that you will also come to understand how He is also working in you.

*Romans 1:20, Genesis 1:1

# GOD CREATED THE WORLDS

In the beginning, God created the heavens and the earth.

Genesis 1:1

## HOW DID THE WORLD COME INTO BEING?

Mankind would have us to believe that the earth was a result of a cosmic bang, but Scripture declares that God spoke the worlds into existence.* We can either suppress that truth in unrighteousness or we can bow in majesty to our great God.

Dear friend, do you suppose that all things came into existence by chance? If so, consider what the Psalmist said: "The heavens declare the glory of God, and the sky above proclaims his handiwork." * Nature has given us plenty of evidence for the existence of God. For since the creation of the world, God's invisible attributes are clearly seen.*

Do not doubt, but rather believe the testimony of Scripture concerning God, who at various times and in various ways spoke in time past to the fathers by the prophets, has in these last days spoken to us by His Son, whom He has appointed heir of all things, through whom also He made the worlds.*

———————◆———————

*Father, Your hands have made all that we see. Help me to continually bow down in majesty to Your great name.*

*I pray these things in Jesus' name. Amen.*

*Psalm 33:9, Psalm 19:1, Romans 1:20, Hebrews 1:1-2

# GOD'S WISDOM IN CREATING THE WORLDS

The Lord possessed me at the beginning of His work,
the first of His acts of old.
Proverbs 8:22

## WHERE WAS WISDOM IN THE BEGINNING?

The Lord by wisdom founded the earth; by understanding he established the heavens.* God framed the worlds, and set their orbits in motion. He fashioned the stars in the heavens and fixed their galaxies. When considering these celestial lights we cannot fathom the breadth of their distance from one another. Yet at a glance, it appears that all of them are in close proximity.

One can only sense beauty when they gaze at a golden sunset or feel complete delight in making snow angels in crystal white, snow-covered mountains. We see the poetic artistry of the sea waves, and the graceful eagle as it soars high above in the sky.

Man, in all his glory, can only search out what God has gloriously concealed. Dear friend, don't let your senses be dulled to the wonders around you, but rather be moved to adoration for the King eternal, immortal, and invisible. To God who alone is wise, be honor and glory forever and ever. Amen.*

---

*Father, all of creation testifies to Your infinite wisdom. Help me not to take Your beauty for granted, but rather help me to remain in awe.*

*I pray these things in Jesus' name. Amen.*

*Proverbs 3:19, 1 Timothy 1:17

# CREATION OF MAN IN THE IMAGE OF GOD

Then God said, "Let us make man in Our image, after Our likeness."
Genesis 1:26

## WHAT IS GOD'S TESTIMONY CONCERNING MAN?

We live in a society that has reduced mankind to the beasts of the field, but man is unique in his relation to other creatures. God has created us as personal beings who were made to commune with Him.

The Genesis account tells us that Adam walked with the Lord in the cool of the day.* As an image bearer of God, he enjoyed sweet fellowship with Him. He was made to rule over the lesser creatures, and to tend to the Garden of Eden. When sin entered the world, man's fellowship with his Creator was broken. Ever since the fall, man has not placed a proper value on the sanctity of human life.

It is only through the new birth that I am able to love others with the love of Christ. In light of our glorious redemption, let us be reminded to treat others as image bearers of God.

———————◆———————

*Father, our culture does not treat one another like image bearers. In reality, the Scriptures teach that we were made in Your image.\* Help us to love one another with the love of Christ.*

*I pray these things in Jesus' name. Amen.*

*Genesis 3:8, Genesis 1:27

# CREATED MALE AND FEMALE

So God created man in His own image, in the image of God He created him; male and female He created them.
Genesis 1:27

## HOW DOES GOD IDENTIFY GENDER?

Genesis 1:27 declares that God created two genders. Humans were made to be male and female. In denying this truth, society continues to shake their fists at a Holy and good God. Yet the truth of His Word doesn't change.

In His kindness God created a helper for Adam. The creation account teaches us that God saw that it was not good for man to be alone.* The Giver of good and perfect gifts* provided a companion to be enjoyed. Yet there was also a practical purpose involving procreation. We were to be fruitful and multiply* on the earth. When we twist the gifts of God to serve our own pleasure, we do so to the peril of our own souls. Once we enjoy marriage as God truly intends it to be, a life-long covenant between a man and a woman, then we are truly blessed with a gracious gift.

Let all, who are in Christ, take a stand against the perversions of our day.

◆————————◆————————◆

*Father, You have provided genders and marriage to be a great blessing to us. Grant us much boldness so that we can face the pressures of our rebellious society.*

*I pray these things in Jesus' name. Amen.*

*Genesis 2:18, James 1:17, Genesis 1:28

# MADE TO HAVE DOMINION

And God blessed them. And God said to them,
"Be fruitful and multiply and fill the earth and subdue it,
and have dominion over the fish of the sea and over the birds of the
heavens and over every living thing that moves on the earth."
Genesis 1:28

## WHAT IS THE CREATION MANDATE?

God's original commission to mankind was to spread out and rule over the earth. This was a special honor given to mankind, and it was unique from the other creatures. God blessed and graced all of the people of the earth to watch over this celestial world.

But when sin entered into humanity, this privilege was tarnished, if not lost altogether.

Instead of being keepers of the land, man has largely polluted the world around him. Though creation has been put into futility, Christ has redeemed what had been lost through the fall. We are now looking forward to a new heavens and a new earth.* Now, the Christian waits eagerly for the return of Jesus Christ, Who shall reign forever and ever.* We, who partake in the church militant, shall reign with the church triumphant.

Dear soul, do not be dismayed by the injustices of this present life. Rather rest your hope fully on the eternal glorious rest that awaits us.

*Father, You have given us great and precious promises.* Help us to fix our eyes on Jesus, the Author and Finisher of our faith.*

*I pray these things in Jesus' name. Amen.*

*2 Peter 3:13, Revelation 11:15, 2 Peter 1:4, Hebrews 12:2

# MADE AND GIVEN PROVISION

And God said, "Behold, I have given you every plant yielding seed that is on the face of all the earth, and every tree with seed in its fruit. You shall have them for food."

Genesis 1:29

## HOW IS MAN SUSTAINED?

Man is sustained by the providence of God. He has been providing for our basic needs from the beginning of time.

In the Garden, God sustained Adam and Eve with various herbs, seeds, and fruits. These foods provided great nourishment to the body. As it was in the beginning so it is with us this day. The scope of God's providence extends to the just, and to the unjust alike. He has even ordained humanitarian efforts to feed those who lack food.

These truths should serve as a great comfort to our souls. The God, Who provided for Adam and Eve, is the God Who feeds the birds of the air. Look at the birds of the air: they neither sow nor reap nor gather into barns, and yet your heavenly Father feeds them. Are you not of more value than they?*

Beloved, do you find yourself weighed down by the cares of this life? Trust in the God Who is faithful, not only to clothe the flowers of the field,* but Who has promised to care for you.

---

*Father, You are our great Provider. In times when it seems that my resources are scarce, help me to trust that Your resources are inexhaustible.*

*I pray these things in Jesus' name. Amen.*

*Matthew 6:26, Luke 12:27

# GOD'S JUDGMENT THROUGH THE FLOOD

And God said to Noah, "I have determined to make an end
of all flesh, for the earth is filled with violence through them.
Behold, I will destroy them with the earth."

Genesis 6:13

## IS GOD SLACK CONCERNING HIS PROMISES?

Since the dawn of time, man has taken for granted the kindness and
grace of God. Noah's generation did so too, when, in their wickedness,
they tested the Lord. The earth had become corrupted with the
violence of men. In Genesis, we read that the Lord regretted that He
made man on the earth, and it grieved Him to His heart.* When the
time of testing had run its course, God opened the flood gates.

Thousands of years have passed since that catastrophic event, and people
still test the kindness and grace of God.

Folks mock and scoff, and still they have no fear of God. While judgment
has not returned to the earth, it will come at a time when it is least expected.

The Apostle Peter warns that the present heavens and earth are reserved
for fire, kept for the day of judgment and destruction of ungodly
men.* Judgment is coming. This is an eternal truth. With this in mind,
let us put off sin, and prepare ourselves for the coming of the Lord.

---

*Father, You have been patient and kind to us. You have given us plenty of time
to repent, but sadly many still make light of Your grace. The hour is rapidly
approaching when You will judge the living and the dead. Help us to put off
sloth, and prepare ourselves for the coming of the Lord.\**

*I pray these things in Jesus' name. Amen.*

*Genesis 6:6, 2 Peter 3:7, Romans 13:11

# GOD'S PRESERVATION THROUGH THE FLOOD

If He did not spare the ancient world, but preserved Noah, a herald of
righteousness, with seven others, when He brought a flood
upon the world of the ungodly…

2 Peter 2:5

## WHO WAS NOAH?

According to Peter he was a preacher of righteousness. He was also a man
upon whom the favor of God rested. Genesis tells us that Noah found
favor in the eyes of the Lord.* In an age of rampant wickedness, Noah
was a blameless and upright man.*

Though impending judgment awaited the earth, Yahweh spared this
preacher and his family.

Shall God judge the righteous with the wicked?* By no means! He has
set His seal on His chosen people, and they shall not perish. The basis of
His choosing is His own free and sovereign love. We are not elected by
our own merit, but by His grace.

Noah was a man of like passions just like us, but the Lord showed compassion towards him. In light of the kindness that God has shown us, let
us tell others of the great things that He has done for us.

*Father, You have shown me great kindness, but there is still a judgment that
awaits the unconverted. Help me to be a bold preacher of God's righteousness
in this evil and wicked generation.*

*I pray these things in Jesus' name. Amen.*

*Genesis 6:8, 9, Genesis 18:25

# SCATTERING OF THE NATIONS

*Therefore its name was called Babel, because there the Lord confused the language of all the earth. And from there the Lord dispersed them over the face of all the earth.*

Genesis 11:9

## WHY ARE THERE SO MANY LANGUAGES TODAY?

In the beginning, humans had only one language. It wasn't until the scattering of the peoples that the language was divided. This was the miraculous judgment of God upon a people who openly rebelled against His command.

When the Lord commanded people to spread out, they said, "Let us build ourselves a city and a tower with its top in the heavens, and let us make a name for ourselves, lest we be dispersed over the face of the whole earth."* They sought to build a tower that reached up to the heavens, but Yahweh's purposes would not be thwarted.

All of hell's forces, joined in one accord, shall not prevail against God. As He willed it so it was. All of the people were scattered throughout the world. In the scattering of the nations, the Lord demonstrates His omnipotence over all creation. Though man devises many wicked schemes, he shall not prevail against the Lord of hosts. None of His purposes can be frustrated.

---

*Father, at Your Word, kingdoms are divided and conquered. Your purposes remain steadfast and fixed forevermore. Thank You that the church has been united to worship You, and make Your name known amongst the earth.*

*I pray these things in Jesus' name. Amen.*

*Genesis 11:4

# WORKING THROUGH BELIEF

"I will bless those who bless you, and him who dishonors you I will curse, and in you all the families of the earth shall be blessed."

Genesis 12:3

## WHAT DOES FAITH LOOK LIKE IN ACTION?

It was no small task for Abram to leave his family and home for an unknown destination. He had no map or compass, but only the word of the Lord. Yahweh gave him the promise, and contrary to plain sight, Abram took God at His word. Genesis tells us that Abraham believed God, and it was accounted to him as righteousness.*

Abraham's testimony still speaks to us this day.

The Gospel, which was veiled in mystery, has now been made clear. All those who believe on the Lord Jesus Christ are the seed of Abraham through faith. There is no longer Jew or Gentile, slave or free, male and female. For we are all one in Christ Jesus. And now that we belong to Christ, we are the true children of Abraham. We are His heirs, and God's promise to Abraham belongs to you.*

In light of this eternal truth, let us reflect on the many blessings of God. They are more innumerable than the stars in the sky.

———◦———

*Father, You have given us a Deliverer from our sins. We too, like Abraham, are accounted righteous by faith. Help us to trust You moment by moment.*

*I pray these things in Jesus' name. Amen.*

*Romans 4:3, Galatians 3:28-29

# WORKING IN SPITE OF PRIDE

*"But for this purpose I have raised you up, to show you My power, so that My name may be proclaimed in all the earth."*

Exodus 9:16

## WHAT WAS THE PURPOSE OF THE PLAGUES OF EGYPT?

Six plagues had overtaken the land, but Pharoah's heart had grown hard. He would not let the Israelites go and worship the Lord. By the fourth plague, Pharoah's magicians could no longer duplicate God's signs that they had witnessed.

That's because this was no counterfeit operation, but rather a true work of God.

The signs and wonders in Egypt were so great that many of the Egyptians began to believe. We read later on in Exodus that the Lord caused the Egyptians to look favorably on the Israelites, and they gave the Israelites whatever they asked for.* Moreover, the man Moses was very great in the land of Egypt, in the sight of Pharoah's servants and in the sight of the people.* God's name was made known to a Gentile nation, in spite of Pharoah's rejection.

What about you, dear reader? Have you experienced the goodness of God and yet remained in unbelief? If so, then imitate the faith of those Egyptians who saw the Lord's works and believed.

---

*Father, in spite of Pharoah's rejection Your glory was made manifest in Egypt. Help us not to reject Your purpose, but rather to believe in Your promises day by day.*

*I pray these things in Jesus' name. Amen.*

*Exodus 12:36, Exodus 11:3

# WORKING THROUGH HUMILITY

And the angel of the Lord appeared to him in a flame of
fire out of the midst of a bush. He looked, and behold,
the bush was burning, yet it was not consumed.

Exodus 3:2

## HOW MAJESTIC WAS THE SIGHT OF THIS BURNING BUSH?

Engulfed in holy flames, we read that the bush was not consumed.
God was revealing Himself to Moses as He had in times past to the
ancients of old. Here was a man, Moses, who was doing anything
but the spectacular. He was tending to his father-in-law's
flocks.* This was a task that he had done faithfully for forty years!

It was D.L. Moody who rightly said, "Moses spent forty years thinking
he was a somebody; forty years learning he was a nobody; and forty years
discovering what God can do with a nobody."

We tend to look at Moses as a man of extraordinary talents, and yet God
uses ordinary men in extraordinary ways. Moses was very meek, more
than all people who were on the face of the earth.* This prophet of old
simply made himself a vessel through whom the power of God would be
displayed. Through his humility, Yahweh worked the miraculous.

Dear friend, do not look to the measure of your gift, but rather look to
the God Who empowers ordinary people.

––––––––––◇––––––––––

*Father, so often we mistake credentials for effectiveness in ministry. Let us
not grow weary in Your service, but rather trust You for the fruitfulness of our
work.*

*I pray these things in Jesus' name. Amen.*

*Exodus 3:1, Numbers 12:3

# WORKING THROUGH DEATH

At midnight the Lord struck down all the firstborn in the land of Egypt;
from the firstborn of Pharoah who sat on his throne to the firstborn of
the captive who was in the dungeon and all the firstborn of the livestock.
Exodus 12:29

## IN WHAT WAYS CAN WE, AS BELIEVERS, REMEMBER THE GREAT THINGS THAT GOD HAS DONE FOR US?

There was a terrible outcry in the land. God had killed all the firstborn
of the Egyptians. This was an inevitable outcome of unbelief in the face
of the miraculous. God had revealed signs and wonders to the Egyptians,
but Pharoah would still not let the Israelites go free.

In this final plague of death, God had instructed His people to sprinkle the
blood of a paschal lamb over the doorposts of their dwellings. Yahweh would
pass over all the houses that were sprinkled with blood, and He would spare
the Israelites' firstborn.* In order to celebrate the deliverance of the Israelites
in this way, the Lord would appoint for them a memorial feast. They would
celebrate the feast of Passover, and teach their children to do so as well.

Ultimately we see the Passover fulfilled in Christ, Who is our Passover
Lamb. Now, through the partaking of the Lord's Supper, we can remember what Christ has done for us. Let us be those who, not only remember,
but also pass down this godly heritage to our children.*

---

*Father, You have worked a great and mighty deliverance for us in Christ.
Help us to remember Jesus' work through Your Word, observe it and teach it
to our children.*

*I pray these things in Jesus' name. Amen.*

*Exodus 12:23, Exodus 12:6-27

# WORKING THROUGH THE IMPOSSIBLE

Then Moses stretched out his hand over the sea, and the Lord drove the
sea back by a strong east wind all night and made the sea dry land,
and the waters were divided.

Exodus 14:21

## IS THERE ANYTHING THAT IS TOO HARD FOR THE LORD?

The children of Israel found themselves at an impasse. Pharoah and his
army were on the pursuit, and the Israelites had no further place to run.
They were trapped between a hounding army and the Red Sea. Yet contrary to plain sight, Moses believed more in the saving power of Yahweh.

In faith, Moses stretched out his hands over the waters, and trusted the
Lord to work the miraculous. Thus, the army of Egypt was thwarted and
the Israelites crossed safely onto dry land.

In this one act, God made a way of salvation when there was no way.
Generations have passed, but our great God still works miraculously
on behalf of His people. In our great salvation, God has made a way
in Christ. Even when we were dead in our sins, He made us alive
together with Christ.* The same Lord, Who has orchestrated our salvation, has also ordained all our circumstances.

Dear soul, do you find yourself in a seemingly impossible predicament?
If so, then cast your cares in the hands of the One Who has power over
the seas. God cares for you*

---

*Father, there is nothing that is too hard for You. You are the God Who moves
seas and overpowers my enemies. Help me not to waver in unbelief, but
rather place my impossible circumstances in Your hands.*

*I pray these things in Jesus' name. Amen.*

*Ephesians 2:5, 1 Peter 5:7

# WORKING THROUGH OBEDIENCE

And when they make a long blast with the ram's horn, when you hear the sound of a trumpet, then all the people shall shout with a great shout, and the wall of the city will fall down flat, and the people shall go up, everyone straight before him.

Joshua 6:5

## ARE YOU SEEKING TO WORK FOR GOD IN YOUR OWN STRENGTH OR IN HIS POWER?

The armies of Joshua were not to break down the gates of Jericho nor scale its walls. Instead they were to march around the city and blow their trumpets. At first glance this seems like unconventional wisdom. Surely, there is no way to capture a city without attacking it, but this was exactly what the Lord had commanded.

By faith they walked in obedience and, therefore, Yahweh worked the miraculous.

The Lord often works in ways which confound the wisdom of man. God calls us to trust Him rather than reason with Him. All the work has been prepared for us, and our labors will be blessed if we will simply walk in obedience. Trust in the Lord with all your heart, and do not lean on your own understanding. In all your ways acknowledge Him, and He will make straight your paths.*

---

*Father, we are Your workmanship, created in Christ Jesus for good works, which You have prepared beforehand that we should walk in them.* Help us to walk in obedience, and leave the results up to You.*

*I pray these things in Jesus' name. Amen.*

*Proverbs 3:5-6, Ephesians 2:10

116

# WORKING WITH THE STRENGTH OF ONE

When they blew the 300 trumpets, the Lord set everyman's sword
against his comrade and against all the army.
And the army fled as far as Bethshittah toward Zererah, as far as the
border of Abel-meholah, by Tabbath.

Judges 7:22

## IS THERE STRENGTH IN NUMBERS?

The Midianites liked their chances against a puny Israelite army of only 300. They grossly outnumbered Gideon's men by about 135,000. Surely, the Midianites expected an easy victory. What they hadn't factored into the equation was that the Lord was with Israel. The events, which transpired next, were gloriously remarkable. We read that as the Israelites sounded their trumpets, the Midianites turned on each other and fled from the battle.

Yahweh had given His people a miraculous victory over a seemingly invincible enemy. With God, a few make a majority.

In the trenches of life, we must understand that we are not to rest in our abilities or large numbers, but rather in the strength of only one: Jehovah. The Christian has infinitely more help with the Lord than with tens of thousands of soldiers. Be encouraged. Don't look to the arm of the flesh, but rest in the confidence of the Triune God.

———————◇———————

*Father, in all things You are with me. Help me not to be moved by the trials of life, but rather place all things into Your hands.*

*I pray these things in Jesus' name. Amen.*

# WORKING IN FEARLESSNESS

Then David said to the Philistine, "You come to me with a sword and with a spear and with a javelin, but I come to you in the name of the Lord of hosts, the God of the armies of Israel, whom you have defied."

1 Samuel 17:45

## WHAT REASON DO THE PEOPLE OF GOD HAVE TO FEAR?

David faced a seemingly invincible opponent. Goliath stood to be nine feet tall, and was a man of war from his youth. He stood in opposition to God and His people, and this naturally caused great fear throughout the land of Israel. While many of the people feared, David would answer the call to fight the Philistine Giant. He was an unlikely adversary who was unskilled in the art of war.

In spite of his lack of experience, David remained confident in his God.

David took to battle without the conventional weapons of warfare. He put his hand in his bag and took out a stone and slung it and struck the Philistine on his forehead.* In faith, David slayed a giant, and his testimony still speaks to this generation.

Poor, tired soul, what is it that weighs you down with fear? Is it a financial uncertainty or a confrontation? Whatever your case may be, rest in the goodness of God. The same God, Who stood with David, now stands with you.

———————◦———————

*Father, there are oftentimes when I fear rather than trust. Give me eyes of faith to rest in You when I am most prone to fear.*

*I pray these things in Jesus' name. Amen.*

*1 Samuel 7:49

# WORKING THROUGH LOYALTY

Then the fire of the Lord fell and consumed the burnt offering and the wood and the stones and the dust, and licked up the water that was in the trench. And when all the people saw it, they fell on their faces and said, "The Lord, He is God; the Lord, He is God."

1 Kings 18:38-39

## HOW LONG WILL YOU FALTER BETWEEN TWO OPINIONS?

The Prophet Elijah posed a question of loyalty to the Israelites. "If the Lord is God, follow Him; but if Baal, then follow him." And the people did not answer him a word.* Years had passed since these people split from the Southern tribe of Judah, and afterward had fallen into gross idolatry. In vain, they had honored God with their mouths, but their hearts were far from Him.*

Here in the text we see Elijah standing face to face with the prophets of Baal. His message to them is clear: We cannot worship and serve two gods. Only the True God will hear the petitions of His people and accept their offering. In a bold stroke of faith Elijah prayed, "Answer me, O Lord, answer me, that this people may know that you, O Lord, are God, and that you have turned their hearts back."* Fire came down from heaven, and consumed the sacrifice. In this one miraculous act, Yahweh showed Himself as the True and Living God.

What about you, dear reader? Do you falter between two opinions? Let us be those who keep ourselves from idols to serve the Living God.

---

*Father, help me to have a loyal heart towards You, and to have the courage to serve only You, rather than sit on a fence.*

*I pray these things in Jesus' name. Amen.*

*1 Kings 18:21, Isaiah 29:13, 1 Kings 18:37

# WORKING THROUGH DROUGHT

Make this valley full of ditches.
2 Kings 3:16

## DO YOU WAVER AT THE PROMISES OF GOD IN UNBELIEF?

God had promised water for the men who were to fight against the Moabites. Yet the ground was a howling wasteland and a dry desert. Nevertheless, the instruction that Elisha gave them was "Make this valley full of ditches."

It is easy for me to be spurred on to obedience in seasons of abundance, but God also moves in seasons of drought. The journey is often a weary one full of discouragements, but it is at this place where faith is tested. There are times when the vision is withheld, and contrary to hope I must believe.

The Lord gave no signs to the Israelites that He would make good on His promise. He just asked them to obey Elisha's proclamation: "Make this valley full of ditches." By faith these men obeyed the voice of God, and they received the abundance of showers.

Dear friend, have you overlooked the importance of preparation? Wait patiently on the Lord. Hope in the purest sense is developed when we are in the process of digging the ditches—that is hope in God alone. It is truly then that we are ready to receive the waters of His blessing.

———◇———

*Father, help me to wait on You in faith and not unbelief. Help me to have a faith like Abraham who, contrary to hope, in hope believed.* *

*I pray these things in Jesus' name. Amen.*

*Romans 4:18

# WORKING THROUGH PRAYER

And that night the angel of the Lord went out and struck down 185,000 in the camp of the Assyrians. And when people arose early in the morning, behold, these were all dead bodies.

Kings 19:35

## HOW GREAT IS YOUR PRAYER LIFE?

King Hezekiah enjoyed a great prayer life. He was a man who fully relied on his great God. So when the Assyrians were literally at the front gates of the city, Hezekiah brought the matter before the Lord in prayer. Their intentions were for evil against the people of Yahweh. They boasted against God in defiance. Yet instead of giving an answer to his enemies, King Hezekiah accomplished more on his knees than any army could ever accomplish in battle.

Hezekiah prayed, "So now, O Lord our God, save us, please, from his hand, that all the kingdoms of the earth may know that you, O Lord, are God alone."*

The Angel of the Lord struck down 185,000 men in one night! It surely was a great victory for God's people.

Let us learn from Hezekiah that the battle is not won with sword or javelin, but rather on our knees in prayer. Prayers offered up in faith have stopped the mouths of lions!* Let us therefore tend to our prayer chambers, and spread our case out before the Lord.

---

*Father, my prayer life is often lacking. Give me the faith of Hezekiah to wait on You in my prayer closet this very day.*

*I pray these things in Jesus' name. Amen.*

*1 Kings 19:19, Hebrews 11:33

# WORKING THROUGH RESILIENCE

My God sent His angel and shut the lions' mouths, and they have not
harmed me, because I was found blameless before Him;
and also before you, O king, I have done no harm.
Daniel 6:22

## HOW CAN WE BE RESILIENT IN OUR FAITH?

Resilience is made through the trials of testing. Daniel was a man of
devout faith, and he was a faithful prayer warrior. He would pray three
times a day with his window opened towards the holy city of Jerusalem.
Yet there were those who sought to do the prophet harm.

Daniel's enemies incited the king to issue a decree that would outlaw
prayer for thirty days. Those who failed to uphold this decree were to be
fed to the lions.

In the face of opposition, Daniel remained resilient.

Though Daniel knew that the document had been signed, he went to
his house where he had windows in his upper chamber opened toward
Jerusalem. He got down on his knees three times a day and prayed and
gave thanks before His God, as he had done previously.*

By faith, Daniel feared the Lord rather than man, and his life was preserved. Likewise, the Revelation saints overcame him by the blood of the
Lamb, and by the word of their testimony; for they loved not their lives
even unto death.* Though we may not be delivered from the lion's mouth,
there awaits an eternal reward for those who are not ashamed of their God.

———————◇———————

*Father, it can be tempting to shrink back in moments of testing. Yet Your
Word says that the fear of man is a snare.* Give us the courage of Daniel to
be resilient in times of testing.*

*I pray these things in Jesus' name. Amen.*

*Daniel 6:10, Revelation 12:11, Proverbs 29:25

# WORKING THROUGH THE ORDINARY

And the angel answered her, "The Holy Spirit will come upon you, and the power of the Most High will overshadow you; therefore the child to be born will be called holy—the Son of God."

Luke 1:35

## WHAT CAN WE LEARN FROM MARY, THE MOTHER OF JESUS?

Her womb was chosen to hold our blessed Savior, but she did not con-sider herself worthy of such an honor. In humility, she took the angel at his word believing that nothing will be impossible with God.* By faith, Mary believed that Yahweh could work the miraculous, and on her lips, bore the sweet praise of her Savior.

Mary said, "My soul magnifies the Lord, and my spirit rejoices in God my Savior, for He has looked on the humble estate of his servant."* She rejoiced in unwavering belief in the promises of God, and she was graciously rewarded.

Mary was chosen, not through any merit of her own, but as a means of unmerited favor. Throughout the history of the world, our Great Jehovah has used ordinary people in extraordinary ways. Therefore, let us not elevate Mary beyond the scriptural intent, but rather be imitators of her humility and faith.

---

*Father, I thank You for Your unmerited favor. Blessed is the womb who bore our Savior, but even more blessed are those who walk in humble obedience to Your Word. Help me to be an imitator of Mary's humility and faith.*

*I pray these things in Jesus' name. Amen.*

*Luke 1:37, 46-48

# WORKING THROUGH A CRISIS

When the master of the feast tested the water now become wine, and did not know where it came from (though the servants who had drawn the water knew) the master of the feast called the bridegroom.

John 2:9

## HOW DO YOU RESPOND IN THE HOUR OF CRISIS?

Jesus, His mother, Mary, and His disciples had found themselves in the midst of a minor crisis. They were all attending a wedding in Cana and the hosting family had run out of wine to serve the guests. To run out of wine at a Jewish wedding was a form of social suicide! When Mary discovered this, she made an urgent petition to our Lord.

Jesus said to her, "Woman, what does your concern have to do with Me? My hour has not yet come."*

We tend to think that a crisis demands an immediate response from God, and yet He is more than willing to wait. Everyone was in a hurry for Jesus to be introduced as the Messiah, except Jesus. It was at the appointed time that Christ worked the miraculous by turning water into wine.

Are we more apt to trust or doubt the sovereignty of God during a crisis? My dear soul, if you find yourself in a crisis, then do not take matters into your own hands. Instead, wait patiently on the Lord Who will work with perfect timing.

---

*Father, it is so difficult to put my time sensitive crisis in Your hands. In all things, help me to wait patiently on You for deliverance.*

*I pray these things in Jesus' name. Amen.*

*John 2:4

# WORKING THROUGH FAITH

Jesus said to him, "Go, your son will live." The man believed the word
that Jesus spoke to him and went on his way.

John 4:50

## WHAT IS TRUE SAVING FAITH?

The scene is Cana, where Jesus turned the water into wine. This is where the first recorded miracle in John's Gospel takes place. This would also be the place of Jesus' second recorded miracle, but the circumstances were much different. There is no rejoicing or celebrating, but rather concern and sadness.

A certain nobleman came to Jesus with a great burden. His son had gotten sick and was on the verge of death. He begs the Lord for help, but he is first met with an unusual response. "Unless you see signs and wonders you will not believe."*

Undaunted by Jesus' response, the man remains steadfast, and petitions for his son's healing again. Then upon receiving the blessed promise, "Go, your son will live" the nobleman believed. He took Christ at His word, without seeing, and therefore received the reward.

Am I more apt to walk by faith or by sight? The problem with many people in Jesus' day was that their belief was predicated on outward manifestations. Their faith lacked any inward substance. We are blessed if we take God at His Word without seeing. This is an eternal truth. Let us rest fully on the promises of God, without seeing, to the believing of our souls.

---

*Father, we are blessed if we walk by faith not by sight.\* Help me not to look to the things which are seen, but rather believe fully in your covenant promises.*

*I pray these things in Jesus' name. Amen.*

\*John 4:48, 2 Corinthians 5:7

# WORKING THROUGH STORMS

When they had rowed about three or four miles, they saw Jesus walking on the sea and coming near the boat, and they were frightened. But he said to them, "It is I, do not be afraid."
John 6:19-20

## WHY DOES GOD PUT US THROUGH STORMS?

The hour was about three o' clock in the morning, and the disciples had been rowing all evening. Mark tells us, in his Gospel, that Jesus had instructed the disciples to get into the boat and cross the sea.* They were experienced fishermen, and knew that this was no ordinary storm.

Now in the midst of their straining at rowing, for the wind was against them, they saw a figure walking on the water. John tells us that the initial sight of Jesus frightened the disciples, but our Lord meets them with faithful words. "It is I; do not be afraid."

We tend to think that being in the will of God will exempt us from storms, but quite often this is right where the Lord is. In the midst of the storm, Jesus taught His disciples a valuable lesson about faith. Storms are the means by which our faith is tested and purified.

Dear friend, do you find yourself in the midst of a storm? If so, then take comfort in the fact that you are not alone. The Lord, Who ordains all your circumstances, remains with you.

*Father, Your will does not exempt us from difficulty. Please help me to take comfort in Your presence even when I am in the midst of a storm.*

*I pray these things in Jesus' name. Amen.*

*Mark 6:45

126

# WORKING THROUGH SICKNESS

Jesus said to him, "Get up, take your bed, and walk." And at once the man was healed, and he took up his bed and walked.

John 5:8-9

## "DO YOU WANT TO BE HEALED?"*

It seems like a strange question, but this is exactly the question that Jesus posed to the crippled man. The response given to the question is telling. "Sir, I have no one to put me into the pool when the water is stirred up, and while I am going another steps down before me."*

Perhaps the sick man had given up hope or perhaps he thought that only the waters could heal him. Nevertheless, the Divine response was: "Get up, take up your bed, and walk."

He was healed by the words of Jesus apart from any ability of his own. Thus it is with the sons of God. They are saved apart from any merit of their own. For by grace you have been saved through faith. And this is not your own doing; it is the gift of God.*

The Holy Spirit is not limited in any way, but moves in the hearts of men as He sovereignly wills. It was faith in Christ, not in the waters, which God used to work the miraculous. The question which was posed to the sick man is also posed to you. "Do you want to be healed?" If so, then look not to your own devices, but rather look to the Lord Jesus Christ.

---

*Father, salvation is a sole work of Your hands. Help me to rely only upon You for my deliverance.*

*I pray these things in Jesus' name. Amen.*

*John 5:6, 7, Ephesians 2:8

# WORKING THROUGH LIMITATIONS

Jesus then took the loaves, and when he had given thanks, he distributed them to those who were seated. So also the fish, as much as they wanted.

John 6:11

## ARE YOU OPERATING WITH LIMITED RESOURCES?

Crowds had gathered to see Jesus. The day grew long, and there was very little food for the 5,000 who remained there with them. But the disciples said, "Send the multitudes away, that they may go into the villages and buy themselves food."*

But Jesus had a very different idea. Mark tells us that Jesus was moved with compassion, and therefore ordered the disciples to feed them.* This presented a great dilemma, because in the crowd of 5,000, there was only one lad who had five loaves and two fish. Nevertheless, the command was given, "Have the people sit down."*

In miraculous fashion, our Lord turned a small meal into an insurmountable feast! The feeding of the 5,000 demonstrates the power of God over the limitations of man. The disciples were tested to see if they would trust in Divine providence.

Dear soul, do you find yourself with limited resources? If so then look to our great God Who possesses inexhaustible resources.

———◇———

*Father, so often my resources are limited. Help me to look to You for all my daily needs.*

*I pray these things in Jesus' name. Amen.*

*Matthew 14:15, Mark 6:34, John 6:10

# WORKING THROUGH BLINDNESS

Jesus answered, "It was not that this man sinned, or his parents, but that the works of God might be displayed in him."

John 9:3

## HOW DO YOU PERCEIVE SUFFERING?

When Jesus and His disciples passed by and saw a blind man, the disciples laid the fault of this man's blindness on his sin. They perceived his suffering to be the direct judgment of God. But our Lord corrects their misunderstanding. This man's blindness was not the direct result of a specific sin, but rather the occasion for the power of God.

Making use of the natural, our Lord worked the supernatural.

Jesus said to him, "Do you believe in the Son of God?" He answered, "Lord, I believe!" And he worshiped Him.* Jesus used this man's blindness for the believing of his soul.

What do you make of the suffering in which you see? Are you quick to formulate opinions? Oftentimes, our Lord will use pain to reach a lost soul. It is His means to work a far more needed healing. Let us not be quick to come to false conclusions, but rather be quick to identify with the needs of those around us.

——◆——◆——◆——

*Father, it is not in a man to understand Your ways. Help us not to be rash in our judgments, but rather to discern the real need and then be full of compassion.*

*I pray these things in Jesus' name. Amen.*

*John 9:35-38

# WORKING THROUGH DOUBT

"I knew that You always hear me, but I said this on account of the people standing around, that they may believe that You sent me."

John 11:42

## HOW DO WE SEE THE GLORY OF GOD?

Lazarus' sisters followed Jesus. Loved Jesus. But in their grief, they doubted.

"Take away the stone from the tomb" Jesus said. But Martha, Lazarus' sister, said, "Lord, by this time there will be an odor, for he has been dead four days." Jesus said to her, "Did I not tell you that if you believed you would see the glory of God?"

Even though Jesus was going to raise Lazarus back to life, John tells us that our Lord wept.* Jesus identified with the pain and suffering of those around Him. Yet this was such the occasion for the glory of God to be manifested. Jesus' petition here is offered up to His Father, and the call is given—"Lazarus, come out."*

In a demonstration of Divine power we see a dead man raised back to life. Who was this Man Who could call the dead out of the grave? That was the question that the Pharisees and the Sadducees pondered.

What do you make of Christ? Is He just a teacher or is He the Son of God? Let us be those who do not waver in doubt, but believe on the One Who raises the dead.

———————◆———————

*Father, You have raised us and seated us with Christ.* Help us to walk in Your resurrection power.*

*I pray these things in Jesus' name. Amen.*

*John 11:39-40, John 11:35, 43, Ephesians 2:6

# WORKING THROUGH THE LIFE OF CHRIST

Now Jesus did many other signs in the presence of the disciples,
which are not written in this book; but these are written so that
you may believe that Jesus is the Christ, the Son of God,
and that by believing you may have life in His name."
John 20:30-31

## DO YOU BELIEVE?

The Gospel of John was written so that many would believe and have life in the name of Jesus. Christ is not just another teacher or prophet, but rather the Son of God. Jesus did many signs and wonders, but there were still many who remained in their unbelief. How can this be?

How can so many, who saw Jesus' deeds, petition for His death, and cry out with the rest of the world, "Away with Him, away with Him, crucify Him!"?* This was the case with many in Jesus' day, and it rings true for the unbeliever today.

The reality is that man suppresses the truth in unrighteousness, and only a Divine intervention can open his or her eyes. While the miracles of Christ bore witness to His claims, it is ultimately the power of God that saves a man. Even Thomas saw the works of God, and said, "Unless I see, I will never believe."* Dear friend, what do you make of Jesus? The answer to that question has eternal implications.

———————◇———————

*Father, You have given us the very words of life. Give us a heart of worship and adoration for the risen Christ.*

*I pray these things in Jesus' name. Amen.*

*John 19:15, John 20:25

# MAY

## WHAT IS THE KINGDOM OF GOD?

Amongst the various theological debates in circulation, one of the most contested has to do with the Kingdom of God. Depending on who you ask, you are likely to hear diverse viewpoints.

In the next 31 days, I'd like to reflect on the condition of our hearts, rather than stir up controversy. We, who are of the kingdom, have been renewed from the inside-out. We are not merely interested in reforming our outward religion, but rather desire a heart that is pleasing to the Lord. Jesus said, "I am the vine; you are the branches. Whoever abides in Me and I in him, he it is that bears much fruit, for apart from Me you can do nothing."* These are characteristics of those who have been transformed by the saving work of Christ.

My prayer for you, as you read these devotions in May, would be that you are driven to self- examination. All of us need to examine our hearts on a regular basis. Also, keep in mind that salvation is a process. None of us have attained perfection in these principles, but should be noticing growth in these areas.

Let us therefore prepare our hearts so that we can understand the things that are written here for our instruction about the kingdom of God.


*John 15:5

# A KINGDOM OF REPENTANCE

From that time Jesus began to preach, saying,
"Repent, for the kingdom of heaven is at hand."
Matthew 4:17

## WHO BRINGS LIGHT INTO THE WORLD?

Here, within this text, we find the prophetic utterance of Isaiah coming to life. The Gentiles had occupied Galilee, and it is to these people that we find the kingdom proclaimed. It is interesting to note that the very first recorded proclamation is given to a people who were without the covenant promises. Jesus Christ came for the true Israel, not by birthright, but through the seed of faith. His message of repentance has always been a matter of chief importance for the sinner, but sadly, it is an often-neglected message in our day.

Many would suppose that there might be an easier way to enter into heaven—a way without the cross. Yet, if we are going to enter into the kingdom of heaven, then it can only be through the gracious gift of repentance.

Dear friend, have you experienced real repentance? Let us be those, who in humility, correct those who are in opposition, if God perhaps will grant them repentance, so that they may know the truth.*

---

*Father, the heavenly citizens of Your kingdom are marked by repentance. Give us the grace to die daily to the corruptions of our flesh, and put on the Lord Jesus Christ. Help us repent, and believe in the gospel.*

*I pray these things in Jesus' name. Amen.*

*2 Timothy 2:25, Mark 1:15

# A KINGDOM OF POVERTY

"Blessed are the poor in spirit, for theirs is the kingdom of heaven."
Matthew 5:3

## HAVE YOU BEEN EMPTIED OF YOUR SELF-RIGHTEOUSNESS?

Here in the text, Jesus associates a blessing with the poor. Those who "are poor in spirit" shall inherit the kingdom of heaven. Yet how can the poor in spirit possess the covenant blessings of God?

The Pharisees were admired for their devout piety, and they sat in positions of power and affluence. However, they used religion as a cloak for fraud and extortion. Their motives in religion were not for the glory of God, but rather for their own self-aggrandizement.

Jesus provides His hearers with a radically different understanding of worship. Those, who will enter into heaven, must be made aware of their sinful condition before a holy God. They must strip themselves of any claim that seeks to promote their good works at the expense of grace.

Has the Holy Spirit awakened you to your own moral depravity? Let us be a people who humble ourselves in Your sight.*

---

*Father, so often it is easy to think of myself in a better light than I ought. Help me to walk in true humility and poverty of soul.*

*I pray these things in Jesus' name. Amen.*

*James 1:10

# A KINGDOM OF SORROW

"Blessed are those who mourn, for they shall be comforted."
Matthew 5:4

## ARE YOU AMONG THOSE WHO MOURN?

Those, who have been made poor in spirit, exemplify a true sorrow for their sin. It was the sin of the world that put Jesus Christ on the Cross; and therefore, we must experience brokenness if we are to have fellowship with Him. It is important to note that this type of sorrow is not rooted in self, but rather in the grim reality that an individual has personally sinned against God.

Paul speaks of this godly sorrow as a sorrow that "leads to repentance." This sorrow is quite different than a worldly sorrow that "leads to death."* The sorrow of the world does not concern itself with the matters of the heart, but rather seeks to reform its shallow exterior. Those, who are only concerned about the approval of man, will never come to grips with grace. Accordingly, we need the type of mourning that penetrates deep into the heart. Those who experience this type of brokenness will be given a true comfort from above.

In light of this eternal truth, let us seek the Lord for the gracious gift of godly sorrow.

———————◎———————

*Father, You lift up the heavy hearts of those who are contrite in spirit. Please help me to give You a sacrifice of a broken spirit and a broken and a contrite heart—these, O God, You will not despise.**

*I pray these things in Jesus' name. Amen.*

*2 Corinthians 7:10, Psalm 51:17

# A KINGDOM OF MEEKNESS

"Blessed are the meek, for they shall inherit the earth."
Matthew 5:5

## WHAT DOES IT MEAN TO BE MEEK?

A.W. Pink describes meekness as "being made pliant, tractable, submissive, teachable."[5] The Apostle James provides us with a little more insight on the essence of meekness, "But the wisdom from above is first pure, then peaceable, gentle, open to reason, full of mercy, and good fruits, impartial and sincere."*

Those, who are characterized by meekness, exude a sweet and tender disposition towards God. They no longer insist on their own way, but rather submit all their ways to Christ. Thus, the virtue of meekness is the rarest of treasures, and a crown jewel for those who wear it.

Jesus said, "Take my yoke upon you. Let me teach you, because I am meek and lowly in heart." If we can learn the art of meekness, then we will one day reap the rewards of reigning with Christ. This eternal truth instructs us be a people who do not insist on our own rights, but are tenderhearted and lowly before our God.

———————————

*Father, it can be tempting to insist on my own way, but You have shown me a more excellent example. Give me the rarest of virtues so that I can exemplify a Christ-like disposition toward others.*

*I pray these things in Jesus' name. Amen.*

*James 3:17, Matthew 11:29

136

# A KINGDOM OF RIGHTEOUSNESS

"Blessed are those who hunger and thirst for righteousness,
for they shall be satisfied."
Matthew 5:6

## WHAT ARE THE DESIRES OF YOUR HEART?

It seems as though people are never satisfied in their pursuit of happiness. Many always seem to want more than what they possesses. But what causes someone to be so unfulfilled?

King Solomon, upon further reflection of this matter, imparted some wisdom to us. He came to the conclusion that all of life apart from God is vanity and grasping for the wind.* Likewise, if you truly want to be content in this life, then heed the words of Jesus: hunger and thirst for righteousness.

Here we are taught that true life is not found in the trivial pursuits of this world, but rather in the possession of the living God. If all those, who are citizens of the heavenly kingdom, delight in the Law according to the inward man,* they are promised to be satisfied with the good things that are from above. They have their hope set on the New Jerusalem, and they have a sure anchor for their souls.

Is that where your hope lies? If so, do not spend your time pursuing the temporal things of this life, but rather occupy your time pursuing the One Who promises true and lasting fulfillment.

---

*Father, You have made us joint-heirs with Christ. Give me a distaste for the things of this life, but rather to hunger and thirst for righteousness.*

*I pray these things in Jesus' name. Amen.*

*Ecclesiastes 4:16, Romans 7:22

# A KINGDOM OF MERCY

"Blessed are the merciful, for they shall receive mercy."
Matthew 5:7

## WHAT IS YOUR GRASP ON THE CHARACTER OF GOD?

Hypocrisy can cloak itself in deceptive disguises. The Pharisees thought themselves to be religious, but yet they neglected the weightier matters of the Law.* In their zeal for outward observances, they completely missed the heart of Christ. Their religious spirit manifested itself in pride and arrogance.

On the other hand, this is contrary to the spirit of our Lord.

Those, who have been shown the mercy of God, will also deal mercifully with others. Here we are taught the principle of sewing and reaping. If I take a hard line with others, than I can expect to be given a hard line in return. However, if I extend mercy towards others, then I can also expect to receive mercy in return. For judgment is without mercy to the one who has shown no mercy. Mercy triumphs over judgment.*

Am I more apt to be merciful or harsh in my dealings with others? Let us be a people who extend the same mercy to others that God has extended to us.

———————◆———————

*Father, You have not dealt with me according to what my sins deserved. Instead of judgment you have extended mercy. Help me to also extend that same mercy towards others.*

*I pray these things in Jesus' name. Amen.*

*Matthew 23:23, James 2:13

# A KINGDOM OF PURITY

"Blessed are the pure in heart, for they shall see God."
Matthew 5:8

## IS YOUR HEART PURE BEFORE GOD?

Here in this beatitude, Jesus continues to address the matters of the heart. The Pharisees only concerned themselves with an outward conformity to laws. They boasted in their obedience to the Torah, but Jesus referred to them as white-washed tombs.* Outwardly, they appeared clean before others, but inwardly they were filled with all sorts of evils.

If I am going to enter into the kingdom of heaven, I am going to need to be washed from my sins. This type of washing can only happen through the blood of Christ. Once my heart has been renewed then I will have an inward disposition that is geared towards holiness. Have I experienced such an inward change?

To the pure all things are pure, but to those who are defiled and unbelieving nothing is pure; but even their mind and conscience are defiled.* So let us draw near with a true heart in full assurance of faith, having our hearts sprinkled from an evil conscience and our bodies washed with pure water.* Then, let us pursue God with all sincerity and purity of heart.

---

*Father, help me never to be satisfied with outward reformation, but rather to desire purity in my most inward being.*

*I pray these things in Jesus' name. Amen.*

*Matthew 23:27, Titus 1:15, Hebrews 10:22

# A KINGDOM OF PEACEMAKERS

"Blessed are the peacemakers, for they shall be called sons of God."
Matthew 5:9

## ARE YOU A PEACEMAKER?

The wisdom of the world looks at a contentious spirit as a badge of honor, but this is contrary to the spirit of Christ. Those, who have been trained by godly wisdom, seek to live in peace with everyone. They understand that peace is not always attainable, but as much as possible, to live peaceably with all people.*

Notice the promise that is given to peacemakers in this text. Jesus says of them that "they shall be called sons of God." Those, who strive to maintain the unity of peace, have first experienced the peace of God in their own lives.

The gospel has radically transformed their disposition toward others, and instead of pursuing conflict they pursue harmony. This does not mean that they are always perfect in their pursuit of peace, but their desire is for unity amongst the brethren.

Dear friend, is conflict lurking at your door? If so, then do not entertain it, but rather pursue what leads to peace and to mutual edification.* Seek that peaceable fruit of righteousness which is from above.*

———————◇———————

*Father, in a world of wars and rumors of wars,* help me to live a quiet and peaceable life amongst others. Give me the grace, not only to maintain unity, but to share the good news of the gospel with all.*

*I pray these things in Jesus' name. Amen.*

*Romans 12:18, Romans 14:19, Hebrews 12:11, Matthew 24:6

# A KINGDOM OF SUFFERERS

"Blessed are those who are persecuted for righteousness' sake,
for theirs is the kingdom of heaven."
Matthew 5:10

## IS A SERVANT GREATER THAN THEIR MASTER?

Jesus, in this text, is laying down the terms of discipleship in a very clear manner. If the Son of God endured such hostility from sinners,* then what makes me think that I will fare any differently?

Many have gone before us, who have suffered greatly for the sake of the kingdom. In the same way, if we are going to follow Christ, then we can expect much suffering from the hands of the wicked. There are so many troubles in this life, but the citizens of the heavenly kingdom have placed all hope in their everlasting God. They will possess a kingdom that is not made with hands, but one that is eternal in the heavens.*

Notice, though, that Jesus does not just lay down the conditions for discipleship, but He also gives us a blessed promise. All those, who have suffered with Christ, will also reign with Him.

Dear friend, do not be disheartened by your present sufferings, but rather take heart! Though we suffer in this life, we shall receive a hundred-fold now in this time—and in the age to come, eternal life.*

———————◆———————

*Father, it is so tempting to be given over to compromise. Help me not to forsake the eternal joys of heaven for the temporary relief of this life, but rather give me the grace to endure hardship as a good soldier.**

*I pray these things in Jesus' name. Amen.*

*Hebrews 12:3, 2 Corinthians 5:1, Mark 10:30, 2 Timothy 2:3

# A KINGDOM OF LIGHT

You are the light of the world. A city set on a hill cannot be hidden.
Nor do people light a lamp and put it under a basket,
but on a stand, and it gives light to all in the house."
Matthew 5:14-15

## DO YOU SHINE IN A DARK PLACE?

The kingdom of heaven brings the light of God to shine in the darkness. It manifests itself in good works, and it serves as a testimony against a dark and fallen world. However, in our zeal for good works, we need to be very careful to discern between mere religious orthodoxy and true kingdom living. It is entirely possible for me to do my good deeds with the wrong motivation.

The Pharisees prided themselves in their good works, but they did these things to merit the praise of men. So Jesus is communicating the importance of living in such a way that God will be glorified. He encouraged, "In the same way, let your light shine before others, so that they may see your good works and give glory to your Father Who is in heaven."

Is your life a testimony of God's redeeming grace for others to witness? If not, then let this be a reminder to do good works, not for the praise of men, but to the glory of God.

---

*Father, we live in very dark times. Help me to shine a light in a way that others would glorify You in heaven.*

*I pray these things in Jesus' name. Amen.*

*Matthew 5:16

# A KINGDOM OF HOLINESS

"For I tell you, unless your righteousness exceeds that of the Scribes and Pharisees, you will never enter the kingdom of heaven."
Matthew 5:20

## WHAT IS YOUR STANDARD OF RIGHTEOUSNESS?

The Pharisees sought to measure themselves by the Law of Moses. Yet they failed to see the "forest for the trees." A blind superficiality to the outward observances of the Law fueled their motivation.

In dealing with the topic of the Law, Jesus completely dismisses their efforts. The outward expression of religion can never deal with the deep matters of the heart. Apart from the new birth a man will always lower the standard of righteousness to something which is attainable, but that is a grave error. The Law, which is perfect, will always bare light on our imperfections. Therefore, the Law must be written on our hearts to be holy.

For this is the covenant I will make with the house of Israel after those days, declares the Lord. I will put My laws in their minds, and inscribe them on their hearts. And I will be their God, and they will be My people.*

Once I understand this truth, then all boasting comes to an end. Instead of trying to conform myself to the standard of the Law, I will become a conduit for the Spirit of holiness.

In light of this truth, let us be those who desire a righteousness that transforms the inward person.

---

*Father, sacrifices and appointed feasts are not Your delight. You desire a reformation from within. Help me not to be merely clean on the outside, but rather holy on the inside. Help me to delight to do Your will, O my God; Your law is within my heart.*

*I pray these things in Jesus' name. Amen.*

*Hebrews 8:10, Psalm 40:8

# A KINGDOM OF FORGIVENESS

"So if you are offering your gift at the altar and there remember that your brother has something against you, leave your gift there before the altar and go. First be reconciled to your brother, and then come and offer your gift."
Matthew 5:23-24

## WHAT IS A TRUE ACT OF WORSHIP?

Worship is an outward expression of an inward reality. Again, Jesus is dealing with the matters of the heart. He does not merely delight in outward observances, but rather in a disposition of love and compassion towards others.

In the previous verses our Lord deals with the issue of murder. Jesus said, "You have heard that it was said to those of old, 'You shall not murder, and whoever murders will be in danger of the judgment.' But I say to you that whoever is angry with his brother without a cause shall be in danger of the judgment."*

This destructive sin takes root in a heart that harbors anger and hatred. So Jesus puts a premium on being reconciled to the offended party. We, as believers, ought to be people who enable others to worship. When we sin against our brothers and sisters, we put a stumbling block in their way. It is entirely impossible to worship the Lord with anger and bitterness weighing on our hearts.

Therefore, let us stop judging one another. Instead, make up your mind not to put any stumbling block or obstacle in your brother's way.* Let us be reconciled to our brothers and sisters. In doing so, this will ensure that our worship will be offered in truth and sincerity.

———————◆———————

*Father, You desire mercy and not sacrifice in Your kingdom. Help me to have a tender heart towards those whom I have offended.*

*I pray these things in Jesus' name. Amen.*

*Matthew 5:21-22, Romans 14:13

# A KINGDOM
# OF MORTIFICATION

"If your right eye causes you to sin, tear it out and throw it away.
For it is better that you lose one of your members than that
your whole body be thrown into hell."
Matthew 5:29

## HOW SERIOUSLY DO YOU TAKE THE WARNINGS OF JESUS?

Our Master, by way of illustration, is communicating the importance of mortification. The eye is a member of great value to the body, but it is also the window into the soul. Jesus is adding emphasis to His previous statement regarding lust.

"You have heard that it was said, 'You shall not commit adultery.' But I say to you that everyone who looks at a woman with lustful intent has already committed adultery with her in his heart."* Moreover, Jesus extends a further exhortation. Those who make a practice of lusting are in danger of eternal judgment.

We must take great care in what we view with our eyes. There is no member of the body, regardless of value, which is worth an eternity in hell.

Now note, Jesus' teaching is to be understood metaphorically and not literally. He is simply emphasizing the importance of mortifying or putting to death our fleshly lusts. This is a kingdom principle, and along those lines, we are commanded to make our calling and election sure.* This is not a means of earning our salvation, but rather a sign of our growth in grace. Let us therefore seek to fight valiantly against temptations.

———◆———◉———◆———

*Father, sin claims many souls, but You have set Your citizens free from its grip. Help me to walk worthy of my calling* by fleeing youthful lusts.*

*I pray these things in Jesus' name. Amen.*

*Matthew 5:27-28, 1 Peter 1:10, Ephesians 4:1

145

# A KINGDOM OF INTEGRITY

"Let what you say be simply 'Yes' or 'No';
anything more than this comes from evil."
Mathew 5:37

## WHAT VALUE DO YOU PLACE ON YOUR WORD?

The Jews were accustomed to making oaths. This tradition went all the way back to the days of Abraham. However, our Lord warns us of its dangers.

Citizens of the heavenly kingdom should not make themselves a surety for their word if they do not intend to carry it out. Jesus teaches us a better way. In a world of covenant-breakers, He calls us to something that is radically different. We, as citizens of the kingdom, are warned to first weigh out the costs of making a commitment to others.

Are we going to be able to keep our word? If not, then we should not even make an oath in the first place. But above all, my brethren, do not swear, either by heaven or by earth or with any other oath. But let your "Yes" be "Yes," and your "No," "No," lest you fall into judgment.*

In a society that does not place a value on keeping his or her word, let us be those who let our "Yes" be "Yes," and our "No" be "No."

---

*Father, You have called us to a radically different way of life. We are to be a people who keep our word to others. Help me to guard against the danger of making rash oaths.*

*I pray these things in Jesus' name. Amen.*

*James 5:12

# A KINGDOM OF LOVE

"But I say to you, love your enemies and pray for those who persecute you, so that you may be sons of your Father Who is in heaven."
Matthew 5:44

## WHAT IS UNCONDITIONAL LOVE?

The Jews were taught to love their neighbors and hate their enemies,* but our Lord takes occasion here to show us a more excellent way.* It is a lot easier to love those who love us back, but it is rather impossible for the natural person to love his or her enemies.

Nevertheless, this is exactly what Jesus is calling us to do.

Our culture has a superficial understanding of love, but God truly loves the unlovable. Paul says in Romans, "God demonstrates his love for us in that while we were yet sinners Christ died for us."* This teaching flies in the face of any man-made standard of righteousness. Only through the power of the Holy Spirit am I able to love in this way.

In light of this eternal truth let us, who have been shown unconditional love, show the love of Christ to our enemies.

———◦———

*Father, though I speak with the tongue of angels, I am nothing without love.* Help me to show the same unconditional love towards others that You have shown me.*

*I pray these things in Jesus' name. Amen.*

*Matthew 5:43, 1 Corinthians 12:31, Romans 5:8, 1 Corinthians 13:1

# A KINGDOM OF CHARITY

"Beware of practicing your righteousness before other people in order to be seen by them, for then you will have no reward from your Father who is in heaven."
Matthew 6:1

## WHAT IS THE PURPOSE OF CHARITY?

There were many in Jesus' day who boasted in their giving before men. They turned charity into a theatrical performance, yet Jesus warns us against this type of giving.

Thus, when you give to the needy, sound no trumpet before you, as the hypocrites do in the synagogues and in the streets, that they may be praised by others. Truly, I say to you, they have received their reward.* All their deeds are done for men to see.*

Our works are to be done in such a way that will direct all glory to God. Yet again, this can only be accomplished through the new spiritual birth.

It is wrong to put on a good show before men. We must concern ourselves with the matters of the heart. Where do your affections lie? Are they rooted in the glory of God or are they rooted in self-importance? A person, who is truly given over to the will of the Lord, only seeks to make Jesus famous. In light of this eternal truth, let us seek to offer up our good works solely for the glory of God and His kingdom.

---

*Father, let my love be without hypocrisy. Help me to abhor what is evil and cling to what is good.* Help me not to seek the approval of men, but rather to do all things for Your glory.*

*I pray these things in Jesus' name. Amen.*

*Matthew 6:2, Matthew 23:5, Romans 12:9

# A KINGDOM OF TRUTH

"But when you pray, go into your room and shut the door and pray to
your Father who is in secret. And your Father
who sees in secret will reward you."
Matthew 6:6

## WHAT IS THE PURPOSE OF PRAYER?

Prayer is one of the deepest expressions of worship to God. Believers are
granted this holy privilege for the purpose of communion with Him. Yet,
as with any other form of worship, it can be misguided if not offered up
with the proper motivation.

There were many in Jesus' day who prayed in order to be heard by men.
Jesus cut right to the heart of the matter. He said, "And when you pray,
do not be like the hypocrites. For they love to pray standing in the synagogues and on the street corners to be seen by men. Truly I tell you, they
already have their full reward."*

Prayer is to be offered up to God Who hears us, and answers
according to His will. He is a discerner of the secrets of our hearts, and
there is no hidden motive or ambition, which can be concealed from
Him.

This eternal truth has implications. It is very important that we examine our hearts to see if there is any crooked way in us. The Lord, Who
knows all things, knows our hearts and what is exalted among men is an
abomination in the sight of God.*

---

*Father, You are a Discerner of all the intents of my heart. Help me to offer up
my prayers to You in sincerity and in truth.*

*I pray these things in Jesus' name. Amen.*

*Matthew 6:5, Luke 16:15

# A KINGDOM OF REVERENCE

"Our Father in heaven, hallowed be your name."
Matthew 6:9

## HOW SHOULD WE APPROACH GOD IN PRAYER?

Jesus provides us with two revelations as He begins His discourse on the model prayer. Kingdom citizens should approach God boldly. We are no longer strangers, but heirs with Christ. The privilege of prayer is given to us who are now sons and daughters of the Most High. As a child of God, we are to address Him as our Father in heaven.

Yet it is important to note that those, who approach God's throne boldly, must also approach it reverently.

Do you not know? Have you not heard? The LORD is the everlasting God, the Creator of the ends of the earth. He will never grow faint or weary; His understanding is beyond searching out.* He is the High and Lofty One Who inhabits eternity.*

All His angels praise Him, and all His heavenly hosts. The sun and moon praise Him, and all the shining stars. The highest heavens praise Him, and all waters above the heavens!* If all creation praise God in reverence, then how much more should we consider our lowly state before Him? In light of this truth, let us approach God with both reverence and honor.

———◆———◉———◆———

*Father, I am your child by adoption, but Your name is also holy. Help me to approach You, not only with boldness, but also with a godly reverence.*

*I pray these things in Jesus' name. Amen.*

*Isaiah 40:28, Isaiah 57:15, Psalm 148:1-4

# A KINGDOM OF GOD'S WILL

"Your kingdom come, Your will be done, on earth as it is in heaven."
Matthew 6:10

## WHAT IS YOUR HEART IN PRAYER?

Is it to accomplish your will or God's will?

Citizens of the heavenly kingdom have had their desires realigned. They are no longer seeking their own way, but rather the way of the Lord. Their purpose in prayer should be for the advancement of the kingdom.

Here, in this text, Jesus is communicating the importance of praying according to the will of God. Thus we have three important keys to unlocking the heart of the Father in prayer.

First, we see Jesus' emphasis on the Kingdom. Those, who are born again, long for the kingdoms of this world to be the kingdoms of Christ. Secondly, we see our Lord's emphasis on the will of God. People of the heavenly kingdom desire the things of their Father. They put their lives in the hands of Divine Sovereignty, trusting that whatever He wills is safest and best. Finally, Jesus places a tension on this present age, and the age to come. We, who long for His return, ought to desire true righteousness both in the present, as well as in eternity. Is this your desire? If so, then make sure you are seeking the will of the Lord in prayer.

---

*Father, help me to pray with a passion to see Your purposes accomplished both in heaven and on earth.*

*I pray these things in Jesus' name. Amen.*

# A KINGDOM OF FAITHFUL PROVISION

"Give us this day our daily bread."
Matthew 6:11

## ARE YOUR PRAYERS OFFERED UP IN FAITH?

The Apostle James warns us of the dangers of being double-minded. He said, Let a man ask in faith, with no doubting, for he who doubts is like a wave of the sea driven and tossed by the wind. For let not that man suppose that he will receive anything from the Lord; he is a double-minded man, unstable in all his ways.*

We are not to waver in unbelief, but rather remain quietly assured in the faithfulness of God. Citizens of the heavenly kingdom trust Him in the present moment. They have come to realize that it is foolish to worry about the uncertainties of tomorrow, because wisdom has taught them the importance of focusing on the task at hand.

Jesus reminds us to rely on the Father's daily provisions for our lives. It is in the present circumstance that grace is renewed. Once I have entered into His rest, then I can be set free from the unnecessary anxieties of this life. In the pressures and toils of the present, have you labored to enter into His rest? If not, then place your cares in the hands of the One Who cares for you.*

---

*Father, You are a faithful provider to Your children. You even send rain on the just and unjust alike.\* Help me to seek You in faith, and deliver me from the anxieties of life.*

*I pray these things in Jesus' name. Amen.*

*James 1:6-8, 1 Peter 5:7, Matthew 5:45

# A KINGDOM OF FORGIVENESS

"And forgive us our debts, as we also have forgiven our debtors."
Matthew 6:12

## ARE YOU HARBORING UNFORGIVENESS IN YOUR HEART?

In the Jewish culture, they understood the importance of paying off their debts to others. Those who could not repay their debts would often sell themselves into slavery. In like manner, we owed an insurmountable debt to God.

It is interesting that Jesus likens sin to a debt. This was a debt that we could have never settled with Him. Yet, in His kindness, He was moved with compassion for us. We were all slaves to sin.* He sent His Son to redeem us from the slavery of sin. For the wages of sin is death. Now that we have been set free from sin, we have the free gift of God, eternal life in Christ Jesus our Lord.* As recipients of His grace, we ought to extend that same forgiveness to others.

In our text, Jesus reminds us of the importance of forgiving one another. For if you forgive others, your heavenly Father will also forgive you, but if you don't, neither will your Father forgive you. Come now, let us reason together.* There is no freedom or assurance in harboring unforgiveness. The only way to experience true freedom and peace is to let go of your past hurts. In doing so, you will be able to enjoy the communion and presence of our ever-present Redeemer.

---

*Father, I owe You an insurmountable debt. Please give me the grace to forgive others as You have forgiven me.*

*I pray these things in Jesus' name. Amen.*

*Romans 6:20, 23, Matthew 6:14-15, Isaiah 1:18

# A KINGDOM DELIVERED FROM EVIL

"And lead us not into temptation, but deliver us from evil."
Matthew 6:13

## HOW DO YOU RESPOND TO TEMPTATION?

Continually, we are surrounded by the snares of the evil one. Temptation remains at our very doorstep, and its desire is to have us.* If we are not careful to ponder our steps, then we may find ourselves entangled in sin.

Those, who are heavenly citizens, desire to be free from the pollutions of the old man. They have been taught by godly wisdom to hate their sin, but the battle rages on in the grind of daily life. We must entreat the Lord's mercy in times of temptation.

It is in light of these present dangers that it is imperative to go to our heavenly Father in prayer. He knows our frame and remembers that we are dust.* No temptation has overtaken you that is not common to man. God is faithful, and He will not let you be tempted beyond your ability, but with the temptation He will also provide the way of escape, that you may be able to endure it.*

Do you rely on the Lord in temptation? If not, then seek Him Who is able to keep you from stumbling.

———◆———◆———◆———

*Father, Satan desires to sift me as wheat. I am constantly being bombarded by temptations on every side. Help me to learn the godly habit of continual prayer that I will not enter into temptation.* *

*I pray these things in Jesus' name. Amen.*

*Genesis 4:7, Psalm 103:14, 1 Corinthians 10:13, Jude 24, Luke 22:40

# A KINGDOM OF PRAYER

"Ask and it will be given to you; seek, and you will find; knock, and it will be opened to you."
Matthew 7:7

## DO YOU BELIEVE THAT GOD ANSWERS PRAYER?

It is said in the book of James that the fervent prayers of the righteous avail much.* Here our Lord is also teaching us the importance of being persistent in prayer. If our prayers are going to be effective, then not only must we be fervent and persistent, there are a few other things that we must come to understand.

First, our heavenly Father is faithful in keeping His promises. The citizens of His kingdom must expect that He will reward those who diligently seek Him.*

Secondly, we must also believe that He is able to answer our prayers. If we do not ask in faith, but doubt,* then how are we to expect an answer? Finally, we must believe that He is a Giver of good and perfect gifts.* When we pray, according to His will, we will find that He is gracious in His answers to us. He gives all good things to His children, not begrudgingly, but willingly. For all these reasons, let us not lose heart in prayer, but rather pray earnestly with expectation.

---

*Father, You are a Giver of good and perfect gifts. Help me to persist in prayer, like the Prophet Elijah who prayed earnestly for rain.**

*I pray these things in Jesus' name. Amen.*

*James 5:16, Hebrews 11:6, James 1:6, 17, 2 Corinthians 9:7, James 5:17

155

# A KINGDOM OF TREASURE

"But lay up for yourselves treasures in heaven, where neither moth nor rust destroys, and where thieves do not break in and steal."
Matthew 6:20

## WHAT ARE YOUR PRIMARY MOTIVATIONS?

Jesus is about to shift focus to the topic of money. He has a great deal to say on the topic of finances, not only in this passage, but in the parables as well. The Jews viewed wealth as a sign of favor from God, but Jesus cuts to the heart. As the heavens are higher than the earth, so are the Lord's ways higher than ours.*

The choice is laid bare before us. We can either live for the passing pleasures of a season or we can invest our lives in the things of eternity. Those, who possess godly wisdom, do not squander their money on things which do not last. Citizens of the kingdom treasure up for themselves a firm foundation for the future, so that they may take hold of that which is truly life.*

What are the treasures of your heart? Do not set your heart on the things of this earth, but rather set your heart on the things which are from above.*

———◆———

*Father, so often I waste my resources on corruptible things. Help me to treasure eternity and set my affections on the things which are above.*

*I pray these things in Jesus' name. Amen.*

*Isaiah 55:9, 1 Timothy 6:19, Colossians 3:2

# AN INCORRUPTIBLE KINGDOM

"For where your treasure is, there your heart will be also."
Matthew 6:21

## WHAT DOES YOUR HEART TREASURE?

The Pharisees did not treasure things from above. They used religion as a means of acquiring influence and money. Knowing this, Jesus warns us to examine our hearts in our pursuit of material possessions.

Citizens of the heavenly kingdom are true worshipers of God. They have set their aim on His glory, and their goal is to enjoy Him. The heart is the seat of affections and motivations, and we will worship what we adore. If pursuing wealth is the passion of my heart, then it will manifest itself in my actions.

The world pursues those things that perish, but this is not to be so with us. We, as kingdom citizens, are to pursue an inheritance incorruptible and undefiled and that does not fade away, reserved in heaven for us.* Beloved, let us not strive and labor for those things which perish, but I urge you, be as sojourners and exiles to abstain from the passions of the flesh, which wage war against your soul.*

———————◆———————

*Father, You have shown us that our treasure is to hope in eternity, and not to live for the temporary things of this life. Help me to live for those things that will not fade away.*

*I pray these things in Jesus' name. Amen.*

*1 Peter 1:4, 1 Peter 2:11

# A KINGDOM OF ONE MASTER

"The eye is the lamp of the body. So, if your eye is healthy, your whole body will be full of light, but if your eye is bad, your whole body will be full of darkness. If then the light in you is darkness, how great is the darkness!"

Matthew 6:22-23

## ARE YOUR EYES WORKING?

Jesus, by means of illustration, is warning us against the dangers of idolatry. He has been teaching us about the proper place of money in the believer's life. Now He continues to drive that point home with the example of the eye.

If we are blinded by the corruptions of greed, then we will be children who walk to and fro in darkness. As citizens of the heavenly kingdom, we have been blessed with provisions for our daily needs. Accordingly, we are to be whole-hearted in our devotion to the One Who showers us with gifts.

Dear friend, are you torn between the light and the darkness? If so, Jesus has made it clear. No one can serve two masters, for either he will hate the one and love the other, or he will be devoted to the one and despise the other. You cannot serve God and money.*

This eternal truth, should cause us to worship and serve the Lord with a singleness of heart.

———————◆———————

*Father, You have made it very clear that we cannot serve two Masters. Help me to love You with all my heart and with all my soul and with all my mind.*

*I pray these things in Jesus' name. Amen.*

*Matthew 6:24, Matthew 22:37

# A WORRY-FREE KINGDOM

"Therefore I tell you, do not be anxious about your life, what you will eat or what you will drink, nor about your body, what you will put on. Is not life more than food, and the body more than clothing?"
Matthew 6:25

## WHAT IS YOUR LIFE IN LIGHT OF ETERNITY?

God has placed us on this earth for such a short period of time. Our lives are, but a moment in light of eternity. For we are a mist that appears for a little time and then vanishes.* We are commanded not to waste a minute of our lives worrying about our daily provisions.

Jesus drives home this point of faith in three key ways. First, he addresses the birds of the field. He said, "Look at the birds of the air: they neither sow nor reap nor gather into barns, and yet your heavenly Father feeds them. Are you not of more value than they?"* Secondly, our Lord considers the lilies of the fields. They neither toil nor spin for their clothing, and yet our Lord arrays them in beautiful colors.* Finally, Jesus mentions the heathen who spend their days laboring for perishable things.* Many are their anxieties, but the Lord cares for His sheep.

Let us not absorb our lives in the sin of worry. Our God, Who feeds the birds and clothes the lilies, will surely provide for you.

---

*Father, many are the anxieties of life. Help me not to waste one minute of my life in fear, but rather help me to place my trust entirely in Your loving hands.*

*I pray these things in Jesus' name. Amen.*

*James 4:14, Matthew 6:26, 28, 32

# A KINGDOM OF PRIORITIES

"But seek first the kingdom of God and his righteousness,
and all these things will be added to you."
Matthew 6:33

## WHAT ARE YOUR PRIORITIES?

Jesus has been warning us about the dangers of money, idolatry, anxiety, and now He gives us a gracious promise. Millions around the globe have set their focus on earthly money. They busy themselves with their own kingdom, but heavenly citizens seek to advance God's kingdom.

Kingdom folk are strangers and sojourners on the earth. Their pursuits are of a different order than the unbeliever. They are resting confidently in the Lord's provisions for their lives. This frees them up from the worries of life so that they can focus on the service of the King.

Do you prioritize your life that way? If not, then stop allowing the cares of this life to choke away your effectiveness for Christ. Rather trust and wait patiently for Him Who will add these things to you. More than anything else, put God's work first and do what He wants. Then the other things will be yours as well.

---

*Father, Satan would have me to be distracted from the service of Your kingdom. Give me an unwavering faith in Your promises so that I can be free to serve You.*

*I pray these things in Jesus' name. Amen.*

# A KINGDOM OF SINCERITY

*"Why do you see the speck that is in your brother's eye,*
*but do not notice the log that is in your own eye?"*
Matthew 7:4

## HOW CLEARLY DO YOU SEE?

In this text, Jesus warns us against the dangers of short-sighted judgments. How can we, who have not dealt with our own sin, see clearly enough to point out the faults in others?

Godly wisdom teaches the importance of righteous judgments. Jesus provides us with a clear path in restoring others. First, we are taught to be mindful of our own sins against God. In order for us to see clearly we must seek repentance for ourselves. Hypocrisy finds it much easier to point out the faults in others, but it is much more difficult to examine the faults in ourselves.*

It is only through the crucible of self-examination that we are able to clearly discern the sins of others. Then, once we have dealt with our own sins, may we lovingly help our brothers and sisters with their sins. Beloved, if anyone is caught in any transgression, you who are spiritual should restore him in a spirit of gentleness. Keep watch on yourself, lest you too be tempted.*

This eternal truth deals first with the plank in my own eye so that I can restore others with all humility and gentleness, with patience, in a spirit of meekness and love.*

---

*Father, self-examination is very difficult, but it is absolutely essential for the benefit of our souls. Grant me the grace to deal with the plank in my own eye before I tackle the speck in my brother's eye.*

*I pray these things in Jesus' name. Amen.*

*Matthew 7:5, Galatians 6:1, Ephesians 4:2

# THE KINGDOM GATE IS NARROW

"Enter by the narrow gate. For the gate is wide and the way is easy that leads to destruction, and those who enter by it are many. For the gate is narrow and the way is hard that leads to life, and those who find it are few."
Matthew 7:13-14

## WHICH PATH ARE YOU ON?

In a world of post-modern thought, our society has blurred the lines. However, the lines of demarcation have been drawn, and the ax has been laid to the root.

Jesus tells us that we can only go one of two ways. Either we are on the way that leads to life or we are on the way that leads to death. Folly deceives us to think that the gate which leads to life is an easy and broad path, but wisdom teaches us that the true gate opens up to a narrow and difficult way.

Therefore, we are invited to come, but we are warned to count the cost. For which of you, desiring to build a tower, does not first sit down and count the cost, whether he has enough to complete it?* So any one of us who does not renounce all that he has cannot be Christ's disciple.*

Dear friend, think it not strange that your commitment to Christ has caused you great suffering. While this Kingdom road is marked with great difficulty, it will eventually lead you to your eternal rest.

---

*Father, there is only one of two ways which lead to life. Help me to ignore the lies of this culture, and remain fixed on the hope of eternity.*

*I pray these things in Jesus' name. Amen.*

Luke 14:28, 33

# A KINGDOM OF DOERS

"Everyone then who hears these words of mine and does them will be like a wise man who built his house on a rock."

Matthew 7:24

## ARE YOU STANDING ON A FIRM FOUNDATION?

Our culture has made obedience the enemy of faith, but these two principles are really the best of friends. True faith leads to action. If I truly believe that Jesus is the Son of God, then it will manifest itself in the fruit of the Spirit. If we live by the Spirit, let us also keep in step with the Spirit.*

Our Lord alerts us against an insincere profession of faith. We are to be doers of the Word, and not hearers only.* There were many, in Jesus' day, that honored Him with their lips, but their hearts were far from Him.*

Citizens of the heavenly kingdom not only profess faith with their mouths, but also demonstrate it with their actions. They are those who have been reformed inwardly.

The warning in this passage is made clear to all those who hear it. I have no reason to think I have been made right with God if my life does not reflect it. This eternal truth urges you to walk in a manner worthy of the calling to which you have been called.*

---

*Father, help me to be a kingdom citizen who not only honors You with my lips, but also honors You with my heart.*

*I pray these things in Jesus' name. Amen.*

*Galatians 5:25, James 1:22, Matthew 15:8, Ephesians 4:1

# JUNE
## WHAT IS THE WORD OF GOD?

What value do you place on God's Word?

God's Word guides us. It gives us wisdom. It comforts us. It brings joy. It gives peace. It is our salvation.

Many of us live in a country where we can worship freely without worry of persecution, but there are many countries where the Bible is outlawed. We all have wanted to hear from God at some point in our lives, and it is through the Word of God that He speaks to us. Those, who own a Bible, have the words of eternal life.

This June, as we study Psalm 119 together, we will not be able to escape the Psalmist's desire for God's Word. He not only wants to understand it, but he wants it to transform him from the inside out.

Sadly, though, there are those who only want to study the Scriptures for the academic knowledge. God's Word bears no weight on the way in which they live, and they find themselves without hope in this world.

Dear friend, my prayer for you is that you would not only treasure the knowledge of the Word, but also the Author. My hope is that you will be transformed by the renewal of your mind that by testing you may discern what is the will of God, what is good and acceptable and perfect.*

*Romans 12:2

# WALKING IN THE WORD

Blessed are those whose way is blameless,
who walk in the Law of the Lord!
Psalm 119:1

## WHAT DOES IT MEAN TO BE BLESSED?

According to the psalmist, he describes blessedness as those whose ways are blameless, or undefiled and upright, and whose feet walk in the Law of the Lord. They whole-heartedly seek to walk in the ways of God. The Law, which once brought fear and dread, now brings delight to a soul because he or she knows it's the path to blessing.

We live in a culture that views blessing as a means of material gain. Yet those, who have been trained by righteousness, possess the Lord as their exceedingly great reward.* The Word of God is our sustenance.

It has been written in plain language for all who desire God's guidance. Those, who walk uprightly in the Law of the Lord, have the blessing now and of eternal life.

This eternal truth instructs us to be those whose feet have been made to travel on the path of righteousness.

———◆———

*Father, Your word is a lamp to my feet and a light to my path. Help me to be someone who travels on the true path of Your Law.*

*I pray these things in Jesus' name. Amen.*

*Genesis 15:1, Psalm 119:105

# LEARNING THE WORD

Blessed are you, O Lord; teach me your statutes.
Psalm 119:12

## HOW CAN A YOUNG MAN KEEP HIS WAY PURE?*

The Psalmist directs us to the Scriptures. If I am to keep my way pure before God, then I must take careful heed to learn His Word. A person cannot properly navigate his or her way through life without an understanding of the Law of God. Therefore, it is absolutely essential that I am taught in the way of righteousness.

Notice that the psalmist is not requesting only a mere academic understanding, but his desire is to be transformed by its truths. It is not enough to have an intellectual understanding of the Word, but rather my entire life must be conformed to it.

Do you share in the psalmist's desire? If so, then let the Word of God transform your life.

◆————————◆————————◆

*Father, I have stored up your word in my heart, that I might not sin against you.\* Help me not to be only a hearer of Your Word, but also to do Your Word. I pray these things in Jesus' name. Amen.*

*Psalm 119:9, 11

# MEDITATING ON THE WORD

I will meditate on your precepts and fix my eyes on your ways.
Psalm 119:15

## WHERE DO YOU FIX YOUR THOUGHTS?

The heart of a man is a deep well. If it is polluted, then it will manifest itself in ungodly thoughts and actions.

It has been the desire of the psalmist to cleanse his way, and he finds the solution in God's Word. Yet he does not seek merely an intellectual study, but an inward conformity to its truths. He has said, "With my whole heart I have sought You; oh, let me not wander from Your commandments!"*

The psalmist's desire for knowledge moves him to meditation.

Our modern-day culture identifies meditation with the practices of Eastern religion, but the Scriptures illustrate for us the idea of deep reflection. Stillness is an art form that has fallen by the wayside in our day. Yet if we are to fix our minds on the things of God, then we must pause and reflect on His Word. Let's delight in the law of the Lord, and on His law meditate day and night.* This will anchor your soul, and ease your mind in the everyday grind of life.

In light of this eternal truth, let us be those who both study and meditate on the Word of God.

*Father, this culture is always on-the-go. Help me to be a person who slows down, and reflects on the deep truths of Scripture.*

*I pray these things in Jesus' name. Amen.*

*Psalm 119:10, Psalm 1:2

# DELIGHTING IN THE WORD

*Your testimonies are my delight; they are my counselors.*
Psalm 119:24

## WHAT BRINGS JOY TO YOUR HEART?

The psalmist has been on a relentless pursuit after God. He possesses an insatiable thirst, not only to know the Commandments, but also to be transformed by them. The Lord has captivated him with His wonderful ways, and therefore the Psalmist is moved to delight.

We are a people who gravitate toward worship. We worship what we love, and pursue what we adore. C.S. Lewis called us a people who are "too easily pleased."[6] So many set their affections on the lesser things in life, and they wonder why they are discontent. The truth is, God has created us for the purpose of worship. All things were created through Him and for Him.*

Our greatest happiness consists, not in the abundance of our possessions, but in possessing the living God. The study of Scripture, in-and-of-itself, will never yield this type of happiness. Our hearts must be stirred up to adoration for the God that reveals it to us. Now may the God of hope fill you with all joy and peace in believing, that you may abound in hope by the power of the Holy Spirit.*

———◆———

*Father, we are a people who are too easily pleased. Give me a heart that longs and pants after You.*

*I pray these things in Jesus' name. Amen.*

*Colossians 1:16, Romans 15:13

# REVIVED IN THE WORD

My soul clings to the dust; give me life according to your word!
Psalm 119:25

## HOW DO YOU NAVIGATE THROUGH TIMES OF DESPAIR?

The psalmist finds solace in God's Word. In the difficulties of life, he finds no other comfort or strength. This world is filled with various trials and unimaginable griefs. It is only when I meditate on the sure promises of scripture, that I will be anchored in true peace.

This is a sure and steadfast anchor of the soul:* we know that all things work together for good to those who love God, to those who are the called according to His purpose.*

The psalmist is struck down, but he is not forsaken. His knowledge of the Word has worked itself out in the crucible of testing. Instead of despair, he finds revival. All those who find deep sorrow need not remain as those who have no hope. Our God has provided a refuge to those who find themselves in great distress. The map is laid out before us if only we will come to it by faith.

Dear friend, do you find yourself weighed down by insurmountable grief? If so, then look not to the moveable things of this life, but rather set your mind on the sure promises of God.

———————◆———————

*Father, this world is broken. The billows of life can tend to overwhelm me. Help me to be like this psalmist who finds comfort in Your Word.*

*I pray these things in Jesus' name. Amen.*

*Hebrews 6:19, Romans 8:28

# STEADFAST IN THE WORD

I cling to your testimonies, O Lord; let me not be put to shame!
Psalm 119:31

## HAVE YOU RESOLVED TO KEEP GOD'S WORD?

In the midst of trials, the writer finds a faithful companion in the Holy Scriptures. While his soul clings to the dust,* he clings to God's faithful testimonies. Times of testing often accompany great temptations. Though, it is the person who commits themselves to God's Word, who will be preserved in the hour of trial.

Jesus promises, "Because you have kept my word about patient endurance, I will keep you from the hour of trial that is coming on the whole world, to try those who dwell on the earth.*

The psalmist has resolved to keep the testimonies of Yahweh. This keeps him afloat in times of great difficulty. The eyes of faith behold the promises of God without wavering or doubting. It speaks in this way, "Though He slay me yet I will still trust Him."*

Have you found yourself vulnerable to temptation? Faint not, but rather hold fast to God's Word. Satan will seek to fill your mind with doubt, but the Scriptures will flood your mind with peace.

---

*Father, times of testing often lead me to vulnerability. Give me the grace to fill my mind with the Gospel of peace.*

*I pray these things in Jesus' name. Amen.*

*Psalm 119:25, Revelation 3:10, Job 13:15

# SALVATION IN THE WORD

Let your steadfast love come to me, O Lord,
your salvation according to your promise.
Psalm 119:41

## DO YOU TAKE GOD AT HIS WORD?

Often times the promises of Scripture do not manifest themselves in plain sight, and yet the psalmist finds assurance in God's Word. He is not left in despair, but rather hopes in the promises of Yahweh. The Christian life is one that is marked by faith.

Times of testing will reveal the condition of our hearts. Will we waver in unbelief or will we remain steadfast in God's love? When you endure, your joyful perseverance in trials reflects the glory of God to an unbelieving world. It echoes hope of eternity to those who remain in despair.

In a world that seeks answers for the problems which it faces, the Christian has found its answers in God's Word. Therefore, let us be those who have our perspective on trials shaped by His faithful testimonies.

———————

*Father, in your abundant mercy, You have begotten us again to a living hope.\* Your Word reveals the answers to life's greatest challenges. May Your loving devotion comfort me, I pray, according to Your promise to Your servant.\**

*I pray these things in Jesus' name. Amen.*

\*1 Peter 1:3, Psalm 119:76

# ANSWERS IN THE WORD

Then shall I have an answer for him who taunts me,
for I trust in your word.
Psalm 119: 42

## HOW SHOULD YOU RESPOND TO YOUR CRITICS?

Sinful people have always scoffed at the Word of God, because their unbelief has blinded them to the Gospel. Here in the text, the psalmist finds himself to be no stranger to these scoffers, but he comes prepared with answers.

His tongue is the pen of a ready writer.* He does not rest on the convention of worldly wisdom, but rather he commits his trust to the wisdom of God.

The Apostle Paul teaches us that the weapons of our warfare are not carnal, but spiritual.* The high places of worldly wisdom shouted out by scorners are silenced by a soldier who rightly wields the sword of the Spirit, which is the Word of God. The psalmist has been put on the defensive, nevertheless, he is emboldened by the testimonies of Yahweh.

Dear Christian, if you find yourself attacked by the forces of evil, then rest in the promises of Scripture since God has given you a mighty weapon.

*Father, many seek to ensnare me with their words. Give me wisdom to wield the Word of God so that I can share the hope that lies within me.*

*I pray these things in Jesus' name. Amen.*

*Psalm 45:1, 2 Corinthians 10:4, Ephesians 6:17

# LIBERTY IN THE WORD

And I shall walk in a wide place, for I have sought your precepts. Psalm 119:45

## WHAT IS TRUE LIBERTY?

Satan would have us believe that there is no freedom on the path of righ-teousness, but this is quite contrary to the truth. The psalmist finds true liberty in God's Word. He continues, "I will speak of Your testimonies before kings, and I will not be ashamed. I delight in Your command-ments because I love them".*

This is not merely an outward conformity to laws, but rather an inward love in truth. He has set his whole being toward God in a spirit of adulation. Instead of being enslaved, he is enjoying a joyous freedom which comes from above.

This is so contrary to the ways of unrighteousness. Those who tread on the unrighteous path find themselves enslaved under a heavy yoke. Instead of true life and freedom, they find a road that leads to death. As my love for the Lord matures, through the Spirit of God, I am able to enjoy the wide places of liberty.

Have you sought the precepts of the Lord? Then do not be entangled again to a yoke of bondage, but rather enjoy the wide fields of God's grace.

———————————————

*Father, Satan would have me to believe that there is no liberty in following You. Help me to have a proper understanding of the true liberty that You offer me in the Gospel.*

*I pray these things in Jesus' name. Amen.*

*Psalm 119:46-47

# ILLUMINATION IN THE WORD

Your hands have made and fashioned me; give me understanding
that I may learn your commandments.

Psalm 119:73

## WHO GIVES UNDERSTANDING?

Is it not the Lord Who formed you in your mother's womb?* The psalm-ist entreats, not the favor of men, but rather makes his petitions to his glorious Creator. Jehovah sits above the circle of the earth.* His hands have made all things with infinite wisdom, and He looks down from heaven on the children of man to see if there are any who understand, who seek after Him.*

The psalmist rests, not on the arm of the flesh, but seeks that pure under-standing which is from above.

Are we seeking man's understanding or God's? For His thoughts are not our thoughts, nor are our ways His ways.* Apart from the supernatural work of the Holy Spirit, the Scriptures will only be a dry intellectual study. It is only through Him that we can discern those things that are spiritual.

Today, let us entreat the Lord for His understanding. It is He, Who sits above the circle of the earth,* Who will illuminate your mind to the truths of Scripture.

———————◆———————

*Father, Your hands have fashioned me. You have given me wisdom and under-standing. Help me not merely to know Your truth, but also to internalize it.*

*I pray these things in Jesus' name. Amen.*

*Jeremiah 1:5, Isaiah 40:22, Psalm 53:2, Isaiah 55:8, Isaiah 40:22

# COMFORT IN THE WORD

Let your steadfast love comfort me according to
your promise to your servant.
Psalm 119:76

## WHERE CAN COMFORT BE FOUND?

The waves of life's storms often come crashing down on us with a relentless fury. If we are not anchored in the sure promises of Scripture, in a moment, we can be easily swept away.

Saving faith rests, not on the uncertainties of life, but on the immovable God. Here in the text, the psalmist finds comfort as he brings to mind the Scriptures. He does not call for Yahweh to act outside of His Word, but rather to act according to His Word. This brings him great solace in the midst of the chaos that surrounds him.

In like manner, Christians can rest assured of God's promises to them. These promises offer them great comfort and hope in the midst of the storms. Many, are His wonderful works which He has done; and His thoughts toward us cannot be recounted. If we would declare and speak of them, they are more than can be numbered.*

With this eternal truth in mind, let us consider the many promises of God. Though we may not know what sorrows will come our way, we have an anchor which keeps us grounded in hope.

---

*Father, the uncertainties of life seek to drown me in despair. Help me to take comfort in Your immutable promises.*

*I pray these things in Jesus' name. Amen.*

*Psalm 40:5

175

# HOPE IN THE WORD

My soul longs for Your salvation; I hope in Your Word.
Psalm 119:81

## HOW CAN ONE HOPE FOR WHAT HE SEES?

The Apostle Paul poses this question: "For in this hope we were saved. Now hope that is seen is not hope. For who hopes for what he sees? But if we hope for what we do not see, we wait for it with patience."*

This question helps us to focus in on the proper perspective. Salvation, though realized in part, will not be fully realized until the end of the age. Similarly, here in the text, the psalmist finds himself in an interesting position. He has treasured God's Word, but he still faces the trials of life. In spite of his present troubles, he places his hope in the promises of Jehovah. This allows him not to lose heart in the midst of a conflict. In like manner, dear Christians, we can look to God's Word as the lighthouse. He will send forth His light and His truth to guide us.* Even though we are weighed down by the various trials of life, we long for what is unseen.

Dear friend, do you find yourself tossed to and fro by the billows of life's uncertainties? Be patient. Look not to the things which are seen, but rather place your hope in God's Word.

————————◆————————

*Father, there are so many things that tempt me to take my eyes off of You. Help me to hope in the sure promises of Your Word.*

*I pray these things in Jesus' name. Amen.*

*Romans 8:24-25, Psalm 43:3

# ENDURANCE OF THE WORD

Forever, O Lord, your word is firmly fixed in the heavens.
Psalm 119:89

## HOW OFTEN DO YOU REFLECT ON THE MEANING OF FOREVER?

God's Word transcends even time itself. It proceeds from the corridors of eternity, and therefore, abides forever.

In this portion of the Scripture, the psalmist is enduring a season of suffering, but he knows that it will last for only a time. In his moment of affliction, he places his hope in God's enduring Word. He understands that it is "fixed in the heavens," and that it cannot be changed or altered. And thus he prays, "Revive me according to Your loving devotion, and I will obey the testimony of Your mouth. Your faithfulness continues through all generations; You established the earth, and it endures."* This gives him the strength to endure in the midst of his current trials.

In such a way, you and I have much to rejoice over. God has given His people great and precious promises.* These promises will never fade away, but are etched in the marble of eternity. For the Lord is good, and His loving devotion endures forever. His faithfulness continues to all generations.*

This eternal truth is forever. He has spoken it, and therefore it shall not fail.

———————◇———————

*Father, we live in a world of change. There are changing seasons and changing kingdoms. In light of this truth, help me to fix my hope in Your unchanging Word.*

*I pray these things in Jesus' name. Amen.*

*Psalm 119:88,90, 2 Peter 1:4, Psalm 100:5

# LIGHT OF THE WORD

Your word is a lamp to my feet and a light to my path.
Psalm 119:105

## WHICH ROAD SHOULD YOU TAKE?

The writer has resolved to follow the light of God's Word. This has been his compass in all matters of life. His desire is for the Lord to guide him in the way that he should go, and he finds that direction in His Word. He does not seek to be led by worldly wisdom or vain philosophies, but rather through the wisdom of God.

In the prior verse, the psalmist declares that he hates every false way. Thereafter, he declares, "I have sworn an oath and confirmed it, to keep your righteous rules.* Those, who have been redeemed by the blood of Christ, have been given a new heart with new desires. God will put His Spirit within you and cause you to walk in His statutes and to carefully observe His ordinances.*

God's redeemed no longer desire to walk in the darkness of this world. Instead, they find their delight in the Law of the Lord. It is their desire that the Lord would direct their steps, and they look for that direction in the Scriptures.

Dear friend, this eternal truth teaches us that God's Word will light the path on which way you should go.

―――――――――◇―――――――――

*Father, Your Word is a lamp shining in a dark place, until the day dawns and the morning star rises in my heart.* Help me not to stumble in the darkness of sin, but rather to find my direction in Your Word.*

*I pray these things in Jesus' name. Amen.*

*Psalm 119:104, 106, Ezekiel 36:26-27, 2 Peter 1:19

# REMEMBERING THE WORD

I hold my life in my hand continually, but I do not forget your law.
Psalm 119:109

## DO YOU HIDE GOD'S WORD IN YOUR HEART?

The psalmist's life constantly hangs in the balance, but he will not stop obeying God's instructions. He remains at rest in the Lord's promises. Instead of being given over to fear he remembers the Law of God, and this keeps him grounded in times of great distress.

This portion of Scripture teaches us the value of remembrance. One of the greatest helps in the life of a Christian is a good memory. Those who hide God's Word in their heart, find a great source of comfort in times of great need and trouble. The Scriptures hold us up, and keep us safe, so we need to remember God's Word continually.*

Dearly beloved, the Helper, the Holy Spirit, whom the Father has given in the name of Jesus Christ, will teach you all things and bring to your remembrance all that Jesus has said to you.*

———————◆———————

*Father, help me not to wonder from Your commandments in times of great distress\*, but rather to keep Your Word ever before me.*

*I pray these things in Jesus' name. Amen.*

*Psalm 119:117, John 14:26, Psalm 119:10

# DEDICATION TO THE WORD

I hate the double-minded, but I love your law.
Psalm 119:113

## DO YOU HAVE DIVIDED INTERESTS?

The psalmist has followed Yahweh with a whole heart, and to that end, his devotion to Him remains unhindered. He is so taken up with the purposes of God that he hates any notion of compromise. In wisdom, he has chosen the true path, and this keeps him from the dangers of sin.

In like manner, our Lord Jesus Christ has warned us of the dangers of compromise. He referred to those who compromise as those who hear the word, but the cares of the world and the deceitfulness of riches and the desires for other things enter in and choke the Word, and it proves unfruitful.* Jesus would rather us be hot or cold, because He spews out those who are lukewarm.* Those, who walk by faith, are not tossed to and fro by various doubts. They remain at rest in His faithful promises, and their resolve is to walk in obedience to His Word. We must cast out arguments and every high thing that exalts itself against the knowledge of God, and bring every thought into captivity to the obedience of Christ.*

Dear friend, when we find ourselves gravitating between faith and unbelief, let us seek the Lord for a whole-hearted resolve to follow His ways.

---

*Father, Your Law is the delight of my soul. In times of trial and temptation, please give me an unwavering faith in Your promises.*

*I pray these things in Jesus' name. Amen.*

*Mark 4:19, Revelation 3:16, 2 Corinthians 10:5

# OBEDIENCE TO THE WORD

You spurn all who go astray from your statues,
for their cunning is in vain.
Psalm 119:118

## WHAT DOES IT MEAN TO FEAR THE LORD?

King Solomon teaches, "The fear of the Lord is hatred of evil. Pride and arrogance and the way of evil and perverted speech I hate."* A healthy fear of the Lord will preserve us from evil.

That's why the psalmist warns us about the dangers of disobedience. Do not be deceived. God cannot be mocked. A man reaps what he sows.* Those, who will not submit themselves to the Lordship of Jesus Christ, will one day bow their knee to Him.* We must be wise to heed the words of this text.

Discretion will watch over you, and understanding will guard you, to deliver you from the way of evil, from the man who speaks perversity, and from those who leave the straight paths to walk in the ways of darkness.*

Dear friend, would you like to receive blessing from the Lord? If so, then Jesus instructed us that we must enter through the narrow and straight gate.*

---

*Father, the heathen rage against You in vain, but You laugh at their plans.\* You see that their day is coming. In light of this truth, teach me to fear You in all my ways.*

*I pray these things in Jesus' name. Amen.*

*Proverbs 8:13, Galatians 6:7, Philippians 2:9, Proverb 2:11-13, Matthew 7:13, Psalm 2:1

# REVERENCING THE WORD

My flesh trembles for fear of you, and I am afraid of your judgments.
Psalm 119:120

## ARE WE MOVED WITH GODLY FEAR?

The psalmist took the Word of God very seriously. He had such a deep feeling of respect and awe, that it moved him with an intense urgency to obey God's commandments. He would rather commit his life into the hands of God, than to commit it into the hands of his oppressors. He said, "Rulers persecute me without cause, but my heart fears only Your Word."*

It is better to fear the Keeper of souls than the rulers of earthly kingdoms. Jesus said, "I tell you, my friends, do not fear those who kill the body, and after that have nothing more that they can do. But I will warn you whom to fear: fear Him who, after He has killed, has authority to cast into hell. Yes, I tell you, fear Him!"*

When we choose the fear of the Lord over the fear of man, we shall find rest in the hands of his Divine Sovereignty. Trust in God and do not be afraid. What can man do?*

———————◆———————

*Father, it is better to trust in You than to place my confidence in man. Help me to learn to place my trust in You and commit my life into Your hands.*

*I pray these things in Jesus' name. Amen.*

*Psalm 119:161, Luke 12:4-5, Psalm 56:11

# VALUING THE WORD

Therefore I love your commandments above gold, above fine gold.
Psalm 119:127

## WHAT IS VALUED MORE THAN GOLD AND SILVER, YET IS PRICELESS?

The psalmist understood the answer to that riddle. He saw the value of God's Word to be far superior to the things of this earth. The words of the Lord are flawless, like silver refined in a furnace, like gold purified sevenfold.* In that day, many chose to pervert justice, but he clung tightly to the testimonies of Yahweh.

In like manner, King Solomon has much to say on valuing God's Word. He exhorts, "How much better to get wisdom than gold! To get understanding is to be chosen rather than silver."* God's wisdom is more precious than rubies, and all the things you may desire cannot compare.*

When we treasure God's Word, He will be a shield to those who walk in integrity, guarding the paths of justice and watching over the way of his saints.* His discretion will watch over you, understanding will guard you, delivering you from the way of evil, from men of perverted speech.*

Wisdom cries aloud to us, and it invites us to its banqueting table. If we prize it beyond any earthly riches, it will serve as a safeguard to us in times of evil. Let us therefore treasure the wisdom of God in the midst of a crooked and perverse generation.

---

*Father, You have given me a treasure trove of wisdom in Your Word. Help me to prize Your testimonies far more than any earthly treasures.*

*I pray these things in Jesus' name. Amen.*

*Psalm 12:6, Proverbs 16:16, Proverbs 3:15, Proverbs 2:7-8, Proverbs 2:11-12

# GUIDANCE OF THE WORD

The unfolding of your words gives light,
it imparts understanding to the simple.
Psalm 119:130

## DO YOU WANT UNDERSTANDING?

Dear friend, listen to the words of this text. Understanding is revealed to us in God's Word. We do not need to travel great distances nor plummet to the depths of the sea. The Word is very near you. It is in your mouth and in your heart, so that you can do it.* And if you confess with your mouth, "Jesus is Lord," and believe in your heart that God raised Him from the dead, you will be saved.* Then understanding is cultivated through the illuminating work of the Holy Spirit.

Even the simple in knowledge can be made mighty instructors of righteousness.

Here in the text, the psalmist knows the unfolding of God's Word imparts understanding. This gives him light to choices and decisions that lay before him. In times of great distress, God's Word grants him much wisdom in times of perplexity.

This eternal truth unlocks the door to understanding. God has provided to us great comfort in the faithful promises of His Word.

＊——————◆——————＊

*Father, You have given me much wisdom in Your Word. Grant me the grace each day to be led by its light.*

*I pray these things in Jesus' name. Amen.*

*Deuteronomy 30:14, Romans 10:9

# PRESERVATION OF THE WORD

Keep steady my steps according to your promise,
and let no iniquity get dominion over me.
Psalm 119:133

## HOW CAN WE GUARD OUR WAYS FROM EVIL?

When the psalmist found himself in the midst of trouble, he turned to God's promises to steady his steps. His enemies were on the pursuit, and they sought to lay a snare for his soul. In faith he makes his petition before God, and is therefore preserved from evil.

He prayed, "Turn to me and show me mercy, as You do to those who love Your name. Establish my steps through Your promise and let no sin rule over me. Redeem me from the oppression of man, that I may keep Your precepts."*

In like manner, the saints of God are kept by faith through the power of His Word. Their delight is in the Law of the Lord,* and their ways are kept from the snares of the enemy.

Dear friend, would you like to be preserved from the hour of testing? If so, then cling to the promises of God by faith. Those, who trust in the Lord, will be preserved from the way of death.

---

*Father, how can a young man keep his way pure? He keeps his way pure by taking heed according to Your Word.* Give me the grace to understand the things which You have written down for my instruction for my protection and safe-guarding.*

*I pray these things in Jesus' name. Amen.*

*Psalm 119:132-134, Psalm 1:2, Psalm 119:10

# ZEAL OF THE WORD

My eyes shed streams of tears, because people do not keep your law.
Psalm 119:136

## HOW DO WE POSSESS A HOLY ZEAL FOR GOD?

The psalmist was not only zealous for God, but he was zealous to see others walk in His Law. This causes him to be moved to tears for those who disobey God's commandments.

Do we share in the zeal of the psalmist?

If so, then it will manifest itself in compassion for the lost. The Prophet Jeremiah wrote, Oh, that my head were a spring of water, and my eyes a fountain of tears, I would weep day and night over the slain daughter of my people."*

This is contrary to the spirit of religious hypocrisy. Those, who only reform themselves outwardly, are only looking to win the argument, like the Pharisees. Yet those, who are in Christ, are to be sound theologians who desire the salvation of sinners. Their orthodoxy should be a living and powerful testimony to a lost and dying world.

The Apostle Paul said, "To the weak I became weak, that I might win the weak. I have become all things to all people, that by all means I might save some. I do it all for the sake of the gospel, that I may share with them in its blessings."*

Has God's Word driven you to be critical or compassionate towards others? Let us be those who are zealous to see sinners spared from the judgment to come.

———◆———◉———◆———

*Father, You have instructed me in the way of righteousness. Help me to be a person whose understanding manifests itself in compassion for the lost.*

*I pray these things in Jesus' name. Amen.*

*Jeremiah 9:1, 1 Corinthians 9:22-23

# RIGHTEOUSNESS OF THE WORD

You have appointed your testimonies in righteousness
and in all faithfulness.

Psalm 119:138

## WHAT DOES THE WORD REVEAL ABOUT THE CHARACTER OF GOD?

The psalmist reveals two key things about God's testimonies. First, we know that these words come directly from the mouth of God. Secondly, we know that these words are consistent with His character.

The Holy Scriptures are God-breathed, and divinely appointed by Him. All of His decrees have been etched in the granite of eternity, and they shall surely come to pass. Yet they are also a revelation of His Divine righteousness. There is no sin or iniquity that proceeds from His mouth, but every word spoken by God is faithful. So what is the purpose?

All Scripture is breathed out by God and profitable for teaching, for reproof, for correction, and for training in righteousness, that the man of God may be complete, equipped for every good work.*

Today, let's rely on God's Word. Let our souls find refreshment as we meditate on His Divine testimonies.

———————◇———————

*Father, Your words are faithful and true. Help me not to meditate on the profane, but rather to fix my thoughts on Your wonderful testimonies.*

*I pray these things in Jesus' name. Amen.*

*2 Timothy 3:16-17

# PURITY OF THE WORD

Your promise is well tried, and your servant loves it.

Psalm 119:140

## IS THERE ANY ERROR WITH GOD?

God's Word has endured the highest scrutiny, and yet it still shows itself to be perfect. Here the psalmist declares God's promises to be "well tried." God's testimonies have proven to be purer than the most refined silver and gold.

This is not so with fallen man.

Contrarily, our words have been weighed in the balances and found wanting.* They are filled with dross, and they reflect the condition of our sinful hearts. All of us would do well to reflect on the pure words of God, rather than our own opinions. To this degree, the psalmist considers the Divine promise, and is moved to adoration. He has whole-heartedly embraced the pure promises of God.

Dear friend, do you love the pure words of Scripture? Every word of God is pure, and He is a shield to those who put their trust in Him.* Cling to the sure promises of Yahweh, and desire the pure milk of the Word, that you may grow thereby.*

---

*Father, there has never been found any iniquity in Your mouth. Help my soul to take delight in Your pure and peaceable words of righteousness.*

*I pray these things in Jesus' name. Amen.*

*Daniel 5:27, Proverbs 30:5, 1 Peter 2:2

# TRUTH OF THE WORD

The sum of your word is truth, and every one of your
righteous rules endures forever.
Psalm 119:160

## "WHAT IS TRUTH?"*

That was the question posed by Pontius Pilot when he interrogated our Lord. It is still a question that is asked by many today.

The psalmist knows two things about truth. First it is found in God's Word. The entirety of it, down to the very jot and tittle, is completely true. Second, he understands that the Word of God endures forever.

The law of the Lord is perfect, reviving the soul; the testimony of the Lord is trustworthy, making wise the simple.* God's testimonies, which He has commanded, are righteous and very faithful. His righteousness is an everlasting righteousness, and His law is true.*

Many philosophies have come and gone, but God's Word never fades away. His Word is eternal truth. What He has spoken will surely come to pass. Knowing this truth, we would do well to make God's Word our perpetual dwelling place. It will serve us as a beacon of hope in all seasons of life.

Let us be those who place our confidence in the sure and unchangeable testimonies of Yahweh.

---

*Father, there have been no truer words spoken, but what has proceeded out of Your mouth. Help me to fix my hope in the true promises of Scripture.*

*I pray these things in Jesus' name. Amen.*

*John 18:38, Psalm 19:7, Psalm 119:138,142

# MAJESTY OF THE WORD

Princes persecute me without cause,
but my heart stands in awe of your words.
Psalm 119:161

## IS YOUR HEART IN AWE OF GOD'S WORD?

It is easy to lose that sense of awe for God in the everyday grind of life. Yet we are to stand amazed in our worship of God—even when persecuted.

The psalmist remains steadfast in the Word of God. His heart beats with a sense of wonder and amazement for the Holy Scriptures. This keeps him grounded in times of trouble. A mere intellectual study of the Word will never keep anyone rooted when they are mistreated. There must be a holy resolve within us that delights in the Law to rise above threats.

In times of great trial, it is God's Word that will keep us quieted in faith. Though rulers may sit and slander you, God's servant meditates on His statutes.*

What about you dear friend? Are you quiet and at peace in the promises of God's Word? If not, then let us seek the Lord for a new sense of wonder and awe in His Holy Word.

————————◆————————

*Father, in times of persecution, so often it is too easy to lose that sense of majesty in worship. Help my heart to remain in adoration of Your Holy Word in good times and in bad.*

*I pray these things in Jesus' name. Amen.*

*Psalm 119:23

# REJOICING IN THE WORD

I rejoice at your word like one who finds great spoil.
Psalm 119:162

## WHAT DOES YOUR HEART TREASURE?

Throughout this portion of Scripture, the psalmist has been encountering persecution from the hands of his enemies. Yet in spite of his conflict, he rejoices and holds fast to God's Word like one who takes great riches from slain kings and chiefs in battle. His discovery was like finding a prize!

The breakthrough of God's Word keeps us in wonder and awe of the Lord's testimonies, and causes our heart to rejoice. Even though enemies pursued the psalmist, we see him satisfied with the good things which are from above.

In like manner we too possess all the promises of God. They are great riches and we can rejoice as one who finds a great prize in times of trial. Our hope is not placed in what the natural eye can see, but rather placed in the surety of things unseen. This allows us to remain unmoved by our present circumstances. In all these things we are more than conquerors through Him who loved us.*

Have you placed your hope in God? If so, then let us be those who rejoice in the great treasure of God's Word.

---

*Father, it can be difficult to keep an eternal perspective in the face of adversity. Give me the grace to treasure the things that the eye cannot see.*

*I pray these things in Jesus' name. Amen.*

*Romans 8:37

# PEACE IN THE WORD

Great peace have those who love your law;
nothing can make them stumble.
Psalm 119:65

## ARE YOU PRONE TO WORRY?

This world strikes fear in the hearts of many, doesn't it. We live in a time of wars and rumors of war. There are natural disasters and earthquakes in various places.* If these things aren't enough to warrant fear, then there are the worries of everyday life. Yet in spite of the many uncertainties that surround us, we can have much peace.

Jesus said, "Peace I leave with you; my peace I give to you. Not as the world gives do I give to you. Let not your hearts be troubled, neither let them be afraid."* This is not a peace that the world gives, but rather an unwavering assurance in the promises of God.

The psalmist loved the law, and found great peace for his heart. This was the peace of walking in righteousness, and it secured his soul during times of trial. In like manner, those who fear God need not fear the mov-ing forces of our day. They, who have been saved from their sins, find true rest for their souls. The peace of God, which surpasses all understanding, will guard our hearts and minds through Christ Jesus.*

Therefore, let us who have the peace of God allow that peace to rule our hearts. It is a chief cornerstone to the elect and precious, and he who believes on Him will by no means be put to shame.*

---

*Father, You offer me a peace that surpasses all understanding. Help me to rest in quiet assurance of Your great and precious promises to me.*

*I pray these things in Jesus' name. Amen.*

*Matthew 24:6-7, John 14:27, Philippians 4:7, 1 Peter 2:6

# LOVING THE WORD

My soul keeps your testimonies; I love them exceedingly.
Psalm 119:167

## WHERE DO YOUR AFFECTIONS LIE?

Salvation is not measured by outward professions or deeds, but rather sources itself in our hidden affections of the soul. Every person worships what he or she loves, and if their heart has been made new they will love the Lord his God.

Here in the text, the Psalmist has resolved to cling to the testimonies of Yahweh. He is not satisfied with a mere outward observance of the Law, but rather desires for these truths to radically transform him. His affections are stirred for the Law of God. He delights in the law of God according to the inward man.*

In like manner, the children of God will be blessed if their soul exceedingly delights in God. The Christian delights to do God's will, and the Law of God is written upon their hearts.* This means going beyond the surface of the academic mind, and penetrating deep into the recesses of the heart.

Do you share in the desire of the psalmist? If so, then engage both your mind and your heart in His worship.

*Father, You desire not only my mind, but all of my affections as well. Help me to be whole-hearted in my devotion to You.*

*I pray these things in Jesus' name. Amen.*

*Romans 7:22, Psalm 40:8

# SINGING THE WORD

My tongue will sing of your word,
for all your commandments are right.
Psalm 119:172

## WHAT ARE YOUR FAVORITE SONGS ON YOUR PLAYLIST?

Throughout this month, we have learned about this psalmist's discourse on the Law of God. God's Law is not only on his mind, but it is deeply hidden in his heart.

The outward obedience of the Law stems from an inward desire to follow God's ways. This delight has naturally flowed into an outward proclamation that keeps him singing the praises of Yahweh. Telling the generation to come the praises of the Lord, and His strength and His wonderful works that He has done.*

In like manner, the Christian has much to rejoice over. We have been given great and precious promises in God's Word. There is no longer any fear in death, but rather an imminent reunion with our Savior. This gives the believer great consolation in the midst of everyday problems.

In light of this eternal truth, let us echo the praises of eternity to a lost and dying world.

＊━━━━━◆━━━━━＊

*Father, You have given me much reason for singing and dancing. Help me to always have a song of praise in my hearts, and on my lips.*

*I pray these things in Jesus' name. Amen.*

*Psalm 76:4

# JULY

## WHAT IS THE GOSPEL?

The Gospel is the greatest message that the world has ever received. Over the course of centuries this most profound message has turned the world radically upside down. In the Gospel we see many lives transformed, but sadly, it is a message that is misunderstood in our culture.

We live in a day when people are gravitating to the conveniences around them. For the time has come when people will not endure sound teaching, but will have itching ears and they will accumulate for themselves teachers to suit their own passions. They will turn away from listening to the truth and wander off into myths.* They do not want to be bothered with the most pressing questions of humanity. So many churches today are settling for a watered down message that bears little or no resemblance to the true Gospel.

So what is the Gospel?

If we are going to truly understand what it means to have eternal life, then we must think critically. There have been countless throughout the ages that have given their lives for the message of the Cross. Paul the Apostle was no different. He likened the Gospel to the power of God unto salvation to everyone who believes. For in it the righteousness of God is revealed.*

My prayer for you, as we study the first eight chapters of Romans, would be that the Holy Spirit grips you with the Gospel that was preached in the First Century. Let us come to the Holy Scriptures with an open mind and an open heart.

2 Timothy 4:3-4, Romans 1:16-17

# SEPARATED UNTO THE GOSPEL

Paul, a servant of Jesus Christ, called to be an apostle,
set apart for the gospel of God.

Romans 1:1

## WHAT DID THE GOSPEL DO FOR THE "CHIEF OF ALL SINNERS?"

Meet the man who zealously persecuted and killed Christians. Saul of Tarsus was no friend of the church. He prided himself on being a keeper of the Law, and he sought the lives of those who were followers of the Way. This religious zealot went to great lengths in his opposition of the saints.

All of that changed one day while he was traveling on the Damascus Road. Suddenly a light from heaven shone around Paul, and falling to the ground, he heard a voice saying to him, "Saul, Saul, why are you persecuting me?" And he said, "Who are you, Lord?" And he said, "I am Jesus, whom you are persecuting."* On that particular day Paul met Jesus, and his life was radically changed.

No longer would Paul persecute the church, but he went out proclaiming the Lord Jesus Christ to all who would listen. In like manner, all of the saints are witnesses to the power of the Gospel. Grace has shown them the depravity of their hearts, and has set them free from the grip of sin.

If you have experienced this grace firsthand, then let your life be a witness to the power of God through the Gospel.

*Father, where would I be without the Gospel? You have graciously shown me my sin, and have delivered me from its curse. Help my life to reflect the Gospel to a lost and dying world.*

*I pray these things in Jesus' name. Amen.*

*Acts 9:3-6

# THE PROMISE OF THE GOSPEL

Which he promised beforehand through His prophets in the Holy Scriptures.
Romans 1:2

## WHAT IS THE SINGLE GREATEST PROMISE GIVEN TO MANKIND?

The greatest promise ever given to man was the coming of the Messiah. He would come to save His people from their sins.*

This is a hope of eternal life which God, who cannot lie, promised before time began, but has in due time manifested His word through preaching, which was committed to the Apostle Paul according to the commandment of God our Savior.*

Here in the text, Paul reminds us that the Gospel was promised beforehand in ancient times. The prophets foretold of the salvation of God's people. Their message was one of exhortation, edification, and comfort. They exhorted God's people to turn from their sin, they encouraged God's people to trust in Him, and they comforted God's people with the hope of a future deliverance.

Yet their eyes never saw the One Who was promised. They embraced the Promise, which was far off, as though it was near.

Many centuries have been removed, and now the saints have been entrusted with this glorious Gospel. The church no longer dwells in the types and shadows of the Old Testament, but it now lives in the substance of its Savior. In light of this truth, let us rest fully in the hope that lies before us.

*Father, You have fulfilled the promise of salvation to Your people. Help me to trust fully in those promises which have been written down for my joy.*

*I pray these things in Jesus' name. Amen.*

*Matthew 1:21, Titus 1:2-3

# THE REVELATION OF THE GOSPEL

Concerning His Son, who descended from David according to the flesh.

Romans 1:3

## CAN GOD BE CONTAINED IN A HOUSE OF WORSHIP?

That was the question which the prophet posed to King David.

David called for his son Solomon and instructed him to build a house for the Lord, the God of Israel. "My son," said David to Solomon, "it was in my heart to build a house for the Name of the LORD my God."* The sweet Psalmist of Israel wanted to build the Lord a house, but the time was not yet appointed. The God, Who cannot be contained, would build David a throne and a house that would be established forever.

Jesus Christ is the fulfillment of that promise. He shall be great, and shall be called the Son of the Highest: and the Lord God shall give unto him the throne of his father David: And He shall reign over the house of Jacob for ever; and of His kingdom there shall be no end.* In Jesus' humiliation He secured our redemption, and in His exaltation He reigns as King of kings. It was through the line of David that God would bring about this everlasting kingdom.

Those, who have been redeemed by the blood of Christ, are now citizens of that heavenly kingdom. Kingdoms may rise and fall, but Jesus is our King Eternal.*

---

*Father, the heaven of heavens cannot contain You,* but You remain faithful to Your servants. Help us to rest fully in the arms of Your everlasting faithfulness.*

*I pray these things in Jesus' name. Amen.*

*1 Chronicles 22:6-7, Luke 1:32-33, 1 Kings 8:27, 2 Chronicles 6:18

# THE POWER OF THE GOSPEL

And was declared to be the Son of God in power according to the Spirit of holiness by His resurrection from the dead, Jesus Christ our Lord.

Romans 1:4

## HOW IS TRUE POWER PUT ON DISPLAY?

According to Paul, true power was put on display in the resurrection of Jesus Christ. God was manifested in the flesh, justified in the Spirit, seen by angels, preached among the Gentiles, believed on in the world, received up in glory.*

The Gospel offers us victory over death. This is not merely a power over physical death, but also a power over sin. All of us, apart from Christ, were dead in our trespasses and sins.* We were under the curse of Adam, but God sent His Son to be accursed for us.* It was in His death that He satisfied the righteous requirements of the Law, but it is through His resurrection that He brings power from the grave.

Therefore, we need not remain as those who have no hope,* but rather rejoice in the victory we now possess in Christ. Let it be known to you, and to all the people, that by the name of Jesus Christ of Nazareth, whom was crucified, God raised from the dead. There is salvation in no other, for there is no other name under heaven given among men by which we must be saved.*

---

*Father, You are not the God of the dead, but of the living.* Can these dead bones live? Surely You know.* Help me to rejoice in the hope of the resurrection, and free me from the fear of death.*

*I pray these things in Jesus' name. Amen.*

*1 Timothy 3:16, Ephesians 2:1, Galatians 3:13, 1 Thessalonians 4:13, Acts 4:10-12, Mark 12:27, Ezekiel 37:1-14

# THE GRACE OF THE GOSPEL

Through whom we have received grace and apostleship...
Romans 1:5

## WHAT ROLE DOES THE SINNER PLAY IN THEIR SALVATION?

The sinner makes absolutely no contribution to their salvation. It is a gift that we cannot merit or earn. For by grace you have been saved through faith. And this is not your own doing; it is the gift of God, not a result of works, so that no one may boast.*

The case has already been spread out against us, and the verdict that is laid before us is "guilty." This is the worst possible news, because the only thing we can merit is judgment. It was only through the undeserved kindness of God that we stand before Him forgiven. He sent His Son to fulfill the righteous requirements of the Law, and suffer the penalty for our sins.

Now all I must do is simply receive this gracious gift by faith. This leaves no room for the boasting of man, but rather gives all glory to God alone. For I say, through the grace given to me, to everyone who is among you, not to think of himself more highly than he ought to think, but to think soberly, as God has dealt to each one a measure of faith.*

Have we truly come to understand what grace is all about? Let's look no further than to the Gospel. It is a precious gift that has been granted to us freely.

---

*Father, You have not dealt with me according to what my sins deserve. Instead of judgment You have given me mercy. Help me not to fall back into a work-righteousness system, but to walk in the grace that I now stand.*

*I pray these things in Jesus' name. Amen.*

*Ephesians 2:8-9, Romans 12:3

# THE DIVERSITY OF THE GOSPEL

...to bring about the obedience of faith for the
sake of his name among all the nations.
Romans 1:5

## WHO ARE THE RECIPIENTS OF GRACE?

Paul the Apostle was born from the tribe of Benjamin. He was circumcised on the eighth day,* and at one time boasted in his Jewish heritage. It wasn't until Divine grace met him that he came to trust in a righteousness that was apart from the Law.

The true Israel of God does not consist in flesh and blood, but rather of those who are the seed according to faith. There is neither Jew nor Greek, slave nor free, male nor female, for we are all one in Christ Jesus. And if you belong to Christ, then you are Abraham's seed and heirs according to the promise.* This grace extends to all peoples, tribes, tongues, and nations.

Yet all of this was done for the sake of God's Son. The Father has given Him the nations for His inheritance, and the ends of the earth as His possession.* In this glorious Gospel, God has gathered all peoples from the corners of the earth to worship Him.

Are you zealous to see the nations glorify Christ? Then go and make disciples of all nations, baptizing them in the name of the Father, and of the Son, and of the Holy Spirit, and teaching them to obey all that Jesus has commanded you. And surely He will be with you always, to the very end of the age.*

*Father, You have united all those across the world who trust in Your Son. Help me to have a heart to see the nations glorify Your Son Jesus Christ.*

*I pray these things in Jesus' name. Amen.*

*Philippians 3:5, Galatians 3:28-29, Psalm 2:8, Matthew 28:19-20

201

JULY 7

# THE CALLING OF THE GOSPEL

Including you who are called to belong to Jesus Christ.
Romans 1:6

## WHAT IS YOUR CALLING?

There is much controversy and confusion around the calling of God. Many view God's calling as a calling to the ministry or to some other vocation. Yet the calling that is discussed in this text deals with the salvation of sinners. To those who are called, sanctified by God the Father, and preserved in Jesus Christ.*

All those, who have tasted the goodness of God, have been called to "belong to Jesus Christ." They no longer walk in the sins and darkness of this world, but have been set apart for the Gospel.

Who else better to teach on this topic of grace than Paul himself? He was a man who was zealous in his persecution of the church, but the Lord graciously opened his eyes. Now, as a witness of this special calling of God, he passionately reminds the saints of their standing in Christ.

Dear Christian, where would you be today without the Gospel? Consider your holy calling, and all the privileges you now have in Christ. You are not only His, but you also possess all the riches of His grace. And we know that all things work together for good to those who love God, to those who are the called according to His purpose.*

*Father, You have called me to be Your own special people. In times of great trial, help me to remember Your deep love.*

*I pray these things in Jesus' name. Amen.*

*Jude 1, Romans 8:28

# THE SCANDAL OF THE GOSPEL

For I am not ashamed of the gospel, for it is the power of God for salvation to everyone who believes, to the Jew first and also to the Greek.
Romans 1:16

## WHAT MAKES THE GOSPEL A SCANDAL AMONG MEN?

The answer to that question lies in the simplicity of the message. It is foolishness to a lost and dying world, but it is the power of God to those who believe. The wisdom of the Cross veils itself to the proud. It pierces through the pride of man, and strips him of his self-righteousness.

Paul was surrounded by the philosophies of the Greeks, but his message remained true to the doctrine of Christ. In the face of his critics he remained unashamed of the Gospel. It was the single greatest message that he had ever received.

What about you, dear friend? Do you find yourself emboldened to speak the truth or are you more concerned with the approval of others? Jesus said, "For whoever is ashamed of Me and My words, of him the Son of Man will be ashamed when He comes in His own glory, and in His Father's, and of the holy angels."*

May we be a people who proclaim the good news of righteousness in the great assembly, without restraining our lips. Oh Lord, You Yourself know.* Let us be unashamed to declare the scandal of the Cross to sinful men.

*Father, the message of the Cross is foolish to those who are perishing, but to those who are being saved it is the power of God. Forgive me for shrinking back in self-preservation, and grant me boldness to preach the name of Christ.*

*I pray these things in Jesus' name. Amen.*

*Luke 9:26, Psalm 40:9

# NO EXCUSE FOR THE GOSPEL

For the wrath of God is revealed from heaven against all ungodliness and unrighteousness of men, who by their unrighteousness suppress the truth.
Romans 1:18-19

## IS GOD UNJUST TO WITHHOLD MERCY?*

That is a question of great importance in our day. In order for man to be brought to a saving faith, he must submit to the testimony of Scripture. The truth of the matter is that man innately knows that there is a God, but he has all together chosen to reject and deny the Holy and Righteous One.* This is consistent with what has been revealed to us in God's Word.

We are not a people who are looking for our Creator, but rather those who suppress what has been made known concerning Him. For what can be known about God is plain to them, because God has shown it to them. For his invisible attributes, namely, his eternal power and divine nature, have been clearly perceived, ever since the creation of the world, in the things that have been made. So they are without excuse.*

Therefore God will be just in the condemnation of sinners, because they have the revelation of nature and their conscience to testify against them.

In light of this truth, how can we doubt the Divine justice of the Lord? The evidence of our sin has been brought before Him, and all of us are without excuse. Let us then abandon all confidence in the flesh, and fly into the arms of our gracious Savior.

---

*Father, every word which proceeds out of Your mouth is pure and true. You, Who are the Just and Holy One, will do right. Help me to have a biblical understanding of my need for the Gospel.*

*I pray these things in Jesus' name. Amen.*

*Romans 9:14, Acts 3:14, Romans 1:19-20

# THE REJECTION OF THE GOSPEL

For although they knew God, they did not honor him as God or give
thanks to him, but they became futile in their thinking,
and their foolish hearts were darkened.

Romans 1:21

## WHAT IS THE CONSEQUENCE OF DISOBEDIENCE?

God will give you over to your strong delusions. There is a direct correlation between sin and blindness.

Paul points out two key elements in dealing with idolatry. The first is that it is birthed out of a rebellious and sinful heart. Rebellion is as sinful as witchcraft, and stubbornness as bad as worshiping idols.*

People reject God's revelation to their own peril, for the heavens declare the glory of God; the skies proclaim the work of His hands.* Ask the animals, and they will instruct you; ask the birds of the air, and they will tell you. Or speak to the earth, and it will teach you; let the fish of the sea inform you.* If God's kindness is rejected, then what is left but futility? Secondly, a person's rebellion leads them to false conclusions. If someone boasts against the truth, then he or she will forge headlong into further darkness.

Who do you know who has exchanged the truth of God for the lie? Pray for them. Ask the Lord to open their eyes for the saving grace that is found only in Jesus Christ.

---

*Father, Your testimony regarding humankind is true. All of us are without excuse. Help me to exchange the lies of this present age for the wisdom of the Cross.* *

*I pray these things in Jesus' name. Amen.*

*1 Samuel 15:23, Psalm 19:1, Job 12:6-8, Romans 1:25

# THE GOSPEL IS REVEALED BY OUR CONSCIENCE

They show that the work of the Law is written on their hearts, while
their conscience also bears witness, and their conflicting thoughts
accuse or even excuse them on that day when, according to my Gospel,
God judges the secrets of men by Christ Jesus.

Romans 2:15

## IS THERE ANYONE WITHOUT EXCUSE?

The testimony of Scripture reveals that a person's condemnation is just.

For the wrath of God is revealed from heaven against all ungodliness
and unrighteousness of men, who suppress the truth in unrighteousness,
because what may be known of God is manifest in them, for God has
shown it to them.*

Whether he or she has been given the Law or not, God will not show
partiality.

Paul is about to address those who were not given the Law of Moses. God
has graciously given all peoples the revelation of nature and conscience.
We innately know when we have violated God's moral law, and Paul
tells us that our conscience serves as "a law unto us."* The reality is that
man has enough light to condemn him before the judgment seat of
Christ. Therefore, all of humankind is without excuse.

Dear soul, are you listening to your conscience or are you suppressing it?
Do not remain unbelieving, but rather heed the words of Christ and live.

◆————————◆————————◆

*Father, Your Word is like a fire, and it is like a hammer that smashes a rock into
pieces.* Give me the boldness to share the biblical message of the Gospel to others.*

*I pray these things in Jesus' name. Amen.*

*Romans 1:18-19, Romans 2:14, Jeremiah 23:29

# PLACING OUR CONFIDENCE IN THE GOSPEL

You who boast in the law dishonor God by breaking the Law.
Romans 2:23

## WHERE IS BOASTING?

After dealing with the Gentile's rejection of the Gospel, Paul now directs his attention to the people of the Covenant.

The children of Israel had boasted in the Law, but their hearts were far from the Lord. This made their obedience to the commandments of no effect.

Here in the text, the Apostle reasons that there can be no confidence in the Law of Moses. His point is clear: God will judge every man, and bring every action into the light. Therefore those, who have been given the Law, are also excluded from boasting. The wise men are ashamed, they are dismayed and taken. Behold, they have rejected the word of the Lord; so what wisdom do they have?*

What about you dear friend? Have you placed your confidence in good works? If so, then your striving is in vain. There will be no works that will pardon you from the wrath to come. The Law has done its work to reveal your sinful condition, and you are guilty before a holy God. In light of this truth, flee all confidence in your good works, and look unto the Lord Jesus Christ for your salvation.

---

*Father, all hope in keeping Your Law is false. You have the evidence laid out against us, and we are guilty before You. Help me not to look to the Law, but rather to entreat the mercy of Christ for my salvation.*

*I pray these things in Jesus' name. Amen.*

*Jeremiah 8:9

# THE GOSPEL IS FAITH IN JESUS CHRIST

For by works of the law no human being will be justified in his sight, since through the law comes knowledge of sin.

Romans 3:20

## WHAT DOES THE LAW REVEAL ABOUT US?

The Law serves as a magnifying glass which exposes our sin.

Paul later declares that he would not have known what it is to covet if the law had not said, "You shall not covet."* The holiness of God requires nothing more than absolute inward purity of heart. Yet the problem is that there is none who have perfectly kept the Law. Therefore all striving is in vain, because we cannot come to understand the wonderful news of the Gospel until we first realize how hopeless our situation is before God. It is only when we come to realize the true state of our soul that Divine grace will bring about true healing.

Where is boasting then? It is excluded. By what law? Of works? No, but by the law of faith. Therefore we conclude that a person is justified by faith apart from the deeds of the law.*

What is the state of your soul, dear reader? Have you come to the end of your boasting? Knowing that a person is not justified by the works of the law but by faith in Jesus Christ, even we have believed in Christ Jesus, that we might be justified by faith in Christ and not by the works of the law; for by the works of the law no flesh shall be justified.*

---

*Father, all striving is really a vanity of epic proportions. That truth helped set Martin Luther free, and sparked the beginning of the Reformation. Help me seek the gracious gift of repentance to enjoy the true freedom found in the Gospel.*

*I pray these things in Jesus' name. Amen.*

*Romans 7:7, Romans 3:27-28, Galatians 2:16

# THE GOSPEL OF GRACE

For all have sinned and fall short of the glory of God.
Romans 3:23

## WHAT IS THE TESTIMONY OF SCRIPTURE CONCERNING A PERSON?

The testimony of Scripture is simply this: that every person is guilty before a holy God. How is a person guilty? A person is guilty by breaking God's Law. Here in the text, Paul lays out the totality of the problem. All of us "have sinned, and fallen short of the glory of God."

The glory of God mentioned here refers to His moral excellence. Yahweh has revealed His character through the Law of Moses. It serves as a testimony to His holy and perfect ways. This has always been the true standard of measurement for every person. We commit a great error by comparing ourselves to one another. Therefore, each of us needs God's grace to see our sinfulness in light of God's holiness. Once our hearts have been gripped by this harsh reality, then we are truly ready to receive the Gospel with open arms.

Let us therefore come boldly to the throne of grace, that we may obtain mercy and find grace to recognize our standing before a holy God.*

---

*Father, there is not a just person on the face of the earth that has not sinned.* *
*Help me to have an accurate assessment of my sinful condition before you so that grace can reign in my heart.*

*I pray these things in Jesus' name. Amen.*

*Hebrews 4:16, Ecclesiastes 7:20

# THE GOSPEL OF JUSTIFICATION

Are justified by his grace as a gift...
Romans 3:24

## WHAT DOES IT MEAN TO BE JUSTIFIED?

In a biblical sense, justification means that God has declared you and me righteous. Yet how can we, who have broken God's Law, be declared righteous? This mystery is a free gift.

And the gift is not like that which came through the one who sinned. For the judgment which came from one offense resulted in condemnation, but the free gift which came from many offenses resulted in justification.*

Sinful man needs a righteousness that is not his own, since he has broken God's Law. He has no acceptable works of his own, and therefore he can only merit the Lord's eternal wrath. This harsh reality of our fallen state is what makes grace such a wonderful gift.

It is through the grace of God that we are given a righteousness that is apart from the Law.

Dear friend, all of us have become like one who is unclean, and all our righteous acts are like filthy rags; we all shrivel up like a leaf, and like the wind our sins sweep us away.* We all need the righteousness that is freely offered to us in Christ.

━━━━━━━━━━━◆━━━━━━━━━━━

*Father, You have given to us a most precious and incorruptible gift. Help us to walk in the freedom that we now have in Christ. I pray these things in Jesus' name. Amen.*

*Romans 5:16, Isaiah 64:6

# THE GOSPEL OF REDEMPTION

Through the redemption that is in Christ Jesus.

Romans 3:24

## WHAT DOES IT MEAN TO BE REDEEMED?

The idea of redemption runs through the sum of the Scriptures. In the Old Testament, a slave could be set free through a particular redemption price. We also see this idea illustrated in the account of Jeremiah's redemption of a field* or in Boaz's redemption of Ruth.* Here in the text, Paul ties the idea of redemption into the Gospel.

All of us were sold under sin, and were by nature children of wrath.* It is only through the shed blood of Christ that we were redeemed from the curse of the Law. No longer do the saints have to fear and tremble the thunder of Mount Sinai, and stand afar off.* But now, God's people can come near to Mount Zion, the city of the living God, the heavenly Jerusalem, and to innumerable angels in festal gathering, and enjoy the fellowship.*

Dear friend, have you placed all your hope and trust in Jesus? If so, then let not the fear of judgment rule your heart, because God has redeemed you from the curse of sin. In light of this truth, let us now enjoy the freedom that is ours through faith.

———————◇———————

*Father, You have redeemed me through the precious blood of Christ. Help me to no longer fear the curse of the Law, but rather to rest in the finished work of Your Son.*

*I pray these things in Jesus' name. Amen.*

*Jeremiah 32:7, Ruth 4, Ephesians 2:3, Exodus 20:18, Hebrews 12:22

# THE GOSPEL OF THE CROSS

Whom God put forward as a propitiation by his blood, to be received by faith. This was to show God's righteousness, because in his divine forbearance he had passed over former sins.

Romans 3:25

## WHAT DOES THE CROSS REVEAL ABOUT THE CHARACTER OF GOD?

The Cross demonstrates the righteousness of God. The common notion of our day is this: God will forgive every person because He is so kind and loving. Yet if God is just, then how can He forgive sinful man?

The Cross reveals that God must do what is right. His holy Law has been broken, and therefore justice must be served. God's purpose in Christ's death was to demonstrate His justice.

This presents mankind's greatest problem, because it implies that he is guilty before God. In light of this truth, he is buried deep in an eternal debt which he could never repay. For the wages of sin is death.*

Therefore, our only hope and remedy is the sinless Lamb Who is without spot or blemish. Only Christ is worthy and able to propitiate or satisfy God's wrath towards sinners. And He Himself is the propitiation for our sins, and not for ours only but also for the whole world.* Divine grace has swept over those who believe, and now they find themselves free from their former sins.

Now by this we know that we know Him, if we keep His commandments.* This should resemble our testimony. We must look to the sinless Lamb Who has satisfied the wrath of God for sinners.

———————◆———————

*Father, it is sad that Your precious gift of grace is despised. Grant me a heart to share the good news of the Gospel with sinners.*

*I pray these things in Jesus' name. Amen.*

*Romans 6:23, 1 John 2:2, 3

# THE GOSPEL DISPLAYED

It was to show his righteousness at the present time, so that he might be just and the justifier of the one who has faith in Jesus.

Romans 3:26

## WHAT IS YOUR UNDERSTANDING OF THE GOSPEL?

There is a tendency to reflect only on the physical sufferings of Jesus, but the testimony of Scripture reveals something more profound.

The reality is that, on the Cross, the righteousness of God was put on display. His wrath for sinners was poured out on His Son. The sinless Lamb, Who bore our sin, did not do this begrudgingly but rather willingly. It was for our sin that He suffered, but His sufferings did not come merely from the hands of lawless men. His sufferings were brought forth through the eternal counsels of God.

Who has declared this from ancient time? Who has told it from that time? Have not I, the Lord? And there is no other God besides Me, a just God and a Savior; there is none besides Me.*

The Scriptures declare that Jesus was a lamb slain before the foundations of the world.* It was according to the Father's pleasure that He crushed His only begotten Son. Now, through the propitiation of Christ, the sinner is no longer under the wrath of God. Instead, he is welcomed into the open arms of grace. Therefore, let there be no boasting in our merit. The Lord has done all the work, and it is marvelous in His eyes.*

---

*Father, Your Gospel is an everlasting Gospel which has been revealed to us in times past. Deliver me from the temptation of glorying in my merit so that I may only boast in the Cross of Christ.*

*I pray these things in Jesus' name. Amen.*

*Isaiah 45:21, Revelation 13:8, Psalm 118:23

213

# THE GOSPEL OF THE SINLESS LAMB

For we hold that one is justified by faith apart from works of the law.
Romans 3:28

## WHERE IS THE JUSTICE OF GOD IN OUR FORGIVENESS?

Man is born in sin, and he has broken the Law of God. Divine justice demands that the convicted sinner be punished. Therefore, how can sinful man find pardon at the judgment seat?

Oh the mystery of mysteries! Only through the wisdom of God can a way be made for our justification. It was by an eternal and holy decree that God provided for Himself a sacrificial Lamb. The sinless Lamb became sin for us, and satisfied Divine anger in our stead. Yet how is it, you ask, that One could justly take the punishment for another?

In times past, through the revelation of the Law of God, provision had always been made for sinful man. Sacrifices were made once a year for sin, and payment was made to redeem those sold under slavery. In Christ, we now have a Kinsman Redeemer, Who has not only satisfied our sins for a moment but forevermore. We, who were sold under sin, are now redeemed and set free. All of this done in such a way, that God could be Just and the Justifier of the one who has faith in Jesus.* Therefore, let the benefactors of His grace go out with joy and be led forth with peace!*

---

*Father, Your wisdom is unfathomable, and Your ways past finding out!* Thank You for Your marvelous work of redemption. Help my life to reflect the glorious truths of the Gospel.*

*I pray these things in Jesus' name. Amen.*

*Romans 3:26, Isaiah 55:12, Romans 11:33

214

# THE BOASTING OF THE GOSPEL

For what does the Scripture say? "Abraham believed God,
and it was counted to him as righteousness."
Romans 4:3

## WHAT WAS GAINED BY ABRAHAM, OUR FOREFATHER ACCORDING TO THE FLESH?*

Paul now opens the fourth chapter of Romans with this all-important question. The point he is making is simply this: Man can bring no boasting to the judgment seat, because his salvation is a gift that he receives through faith. For if Abraham was justified by works, he has something to boast about, but not before God.*

God had promised Abraham that his descendants would be as innumerable as the stars* in the heavens. We read in Genesis that he believed God, and it was counted to him as righteousness.* Therefore, the true descendants of Abraham do not come through flesh and blood, but through the seed according to faith.

Since our righteousness is as filthy rags unto God,* we needed a righteousness that was not our own. Martin Luther refers to this as an "alien righteousness," because this is a righteousness that only God can provide. Where then is boasting? The Gospel has given flesh no room to boast, because it is a sole work of God alone. Let us therefore give all glory unto Him for his wonderful works.

———◇———

*Father, no flesh can glory in Your presence.* You alone are worthy of our praise. Thank You for Your marvelous gift of salvation, and give me the grace to live every moment in light of the Gospel.*

*I pray these things in Jesus' name. Amen.*

*Romans 4:1, 2, Genesis 26:4, Genesis 15:6, Romans 4:22, Isaiah 64:6, 1 Corinthians 1:29

# THE FRIENDSHIP OF THE GOSPEL

That is why it depends on faith, in order that the promise may rest on grace and be guaranteed to all his offspring—not only to the adherent of the law but also to the one who shares the faith of Abraham, who is the father of us all.

Romans 4:16

## WHAT IS GRACE?

Grace is God's unmerited kindness and benevolence toward sinners. Even when we were dead in trespasses, God made us alive together with Christ (by grace you have been saved).*

What did we, as law-breakers, deserve? We deserved nothing but the eternal wrath of God. Yet instead of anger we are offered kindness. Instead of judgment, we are offered mercy. The Gospel not only offers pardon from sin, but it offers friendship with God.

And the Scripture was fulfilled that says, "Abraham believed God, and it was credited to him as righteousness," and he was called a friend of God.* Abraham was considered a friend of God through faith.

Since then, many centuries have been removed, but our story is still the same. The testimony of Scripture reveals that sinful man is unable to merit the favor of God. Therefore, it is not to the one who wills or runs, but to God Who shows mercy.*

Dear friend, have you come to realize that there is no salvation in your works? If so, then cease from your works to enter into the rest of God.

———————— ◆ ————————

*Father, where would be without grace? Bring us into a deeper understanding of the grace You offer us in Christ Jesus. I pray these things in Jesus' name. Amen.*

*Ephesians 2:5, James 2:23, Romans 9:16

# THE PEACE OF THE GOSPEL

Therefore, since we have been justified by faith, we have peace with
God through our Lord Jesus Christ.

Romans 5:1

## WHAT ARE THE GROUNDS FOR OUR PEACE WITH GOD?

The Apostle Paul has been laboring to show us that salvation is all of grace.
He uses the example of Abraham to point out that he believed prior to
circumcision. God had counted him righteous, not after, but before the
ordinance of circumcision.* Therefore, the seed of Abraham are those who
are the seed according to faith. For the promise that he would be the heir of
the world was not to Abraham or to his seed through the law, but through
the righteousness of faith.*

Now, after laboring to make the case for faith, Paul now shifts gears to the
benefits of our standing in Christ. Those who are counted righteous now
have peace with God. In Christ, we are no longer enemies, but friends of
the Most High. His wrath has been propitiated through the death of His
Son, and now we are able to approach Him boldly in worship.

Now may the God of peace who brought up our Lord Jesus from the dead,
that great Shepherd of the sheep, through the blood of the everlasting covenant, make you complete in every good work to do His will, working in
you what is well pleasing in His sight, through Jesus Christ, to whom be
glory forever and ever. Amen.*

*Father, You have given us peace through the death of Your Son. This is not a
peace that the world gives, but a peace that is secured in Christ Jesus. Give me
the grace to enter fully into Your rest.*

*I pray these things in Jesus' name. Amen.*

*Romans 4:11-12, 13, Hebrews 13:20-21

# THE HOPE OF THE GOSPEL

Through him we have also obtained access by faith into this grace in which we stand, and we rejoice in hope of the glory of God.

Romans 5:2

## DO YOU HAVE HOPE?

Paul declares that we, as believers, have a hope which does not disappoint.* This is a hope that is not based on the moving forces of this present world, but rather a hope that is based on our immovable Savior.

In Christ, believers are granted access into the very presence of God by faith. This gives us great reason to rejoice, because no trial or tribulation can ever take our hope away from us. Let us therefore come boldly to the throne of grace, that we may obtain mercy and find grace to help in time of need.* For the law made nothing perfect; on the other hand, there is the bringing in of a better hope, through which we draw near to God.*

*Father, there is nothing that can separate me from Your love. In times of sorrow may I be reminded of the hope that I now have in Christ.*

*I pray these things in Jesus' name. Amen.*

*Romans 5:5, Hebrews 4:16, Hebrews 7:19

# THE GOSPEL OF SUFFERING

Not only that, but we rejoice in our sufferings,
knowing that suffering produces endurance.

Romans 5:3

## WHY WOULD ANYONE REJOICE IN THEIR SUFFERINGS?

That seems like a fair question to ask. There are many around the world that cannot find a reason to rejoice. For the Christian, though, he or she has a hope that does not disappoint.*

The Apostle Paul drives this point home in his letter to the Corinthians. In speaking of trials he writes that while the outward man is perishing, the inward man is being renewed day by day.* The saints can rejoice because they understand that their present trials are strengthening their faith.

A faith that is tried is a faith that endures, because it is a faith that looks beyond the momentary afflictions to the final outcome. If anyone suffers as a Christian, let him not be ashamed, but let him glorify God in this matter.*

Dear friend, do you find yourself discouraged in your present circumstances? If so, then do not waver in unbelief, but rather rejoice in your present sufferings. These momentary afflictions will not overtake you, but will rather conform you more into the image of Jesus Christ.

———————◇———————

*Father, we do not sorrow as those who have no hope.* You have rooted me and grounded me in love. Help me not to be moved in my suffering, but rather to rejoice in the final outcome.*

*I pray these things in Jesus' name. Amen.*

*Romans 5:5, 2 Corinthians 4:16, 1 Peter 4:16, 1 Thessalonians 4:13

# THE RECONCILIATION OF THE GOSPEL

More than that, we also rejoice in God through our Lord Jesus Christ, through whom we have now received reconciliation.

Romans 5:11

## WHAT IS RECONCILIATION?

Reconciliation means a person's relationship with God has been restored. Everything ties back to the Gospel. The God, Who was once against us, is now for us.

God showed His love for us, in that, while we were still sinners, Christ died for us. Since, therefore, we have now been justified by his blood, much more shall we be saved by Jesus from the wrath of God. For if, while we were enemies, we were reconciled to God by the death of his Son, Jesus Christ, much more, now that we are reconciled, shall we be saved by His life.*

All this was the result of His unmerited kindness and benevolence towards us. The anger of the Lord had rested upon us like an impending storm, but then Divine grace swept under us. Not only were the saints rescued from the wrath of God, but they now enjoy all the benefits of being heirs with Christ.*

The Christian has great reason to rejoice. He is no longer an enemy of God, but rather he is an heir of eternal life.

---

*Father, I am no longer Your enemy, but rather Your friend. Grant me a desire to see others reconciled to You as well.*

*I pray these things in Jesus' name. Amen.*

*Romans 5:8-10, Romans 8:17

# THE GOSPEL IS RIGHTEOUS

Therefore, as one trespass led to condemnation for all men, so one act of righteousness leads to justification and life for all men.

Romans 5:18

## WHO OFFERS US ETERNAL LIFE?

After Paul has shown us the blessings of the Gospel, he reminds us that all of these benefits are offered to us in the righteousness of Christ. He does this by drawing a contrast between Adam and the Son of God. In Adam all are dead in their sins. Adam's disobedience in the Garden led to the condemnation of all men. Through Adam we remain under the judgment of God, and there is no hope of recourse.

Here is hope: Christ Jesus succeeded where Adam failed. His righteousness led to the salvation of many. Now the saints are no longer united to Adam under disobedience, but are rather united to Christ by faith. Jesus' death means that I have died to the curse of the Law, and His life means that I am now raised and seated with Him in the heavenly places.*

All of this is granted to me on the basis of my union with Christ. This eternal truth lets us rejoice each day in the free gift that is offered to us in the Gospel.

---

*Father, all the benefits of eternal life our found in Christ. Help me to have a greater understanding of Christ's righteousness and the union I now have with You.*

*I pray these things in Jesus' name. Amen.*

*Ephesians 2:6*

221

# THE GOSPEL OFFERS FREEDOM

For sin will have no dominion over you,
since you are not under law but under grace.
Romans 6:14

## WHAT IS THE BASIS OF OUR FREEDOM FROM SIN?

The basis of this newfound freedom is our union with Christ. He has redeemed us from the curse of the Law, and therefore has set us free from the power of sin.* Yet this is not so with the natural man.

In Adam there is no power over sin, but rather a certain expectation of judgment. It is only through the redemption found in Christ Jesus where I can find true freedom from the corruptions of my flesh. The Apostle's point is clear: as a result of my union with Christ, I no longer am bound by my flesh. In light of that truth, I am commanded to put to death the deeds of the body. This is not something that I do in my own strength, but rather something that is accomplished by relying on the Holy Spirit.

The blood of Jesus Christ has cleansed us, and set us free. What shall we say then? Shall we continue in sin that grace may abound? Certainly not! How shall we who died to sin live any longer in it?* Let us, who are now united with Christ, reckon ourselves to be dead to sin and alive to God.*

———————— ◆ ————————

*Father, if the Son has set me free, then I am free indeed.* Help me to live every moment in light of the newfound freedom that I now have in Christ.*

*I pray these things in Jesus' name. Amen.*

*Romans 8:2, Romans 6:1-2, Romans 6:11, John 8:36

# A NEW MARRIAGE IN THE GOSPEL

Likewise, my brothers, you also have died to the Law through the body of Christ, so that you may belong to another, to Him who has been raised from the dead, in order that we may bear fruit of God.

Romans 7:4

## WHAT IS THE PURPOSE OF THE LAW?

The purpose of the Law is to magnify sin in me, and therefore it serves as a ministry of death. All are brought under the condemnation of the Law.

In the previous chapters, Paul has been communicating the importance of being united to Christ by faith. He then further drives this point home here by means of illustration in the previous verses. A wife is bound by the Law of her husband until he dies, but after his death she is free to remarry.* Likewise we, who have been united to Christ by faith, are no longer under the curse of the Law. We are now married unto another who is the "second Adam." In Christ, the Law no longer brings dread, but rather brings delight to my soul.

But now we are released from the law, having died to that which held us captive, so that we serve in the new way of the Spirit and not in the old way of the written code.* It is now the love of God that compels me to obedience.

Is that the case with you dear friend? Has the Lord written the Law on your heart? If so, then delight yourself in Him, and be at peace.

---

*Father, I am no longer under the curse of the Law. Grant me the grace to walk in the newfound liberty I now enjoy in Christ.*

*I pray these things in Jesus' name. Amen.*

*Romans 7:2, 6

# NO CONDEMNATION IN THE GOSPEL

There is therefore now no condemnation for those who are in Christ Jesus.

Romans 8:1

## IN WHAT WAY HAS CHRIST SET US FREE?

He has set us free by taking upon Himself the curse of the Law. Now, we are no longer under its condemnation.

The original language denotes an emphatic declaration in regards to our sin. In Christ there is absolutely no way, under any circumstance, that we stand condemned before the judgment seat of God. This empowers us to walk freely in the grace that we now stand.

Prior to conversion we found another law working in our members. This was the law of sin and death.* We had no hope or recourse, but rather a certain expectation of judgment. As a result of Christ's meritorious life and death, we stand forgiven and free from condemnation.

The law of the Spirit of life has set you free in Christ Jesus from the law of sin and death.* Since the Spirit of Him who raised Jesus from the dead dwells in you, He who raised Christ Jesus from the dead will also give life to your mortal bodies through His Spirit who dwells in you.*

Therefore, in light of this eternal truth, let us not be weighed down with the guilt of our former sins, but rather enjoy the freedom we now have in Christ.

---

*Father, I am emphatically delivered from the condemnation of the Law. Help me to walk moment by moment through the Spirit of life.*

*I pray these things in Jesus' name. Amen.*

*Romans 7:23, 8:2, 11

# THE GOSPEL OF ADOPTION

For you did not receive the Spirit of slavery to fall back into fear, but
you have received the Spirit of adoption as sons,
by whom we cry, "Abba, Father!"
Romans 8:15

## WHAT DOES IT MEAN TO BE ADOPTED INTO THE FAMILY OF GOD?

It means that all of the covenant promises of God are ours by faith. We
are no longer alienated from the commonwealth of Israel,* but we are
now called sons and daughters of the Most High.

Christ Jesus has set us free from the law of sin and death, and we are no
longer children of wrath. Today we can rejoice knowing that He is for
us, and that He ordains all things for our good. The Spirit himself bears
witness with our spirit that we are children of God.*

Dear Christian, does the accuser of the brethren hurl accusations towards
you? Fear not! He no longer has any accusations against you, because the
blood of Jesus Christ has cleansed you from all sin. You are now a child
of God, the Father.

---

*Father, thank You for adopting me into Your family. I now have an Advocate
in the Lord Jesus Christ. Help me not to dread the darts of the evil one, but
rest assured in Your covenant faithfulness to me.*

*I pray these things in Jesus' name. Amen.*


*Ephesians 2:12, Romans 8:2, Ephesians 2:3, Romans 8;16

# THE VICTORIOUS GOSPEL

No, in all these things we are more than conquerors
through him who loved us.
Romans 8:37

## WHAT SHALL SEPARATE US FROM THE LOVE OF CHRIST?

Shall tribulation, or distress, or persecution, or famine, or nakedness, or danger, or sword?* Paul answers the question. No! In Christ Jesus I have overcome the world.

The essence of Christianity is this: I am loved by God. This reality completely turns all of my circumstances on their head. The trials which once sought relentlessly to derail me now only work for my good. Knowing this, I do not live only for the present reality, but also with the reality that I will one day emerge victorious.

Throughout all the trials of life, we live with the one inescapable truth that we are not alone. The God, Who redeemed us, is always with us, and that will never change. We live and move in a world that is broken and lost. It is only as we hold the inseparable love of God close to our hearts that we will emerge victorious.

Once we are gripped by this Divine love, only then will we realize that this is not all that there is to life. The saints now long for that day when their Savior will wipe away every tear from their eyes.* This eternal truth is a reminder that nothing shall separate us from the love of God which is in Christ Jesus.*

———————◆———————

*Father, there is nothing that can separate Your children from Your love. Help me to realize that these present trials do not define me, but that in all things I am more than a conqueror.*

*I pray these things in Jesus' name. Amen.*

*Romans 8:35, Revelation 21:4, Romans 8:39

# AUGUST
## WHAT IS THE CHURCH?

The Church is a collection of sinners who have been redeemed for the glory of God. Key in on the word "redeemed" for a moment.

How can anyone, who absolutely has no desire for the things of God, become zealous to see His Kingdom come, and God's will be done on earth as it is in heaven?* That can only be accomplished through a miraculous work of God. When you think about it, the story of the Church is a miracle in and of itself. The book of Acts is filled with testimony after testimony of the power of God. Yet these were no extraordinary people. They possessed nothing in and of themselves that could produce the miraculous things that are written down. Isn't that amazing!

What then was the secret to their success? The secret lies in their reliance upon God. The Church in the First Century did not have all the resources that we possess today, but that did not stop them from turning the world upside down.

In our reflections for August, we will look at the book of Acts. My prayer for you is that you will see how the power of the Holy Spirit worked through the Church, and how that is still continuing today.

*Matthew 6:10

# THE COMMISSION OF THE CHURCH

But you will receive power when the Holy Spirit has come upon you,
and you will be my witnesses in Jerusalem and in all Judea
and Samaria, and to the end of the earth.

Acts 1:8

## HOW DID TWELVE FISHERMEN TURN THE WORLD UPSIDE DOWN?

The answer to that question lies in the fact that they were sent by God. It was their commission to preach the good news of the Gospel, but they did not accomplish this task in their own strength. Jesus said, "Behold, I send the Promise of My Father upon you; but tarry in the city of Jerusalem until you are endued with power from on high."*

We read in Acts how that the Holy Spirit came upon them in power from on high.* Once the disciples were empowered, they became bold witnesses of the Lord Jesus Christ.

In like manner, the Church has been empowered by God to share the message of the Cross. She holds the keys to the kingdom* in her hands. Though the world has rejected its Savior, the Gospel is a message that it desperately needs to hear. Therefore, let us go out in the power of the Holy Spirit as we proclaim Christ to the lost.

◆————————◆————————◆

*Father, I have been commissioned to be Your faithful witness to a lost and dying world. Help me to go forth in the power of the Holy Spirit as I preach the Gospel to the lost.*

*I pray these things in Jesus' name. Amen.*

*Luke 24:49, Luke 24:29, Matthew 16:19

# THE GUIDANCE OF THE CHURCH

And they cast lots for them, and the lot fell on Mathias,
and he was numbered with the eleven apostles.

Acts 1:26

## WHO DIRECTS THE CHURCH IN ITS AFFAIRS?

It is He, Who sits above the circle of the earth, who directs the Church.* The Apostles were looking for a man to replace Judas. In their perplexity, we read that they sought the Lord in prayer. Note that the Church should never hasten to make a decision, but should first spread their case before the Lord.

Jesus said, "But seek first the kingdom of God and his righteousness, and all these things will be added to you. Therefore do not be anxious about tomorrow, for tomorrow will be anxious for itself. Sufficient for the day is its own trouble.*

He is the all-wise Counselor Who knows the way in which we should take.

The apostles made their request known to God, and He heard their prayers. Their lot fell on Matthias who was then numbered with the eleven apostles.* In like manner, let us understand that the lot is cast into the lap, but its every decision is from the Lord.* We can take comfort in knowing that God is faithful in directing His Church for His own glory.

---

*Father, it is You Who governs all things for Your Church. Please help us to be a Church who prays to You about all things.*

*I pray these things in Jesus' name. Amen.*

*Isaiah 40:22, Acts 1:26, Proverbs 16:33, Luke 11:9-10

# THE CHURCH IS THE DWELLING PLACE OF GOD

And they were all filled with the Holy Spirit and began to speak in
other tongues as the Spirit gave them utterance.

Acts 2:4

## WHERE DOES THE CHURCH RECEIVE HER POWER?

It is God Who grants power to His Church.

The disciples were commanded to wait in Jerusalem for the promise of
the Father. We read that on the day of Pentecost the Holy Spirit fell on
them like a mighty rushing wind.* This marks a key event in the history
of the Church. It is from this point onward that the book of Acts is filled
with one miraculous testimony after another.

To another the working of miracles, to another prophecy, to another
discerning of spirits, to another different kinds of tongues, to another
the interpretation of tongues. But one and the same Spirit works all these
things, distributing to each one individually as He wills.*

What changed that day in the upper room?

The difference was in the fact that they were now filled with the Holy Spirit.
Once He made His dwelling amongst the saints, the Church became a bold
witness for the sake of the Gospel. What about our Church in the present
day? Do we rely more on our knowledge and our programs or are we continually drawing strength from the Spirit of God? Let us be a Church that is
empowered by the Holy Spirit to be an effective witness in this evil age.

---

*Father, where would we be without the Holy Spirit? Help us to rely daily on
His ministry to us.*

*I pray these things in Jesus' name. Amen.*

*Acts 2:2, Acts 2:6-7

# THE CHURCH IS EVANGELISTIC

And Peter said to them, "Repent and be baptized every one of you
in the name of Jesus Christ for the forgiveness of sins,
and you will receive the gift of the Holy Spirit."
Acts 2:38

## WHAT IS THE MOST IMPORTANT MESSAGE IN THE HISTORY OF THE WORLD?

It's simply: Jesus Christ died to save sinners.* The Church has been entrusted with this imperative message to share it with an unbelieving world.

Here in this text there are three important points to understand. First we need to understand that Peter's Gospel was Christ-centered. He does not appeal to felt needs, but rather makes much of Jesus. Second, Peter's message is saturated with Scripture. If we are going to preach the Gospel, then our presentation ought to be rich in the testimonies of God. Finally, Peter invites others to receive the Gospel in the form of a command. If sinners are going to be invited to the Lord's banqueting table, then we must exhort them to repent and believe in the Gospel.*

Keep in mind that we are only the messengers of the Cross. It is the primary ministry of the Holy Spirit to convict sinners of their sin.

Our speech and preaching should not be with persuasive words of human wisdom, but in demonstration of the Spirit and of power, that our faith should not be in the wisdom of men but in the power of God.* In light of this truth, let us be a Church who not only evangelizes biblically, but is empowered from on high.

*Father, there is no greater message than the Gospel. Help me to reach the lost with the biblical message of the Gospel.*
*I pray these things in Jesus' name. Amen.*

*1 Timothy 1:15, Mark 1:15, 1Corinthians 2:4-5

# THE INSTRUCTION OF THE CHURCH

And they devoted themselves to the Apostles' teaching…
Acts 2:42

## WHAT IS THE MARK OF A HEALTHY CHURCH?

A healthy Church is faithful in accurately teaching the Word of God. The late great Charles Spurgeon once said: "Don't go where it is all fine music and grand talk and beautiful architecture. Those things will neither fill anybody's stomach, nor feed his soul. Go where the gospel is preached and go often."

We read that the believers devoted themselves to the Apostles' teaching. They were instructed solely from the sound doctrine that is from above. In like manner, the Church has been given the teachings of God's Holy Word. It will be well with us if we devote ourselves to these ancient truths. While the philosophies of our day will change, the Word of the Lord will remain forever.

Now, therefore, you are no longer strangers and foreigners, but fellow citizens with the saints and members of the household of God, having been built on the foundation of the apostles and prophets, Jesus Christ Himself being the chief cornerstone.*

Dear friend, let us reason together.* Does your church emphasize and teach God's Word faithfully? If not, then I would encourage you to find a church that will feed you with the wisdom of God. Let us be a people who can rightly divide the word of truth.*

---

*Father, we have no other foundation for truth, but in Your Word. Help me to press on to maturity by leaving the elementary principles\* so that I can discern truth from error.*

*I pray these things in Jesus' name. Amen.*

*Ephesians 2:19-20, Acts 2:42, Isaiah 1:18, 2 Timothy 2:15, Hebrews 6:1

# THE UNITY OF THE CHURCH

And they devoted themselves to …
fellowship, to the breaking of bread and the prayers.
Acts 2:42

## HOW CAN WE KNOW THAT WE ARE OF GOD?

We know that we are of God by our love for one another.

The early Church was not without its problems, but it was unified for one singular purpose. They desired to make the name of Christ known amongst the nations. Therefore we read that they were unified under the apostles' teaching, and that they broke bread together.

The cup of blessing which we bless, is it not the communion of the blood of Christ? The bread which we break, is it not the communion of the body of Christ? For we, though many, are one bread and one body; for we all partake of that one bread.*

In like manner we, as a Church, ought to lay aside our differences for the sake of the Gospel. The First Century Church served as a great testimony of unity and love to the unbelieving world around them. Let us therefore model their simplicity and singleness of heart. It is only through our love for one another that others will know that we are from God.

--------◦--------

*Father, You have called us to one love, one faith, one hope, and one Lord.* Help us to be united under sound teaching, fellowship, the breaking of bread, and prayer.*

*I pray these things in Jesus' name. Amen.*

*1 Corinthians 10:16-17, Ephesians 4:5

233

# THE BLESSING OF THE CHURCH

And day by day, attending the temple together and breaking bread in their homes, they received their food with glad and generous hearts.

Acts 2:46

## WHO CAN COUNT THE MANY BLESSINGS OF GOD?

His blessings to us are as innumerable as the stars in the sky. How precious to me are your thoughts, O God! How vast is the sum of them! If I would count them, they are more than the sand.*

The early Church, though tried, had much to rejoice over. We read how that they fellowshipped with each other through the breaking of bread. Their hearts and minds were impassioned for the Gospel, and their love for one another was made known to others. The New Testament saints gave out of their resources for the good of their fellow brethren, but the blessing of God reached far beyond the scope of the local Church.

In the book of Acts, we read how many came to saving faith on a daily basis. Praising God and having favor with all the people, the Lord added to their number day by day those who were being saved.* Their Christ-like love for one another served as a testimony to an unbelieving world.

Many centuries have been removed from this time in the Church's history, but a demonstration of Christ's love is still one of the most powerful testimonies to an unbelieving world. This eternal truth is a reminder to bless others with a love that is from above.

*Father, thank You for Your Church. She is Your dwelling place. Help me to imitate the faith and love of the First Century Church.*

*I pray these things in Jesus' name. Amen.*

*Psalm 139:17-18, Acts 2:47

# THE COMPASSION OF THE CHURCH

But Peter said, "I have no silver and gold, but what I do have I give to you. In the name of Jesus Christ of Nazareth, rise up and walk!"

Acts 3:6

## WHAT IS THE GREATEST GIFT THAT YOU HAVE EVER RECEIVED?

There was a man in Jerusalem who was lame from birth, who was being carried, whom the people laid daily at the gate of the temple, that is called the Beautiful Gate, to ask alms of those entering the temple.* We are told that he gained the attention of Peter and John.

This man, who looked for alms, was about to receive something far better. In that very hour his legs were healed, and he leaped for joy. Through this miraculous act, both this man and those around him became witnesses to the power of God. Peter and John had no gold or silver, but they were able to make the name of Jesus famous to those around them.

In like manner, the Church possesses infinitely greater treasures than this world has to offer. She has been given the gift of God's Son, Who has redeemed her from her sins. This is a gift that the world desperately needs if only we will be bold enough to share it.

Listen, my beloved: Has God not chosen the poor of this world to be rich in faith and heirs of the kingdom which He promised to those who love Him?* Let us therefore be those who are moved to compassion to see others come to know Jesus.

---

*Father, Your gift to us cannot be measured by human hands. It is infinitely greater than any earthly treasures. Give me a heart to see others introduced to Jesus.*

*I pray these things in Jesus' name. Amen.*

*Acts 3:2, James 2:5

# THE PERSECUTION OF THE CHURCH

And they arrested them and put them in custody
until the next day, for it was already evening.
Acts 4:3

## WHAT IS IT COSTING YOU TO FOLLOW JESUS?

It costs the early Church everything to follow Jesus. Persecution in the First Century was very sporadic, but it was still an ever-present threat for Christians. Those, who did not face death or imprisonment, were seen as the outcasts of society.

We read here how that Peter and John were arrested for the Word of God and for His testimony, but even in the midst of this great trial we see something amazing unfold. In verse four we read, "But many of those who had heard the word believed, and the number of the men came to about five thousand."* In the Church's hour of trial, the Lord still added to their number!

In like manner, we should not count it strange to be persecuted for the sake of Christ. We must come to understand that all who desire to live a godly life in Christ Jesus will suffer persecution.* Yet while the saints suffer in this present age, their suffering is not in vain. On the other side of glory awaits an inheritance for them which is incorruptible and everlasting.*

Therefore let us go to Him outside the camp and bear the reproach He endured. For here we have no lasting city, but we seek the city that is to come. Through Him then let us continually offer up a sacrifice of praise to God, that is, the fruit of lips that acknowledge his name.*

---

*Father, the gates of hell shall not prevail against Your Church.\* She is preserved by Your sovereign hand. Help me not to shrink back in fear of persecution, but rather to be bold for the sake of Christ.*

*I pray these things in Jesus' name. Amen.*

*Acts 4:4, 2 Timothy 3:12, 1 Peter 1:4, Hebrews 13:13-15, Matthew 16:18

# THE BOLDNESS OF THE CHURCH

But Peter and John answered them, "Whether it is right in the sight of God to listen to you rather than to God, you must judge, for we cannot but speak of what we have seen and heard."

Acts 4:19-20

## WHAT DOES IT MEAN TO BE BOLD FOR THE SAKE OF CHRIST?

The New Testament Church was a lot of things, but it wasn't timid. They preached the truth of what they had seen to all who would listen. In their preaching of the Gospel, they encountered great opposition from the enemies of God, but they remained emboldened for the sake of Christ.

Here in Acts, we read how that Peter and John were compelled to share the things that they had seen and heard. Even though they faced the threat of persecution, they had a burden to share the Gospel with others. In like manner, the Church still carries the same burden with her in this present age. We live in a day where many of the saints around the globe endure fierce persecution from the hands of their enemies. Yet in spite of the opposition they face, they are still bold witnesses for the Gospel.

That which we have seen and heard we declare to you, that you also may have fellowship with us; and truly our fellowship is with the Father and with His Son Jesus Christ. And these things we say to you that your joy may be full.*

What about you, dear friend? Are you emboldened to share the Gospel with those in your communities and places of business? Let us be those who are emboldened to share the Gospel with those who are around us.

———◇———

*Father, how can we not preach the things we have seen and heard? Help me to be bold witnesses for Christ in this present and evil age.*

*I pray these things in Jesus' name. Amen.*

*1 John 1:3-4

# THE NARROW WAY OF THE CHURCH

And there is salvation in no one else, for there is no other name under heaven given among men by which we must be saved.

Acts 4:12

## WHAT IS THE VALUE OF A GOOD NAME?

The book of Proverbs says that, a good name is to be chosen rather than riches.*

Here in the text, the Apostles are making known to man the most glorious of names. It is through the name of Jesus that we are saved to enjoy all the blessings of the Covenant of grace.

Notice, though, that there is a narrowness ascribed to this great salvation. The apostles were very clear that there is no other way to get to the Father accept through the name of Jesus. If a person is to be saved, then he or she must enter in by the straight and narrow gate.* Thus, the Church's responsibility is not to broaden the scope of the message, but rather to speak it in all its truthfulness.

Jesus said, "I am the way, the truth, and the life. No one comes to the Father except through Me."* For there is one God and one Mediator between God and men, the Man Christ Jesus.*

This eternal truth  points sinners to the only name under heaven by which they can be saved.

———————◆———————

*Father, the Way of salvation is very straight and narrow. Help me to graciously show sinners the way of the Cross.*

*I pray these things in Jesus' name. Amen.*

*Proverbs 22:1, Matthew 7:14, John 14:6, 1 Timothy 2:5

# THE GODLY WISDOM OF THE CHURCH

Now when they saw the boldness of Peter and John, and perceived that
they were uneducated, common men, they were astonished.
And they recognized that they had been with Jesus.

Acts 4:13

## WHO IS THE GREATEST TEACHER OF ALL?

The hour was approaching, and soon Jesus would go to the Cross.
Knowing that the time of testing was drawing near He still had some
important things that He needed to teach His disciples. Soon He would
leave the earth, and go to His Father in heaven. That was solemn news,
but it did not come without a faithful promise.

Jesus said, "I will not leave you as orphans; I will come to you. If anyone
loves Me, he will keep My word, and My Father will love him, and We
will come to him and make our home with him. The Helper, the Holy
Spirit, whom the Father will send in My name, He will teach you all
things and bring to your remembrance all that I have said to you."*

Our Master is the Giver of perfect gifts, and while He tarries for a while He
has given us a Comforter. The Apostles were ordinary people just like you
and me, but they had an extraordinary Teacher. When they spoke from the
Scriptures, people everywhere knew that they had been with Jesus.

In like manner, that same Holy Spirit, which was given to the Apostles,
is the same Holy Spirit that is given to us. Let us therefore not rely on the
wisdom of men, but rather learn from the wisdom of our great Comforter.

———◆——◉——◆———

*Father, You have not left us as orphans. We have a Teacher Who leads us into all
truth. Please illuminate my heart and mind to the great truths that are in Scripture.*

*I pray these things in Jesus' name. Amen.*

*John 14:18, 23, 26

# THE GENEROSITY OF THE CHURCH

There was not a needy person among them, for as many as were owners of lands or houses sold them and brought the proceeds of what was sold and laid it at the apostles' feet, and it was distributed to each as any had need.

Acts 4:34

## WHAT IS THE ESSENCE OF COMMUNITY?

Community, in a biblical sense, manifests itself in Christ-like love for one another. This type of love was exemplified in the New Testament Church. Many sold their homes and properties to help meet the needs of their brethren.

The text here tells us that there was not a needy person among them. This concept of community is often foreign to our individualistic society, but the early Church sacrificed everything for the sake of Christ. Their sacrificial love and generosity served as a demonstration of the Gospel to others. When the Church models this type of Christ-like love, it becomes an effective witness to an unbelieving world.

Sell what you have and give alms; provide yourselves money bags which do not grow old, a treasure in the heavens that does not fail, where no thief approaches nor moth destroys. For where your treasure is, there your heart will be also.* In light of this truth let us imitate the generosity and community of the New Testament Church so that others would taste and see the goodness of Christ.

---

*Father, what example of community ought we to be to the outside world? Help me to share in the same type of self-sacrificial love that was put on display in the book of Acts.*

*I pray these things in Jesus' name. Amen.*

*Luke 12:33-34

# THE PURITY OF THE CHURCH

But Peter said to her, "How is it that you have agreed together to test the Spirit of the Lord? Behold, the feet of those who have buried your husband are at the door, and they will carry you out."

Acts 5:9

## IS IT A SMALL THING TO LIE TO GOD?

Apparently, this married couple, Ananias and Sapphira, thought it a small thing to tell a lie unto the Lord. They sold their property, but kept back some of the proceeds for themselves. In their craftiness, they decided to lie about how much they actually received from the sale.

This sin was no small thing to the Church, because it threatened its very integrity.

Unfortunately we read that they persisted in their sin, and their fate was sealed. Though they join forces, the wicked will not go unpunished; but the posterity of the righteous will be delivered.* The Bride of Christ is to be kept pure from the deceitfulness of sin. If we are to worship the Lord, then it must be done in the spirit of holiness.

Let us not tempt Christ, as some of them also tempted, and were destroyed by serpents; nor complain, as some of them also complained, and were destroyed by the destroyer. Now all these things happened to them as examples, and they were written for our admonition, upon whom the ends of the ages have come.* In light of this truth, let us be worshipers of God with a sincere and honest heart.

---

*Father, You are of purer eyes than to behold evil.\* Let there be no sin in the camp, but rather keep Your bride holy.*

*I pray these things in Jesus' name. Amen.*

*Proverbs 11:21, 1 Corinthians 10:9-11, Habakkuk 1:13

# THE ORGANIC GROWTH OF THE CHURCH

And more than ever believers were added to the Lord,
multitudes of both men and women.

Acts 5:14

## WHO GIVES THE CHURCH ITS INCREASE?

Great fear came upon many after witnessing the deaths of Ananias and Sapphira, but there were many more signs and wonders to come. We read that the people also gathered from the towns around Jerusalem, bringing the sick and those afflicted with unclean spirits, and they were all healed.* God had moved in the midst of the holy City of David, and many were brought to saving faith.

The early Church did not have any special programs or gimmicks. They were just simply devoted to the apostles' teaching and the fellowship, to the breaking of bread and the prayers.* Then the word of God spread, and the number of the disciples multiplied greatly in Jerusalem, and a great many of the priests were obedient to the faith.*

In like manner, a healthy Church is a church that grows organically. They are not relying on the conventional wisdom of man, but are being faithful to the Word of God. In a day and age when the focus is on Church growth strategies, let us be a people who rely upon the Lord for the increase.

---

*Father, it is not our responsibility to grow Your Church. We are called to be faithful to the commission You have given us. Give me the grace to remain faithful in that calling.*

*I pray these things in Jesus' name. Amen.*

*Acts 5:16, Acts 2:42, Acts 6:7

# THE OBEDIENCE OF THE CHURCH

But Peter and the apostles answered,
"We must obey God rather than men."
Acts 5:29

## IS IT BETTER TO OBEY GOD OR MAN?

The First Century Church pledged their allegiance unto Christ alone. They did not fear man, but rather committed their lives to the Keeper of souls. The apostles had been arrested for the Word, and the testimony of Jesus Christ.* They were warned never to preach the Gospel again, but instead of fearing man they feared God.

We read how that when they were let go they did not cease teaching and preaching that the Christ is Jesus.* In like manner, if the apostles did not escape the persecution of sinners, then what makes us believe that we can escape from its grip? Our society has enjoyed the benefits of religious freedom, but the time of testing is approaching.

Beloved, do not think it strange concerning the fiery trial which is to try you, as though some strange thing happened to you; but rejoice to the extent that you partake of Christ's sufferings, that when His glory is revealed, you may also be glad with exceeding joy.* Let us therefore count it better to suffer for Christ, than to enjoy the passing comforts of a season.*

———◆———◇———◆———

*Father, You have promised that we will suffer persecution.* Give me great boldness to obey Your Word in times of testing.*

*I pray these things in Jesus' name. Amen.*

*Revelation 1:2, Acts 5:42, 1 Peter 4:12-13, Hebrews 11:25, 2 Timothy 3:12

# THE WITNESS OF THE CHURCH

And we are witnesses to these things, and so is the Holy Spirit,
whom God has given to those who obey him.

Acts 5:32

## WHAT DOES IT MEAN TO BE A WITNESS FOR CHRIST?

The Apostles witnessed firsthand the miracles of Christ. He had appeared
to each of them after His resurrection, and now they are compelled to
testify of the things they have seen. Yet their testimony was given at great
costs to themselves.

Many times they were arrested, and they were brought before authorities.
History tells us that they all died at the hands of their persecutors. But in
spite of the dangers they faced, the apostles stayed true to the testimony
of Jesus. Today, we are still called to bear the responsibility of being faithful witnesses of Christ. While the Church will face much opposition for
the sake of the Word, she must be a faithful herald of the good news.

Therefore submit yourselves to every ordinance of man for the Lord's
sake, whether to the king as supreme, or to governors, as to those who are
sent by him for the punishment of evildoers and for the praise of those
who do good. For this is the will of God, that by doing good you may
put to silence the ignorance of foolish men.* In light of this truth, let us
be a Church that remains bold in our witness for Christ.

———◦———

*Father, many have died for the sake of the Gospel. Help us to be faithful
witnesses even unto death.*

*I pray these things in Jesus' name. Amen.*

*1 Peter 2:13-15

# THE POLITY OF THE CHURCH

Therefore, brothers, pick out from among you seven men of good repute, full of the Spirit and of wisdom, whom we will appoint to this duty.

Acts 6:3

## HOW SHOULD THE CHURCH BE GOVERNED?

A complaint had arisen amongst the Hellenists regarding the widows in the church. These widows did not have the provisions needed for their daily needs, and this presented a difficulty for the apostles. The needs of the widows had to be met, but there was also the responsibility to preach the Word of God.

We read here how that the apostles chose seven men, who were of good reputation, to meet the needs of those around them. As a result, the Word of God continued to spread, and many came to faith.

What we learn from this account is that the church is not a one-man show. It is a community, which possesses diverse gifts and abilities. There were elders and deacons who were set over the local churches, and this is a practice which should continue today.

Beloved, let us not love in word or in tongue, but in deed and in truth,* providing honorable things, not only in the sight of the Lord, but also in the sight of men.* In light of this truth, let us be a people who serve together under the structure of a healthy church government.

---

*Father, Your church is not a Fortune 500 company. There should be a plurality of elders who also delegate responsibilities to other gifted men. Please lead Your people to local churches that practice a biblical church polity.*

*I pray these things in Jesus' name. Amen.*

*1 John 3:16-16, 2 Corinthians 8:21*

# THE DIVERSITY OF THE CHURCH

And when they came up out of the water, the Spirit of the Lord carried Philip away, and the eunuch saw him no more, and went on his way rejoicing.

Acts 8:39

## UNTO WHOM SHOULD THE GOSPEL BE PREACHED?

The Gospel is to be preached unto every tongue, tribe, and nation.

Philip was a man of godly character who faithfully preached the Gospel. We read that he was led to a eunuch who was reading the Prophet Isaiah. The eunuch was an Ethiopian who served as a court official to the Queen.

What happens next is truly remarkable. Philip begins preaching the Gospel to him, and then we are told that the eunuch comes to faith in Christ. Upon being baptized, he goes his way rejoicing.

In like manner, the Church of Jesus Christ is comprised of a people with diverse nationalities who are unified under the Gospel. We are called to go into all the world and make disciples of all nations and peoples baptizing them in the name of the Father and of the Son and of the Holy Spirit, teaching them to observe all that God's Word has commanded. And Jesus promised, "Behold, I am with you always, to the end of the age."*

In light of this truth, let us be a Church who preaches the Gospel to all tribes and tongues.

---

*Father, Your Church is made up of peoples from all types of backgrounds. Help me to be a Church that desires to see Christ preached to the nations.*

*I pray these things in Jesus' name. Amen.*

*Matthew 28:19-20

# THE TRIUMPH OF THE CHURCH

And he said, "I am Jesus, whom you are persecuting, but rise and enter the city, and you will be told what you are to do."

Acts 9:5-6

## CAN THE ENEMIES OF GOD PREVAIL AGAINST THE CHURCH?

Saul of Tarsus was one of the greatest enemies to ever oppose the Church. He was zealous to see the saints thwarted in their efforts to advance the kingdom. We read how that Saul went on a journey to capture followers of the Way, but his travels led him to a personal confrontation with the Lord Jesus Christ.*

Now as Paul went on his way, he approached Damascus, and suddenly a light from heaven shone around him. And falling to the ground, he heard a voice saying to him, "Saul, Saul, why are you persecuting me?"* It was on this particular journey that Paul would be radically transformed through the Gospel.

How is it that one of the greatest persecutors of the Church could become its greatest evangelist? Because the Church has an all-powerful Advocate in Christ Jesus. When the saints are persecuted, they are not forsaken. We may be pressed on all sides, but not crushed; perplexed, but not in despair; persecuted, but not forsaken; struck down, but not destroyed. We always carry around in our body the death of Jesus, so that the life of Jesus may also be revealed,*

———————◇———————

*Father, You have given all things into the hands of Your Son. Your Church may suffer many difficulties in this life, but it will experience the final victory in Christ. Help me not to grow weary while doing Your work, but rather to keep my eyes fixed on the glory that awaits me.*

*I pray these things in Jesus' name. Amen.*

*Acts 9:2, 3-4, 2 Corinthians 4:8-10

# THE SANCTIFICATION OF THE CHURCH

And the voice came to him again a second time,
"What God has made clean, do not call common."
Acts 10:15

## WHO HAS GOD CLEANSED?

The Jewish community had very strict laws and ceremonies for the purpose of keeping themselves clean. They would not even associate with one who was a Gentile, since the Gentiles were considered unclean.

We read that there was a certain Italian who was a God-fearing man whose name was Cornelius. He was a centurion who sought the Lord regularly, but he did not know the purification customs of the Law. This portion of Acts tells us that there came a voice to him: "Rise, Peter; kill and eat." But Peter said, "By no means, Lord; for I have never eaten anything that is common or unclean."* Surely this command came as a surprise to Peter. These animals were ceremonially unclean, but nevertheless, this is what the Lord had commanded Peter to do.

Ultimately, we know that God wanted to show Peter that all peoples in Christ, like Cornelius, are cleansed from their former sins. So Peter opened his mouth and said: "Truly I understand that God shows no partiality.* There no longer remains a distinction between nationalities, but rather an invitation for all to come to faith. Therefore let us be reminded that the Church, while she is imperfect in this life, has been washed and cleansed from her former sins.

---

*Father, how can we call common what You have cleansed? Help me to remember that Your Church has been cleansed, and keep me from the sin of making unrighteous judgments.*

*I pray these things in Jesus' name. Amen.*

*Acts 10:14-15, 34

# THE CHURCH IS SACRAMENTAL

And he commanded them to be baptized in the name of Jesus Christ.
Then they asked him to remain for some days.

Acts 10:48

## WHY SHOULD A CHRISTIAN BE BAPTIZED?

There are many reasons why a Christian should be baptized, but the primary reason is that Christ commands us.

Peter had just preached the Gospel to the Gentiles, and many believed in the Word. The Holy Spirit fell on all who heard the word and were amazed, because the gift of the Holy Spirit was poured out even on the Gentiles.* We are told that these new believers were commanded to be baptized.

When news of what happened reached the Church in Jerusalem, there was much conflict. The Jewish community criticized Peter for eating with the Gentiles, because they supposed these new converts to be unclean. But the blessing of Abraham came upon the Gentiles in Christ Jesus, that we might receive the promise of the Spirit through faith.*

All peoples of every nation, upon believing on the Lord Jesus Christ, are to be baptized. The saints, who have been redeemed, proclaim their profession of faith through the sacrament of baptism. All people are to be baptized who have received the Holy Spirit.*Are you a part of a local church that faithfully practices that holy ordinance?

◆——————◆——————◆

*Father, Your Word commands us to proclaim the Gospel through Word and Sacrament. Help us to obey Your command for all believers to be baptized.*

*I pray these things in Jesus' name. Amen.*

*Acts 10:44-45, Galatians 3:14, Acts 10:47

# THE GREAT MYSTERY OF THE CHURCH

When they heard these things they fell silent. And they glorified God,
saying, "Then to the Gentiles also God has granted
repentance that leads to life."
Acts 11:18

## WHAT IS THE GREAT MYSTERY OF THE CHURCH?

Word had gone throughout Judea that many Gentiles had come to
Christ. This created quite a controversy amongst Jewish believers. The
Gentiles had been ceremonially unclean, and there were many who called
for these new believers to be circumcised.

This portion of the book of Acts tells us that Peter, after being filled with
the Holy Spirit, admonished his brethren "not to call common what God
had cleansed." We read that when the Jewish believers heard these things
they fell silent, and then glorified God.

What we witness in the book of Acts is what we see today amongst the
Church. There no longer remains a middle wall of separation between
the Jewish believer and the Gentile believer. Instead of a separation, there
is one new Church united together in Christ. Our unity in the Gospel
is the great mystery that Paul refers to in his letter to the Ephesians.* In
light of this truth, let us worship the Lord together in love and unity.

---

*Father, the Great Mystery of the Church is that You have united all of Your
saints together in Christ. Help me, therefore, to worship You in a spirit of
unity and love with one another.*

*I pray these things in Jesus' name. Amen.*

*Acts 11:9, Ephesians 5:32

# THE AIM OF THE CHURCH

Immediately an angel of the Lord struck him down, because he did not give glory to God, and he was eaten by worms and breathed his last.

Acts 12:23

## SHOULD ANY FLESH GLORY IN THE PRESENCE OF THE LORD?

There was a dispute that had arisen between the people of Tyre and Sidon. The book of Acts tells us that the people requested the voice of a god, and not a man.* We are told that Herod, in addressing this dispute, would not give glory to God. So, the Lord struck and killed him in front of the large crowd.

Herod's tragic error teaches us the importance of giving all glory to God. He is a jealous God Who does not share His glory with any other.* His work of redemption is independent from the merit of human hands. Thus, it is only fitting that man ascribe all greatness and honor to Him Who sits on the throne.

Are we, as a Church, zealous to see God glorified? Because of Him, you are in Christ Jesus, who became to us wisdom from God, righteousness and sanctification and redemption, so that, as it is written, "Let the one who boasts, boast in the Lord."* Let us worship the Lord in such a way that men ascribe all glory to Him alone.

———————◆———————

*Father, salvation is a supernatural work that is given to us from above. Deliver me from the error of Herod, and help me to preach in such a way that no flesh can glory in Your presence.\**

*I pray these things in Jesus' name. Amen.*

*Acts 12:22, Isaiah 42:8, 1 Corinthians 1:30-31, 1:29

# PRAYER WITHIN THE CHURCH

Then after fasting and praying they laid their hands on them and sent them off.

Acts 13:3

## WHAT ROLE DOES FASTING AND PRAYING PLAY IN YOUR CHURCH?

The role of prayer is one of the most important ministries in the local church, but sadly it is often the most neglected ministry. History teaches us that the most fruitful works for the kingdom have been those works that were bathed in prayer.

The early Church was no exception to this normal practice of prayer and fasting.

They placed a key emphasis on the importance of corporate prayer. It was through the act of worship and fasting that the Holy Spirit revealed the calling of Paul and Barnabas to the church at Antioch. We read that while they were worshiping the Lord and fasting, the Holy Spirit said, "Set apart for me Barnabas and Saul for the work to which I have called them."* They had their answer to prayer and laid hands on them and sent them off. In like manner, the practice of corporate prayer is still of great importance to a healthy Church. There should be no decision that is made without carefully seeking the direction of the Lord.

Are you a part of a church that places an emphasis on corporate prayer? Let us be a Church who brings all their decisions, both small and great, before the Lord our God.

———————◆———————

*Father, prayer is one of the greatest privileges that you have granted to Your Church. Help us to be a people who seek You in all decisions regarding our corporate and private worship.*

*I pray these things in Jesus' name. Amen.*

*Acts 13:2

# THE JOY OF THE CHURCH

And the disciples were filled with joy and with the Holy Spirit.

Acts 13:52

## WHAT WAS IT THAT GAVE THE EARLY CHURCH SO MUCH JOY?

The Church in the First Century endured much hardship for the sake of Christ. Yet Acts tells us that these New Testament believers possessed much joy. We read that the Jews incited the devout women of high standing and the leading men of the city, stirred up persecution against Paul and Barnabas, and drove them out of their district.* Nevertheless, the Church continued to experience a great measure of growth.

God was doing great things in and through the lives of these believers at Antioch, and great joy was present in their midst. Many centuries have been removed, but the Holy Spirit continues to dwell amongst the Church. She possesses all the fullness of God, and therefore His people have great reason to rejoice.

In light of this eternal truth, let us be a people who never cease to sing the sweet praises of our great God.

———◇———

*Father, You have given me immeasurable blessings in Christ. Grant me the grace to keep my candlestick of joy burning brighter each and every day.*

*I pray these things in Jesus' name. Amen.*

*Acts 13:50

AUGUST 27

# THE ENCOURAGEMENT OF THE CHURCH

Strengthening the souls of the disciples, encouraging them to continue
in the faith, and saying that through many tribulations
we must enter the Kingdom of God.

Acts 14:22

## WHAT IS THE BENEFIT OF DWELLING WITH GOD'S PEOPLE IN COMMUNITY?

The saints in Lystra and Iconium endured much hardship. Paul had just been stoned, and many supposed him to be dead. In the wake of these trying times, the Apostles offered up much encouragement to the strug-gling believers in Lystra and Iconium. Their message was clear: "through many tribulations we must enter the Kingdom of God." After they had heard these things, we are told that their souls were strengthened.

Dear friend, have you isolated yourself from the Church? If so, then let me reason with you. The Lord has provided you with a community of believers through the local church. In times of great difficulty, our local fellowship can serve as a source of great encouragement and help. In light of this truth, do not seek to isolate yourself, but rather immerse yourself in the service of your local church.

Let us consider how to stir up one another to love and good works, not neglecting to meet together, as is the habit of some, but encouraging one another, and all the more as you see the Day drawing near.*

*Father, where would we be without a strong community of believers? Help me to remain plugged into a healthy local church so that my soul can stay nourished.*

*I pray these things in Jesus' name. Amen.*

*Hebrews 10:24-25

# THE CHURCH IS CONFESSIONAL

*That you abstain from what has been sacrificed to idols, and from blood, and from what has been strangled, and from sexual immorality. If you keep yourselves from these, you will do well. Farewell.*

Acts 15:29

## WHAT DOES IT MEAN TO BE CONFESSIONAL?

There were those who troubled the Gentile believers with strange doctrines. Men were teaching others that they must be circumcised to be saved. This created no small controversy between these false teachers and the Apostles. Therefore, many elders gathered together and formulated a doctrinal statement. This doctrinal statement brought much clarity to the Church, and encouraged its people to remain faithful to sound doctrine.

Many centuries have been removed since this dispute, but the Church continues to be attacked by false teachers. Therefore, it is necessary for believers to have a solid confession of faith. A Church that doesn't define and confess what they believe will be vulnerable to error.

For the time is coming when people will not endure sound teaching, but having itching ears they will accumulate for themselves teachers to suit their own passions, and will turn away from listening to the truth and wander off into myths.* In light of this eternal truth, let us be a people who echo the truths of our historic creeds and confessions.

---

*Father, woe to us if we deviate from the apostles' doctrine and teaching. Help me to be a part of a local church that confesses its historical doctrines and creeds.*

*I pray these things in Jesus' name. Amen.*

*2 Timothy 4:3-4

# THE CHURCH IS MISSIONAL

And when Paul had seen the vision, immediately we sought to go into Macedonia, concluding that God had called us to preach the gospel to them.

Acts 16:10

## DOES YOUR CHURCH HAVE A HEART FOR MISSIONS?

The New Testament Church was very missions-minded. We read that Paul had a desire to minister in Asia, but that he was redirected to Macedonia. It was in Macedonia that the Lord used Paul and Barnabas in mighty ways.

Throughout the ages there have been many Christians who have left their homes, their families, and their lands to reach others for the sake of Christ. Time would fail me to write about the ministries of David Brainerd, Hudson Taylor, and Jim Elliot. However, their testimonies teach us that there is no small cost for sharing the Gospel with the nations.

Jesus said, "All authority in heaven and on earth has been given to me. Go therefore and make disciples of all nations, baptizing them in the name of the Father and of the Son and of the Holy Spirit, teaching them to observe all that I have commanded you. And behold, I am with you always, to the end of the age."*

Is your church passionate about reaching out to the nations with the Gospel? Let us be a people who desire to see Christ's name go to the ends of the earth.

———⬦———

*Father, You desire that all tongues, tribes, and nations sing Your praises. Help me to have a sensitive and tender heart for missions.*

*I pray these things in Jesus' name. Amen.*

*Matthew 28:18-20

# FAITHFUL MINISTERS IN THE CHURCH

For I did not shrink from declaring to you the whole counsel of God.
Acts 20:27

## HOW DO YOU MEASURE SUCCESS?

There is a temptation for churches in our day to measure their success by the size of their congregations, yet there is a danger in only looking at the numbers.

The early Church did experience much growth, but it was the Lord who added to their number daily those who were being saved.* They did not feel a need to appeal to a seeker-sensitive model, but rather sought to faithfully teach the Word of God.

Paul the Apostle was no exception to this rule. In spite of the fierce opposition that he faced, Paul remained faithful in teaching the whole counsel of God. He did not feel a need to compromise the message of the Cross. Instead, he preached Christ boldly to anyone who would listen.

Paul said to the Galatians, "For do I now persuade men, or God? Or do I seek to please men? For if I still pleased men, I would not be a bond-servant of Christ."*

What about your church? Are you currently sitting under the ministry of faithful ministers? If not, then find a church that will faithfully declare the whole counsel of God.

---

*Father, we need faithful shepherds in this current generation. Help me to be a part of a local church that possesses faithful pastors and teachers.*

*I pray these things in Jesus' name. Amen.*

*Acts 2:47, Galatians 1:10

# A CHURCH THAT REMEMBERS

Therefore, O King Agrippa, I was not disobedient to the heavenly vision.

Acts 26:19

## DO YOU HAVE A GOOD MEMORY?

Paul the Apostle had a great memory. Here in the text, he recalls to mind his testimony. Consequently, it was a testimony that he felt compelled to share with others. Paul never forgot where he came from, and to what extent God had saved him. He carried his testimony where ever he went, and he shared it with those around him.

In like manner, all the saints have a story to share with the world. They have conquered the devil by the blood of the Lamb and by the word of their testimony, for they loved not their lives even unto death.* While we may not stand before kings and magistrates, we can share our story with our neighbors or our co-workers.

What about you, dear friend? Do you have a wonderful story that you can share with others? Let us be a Church that remembers the great things that Christ has done for us.

———————◇———————

*Father, how can I not share my testimony with others? Give me a passion to tell others about the great things that You have done for me.*

*I pray these things in Jesus' name. Amen.*

*Revelation 12:11

# SEPTEMBER
## WHO ARE THE SAINTS?

What is a saint? A saint is someone who has received eternal life through the free gift of God.

We read in Ephesians the following passage: "For by grace you have been saved through faith. And this is not your own doing; it is the gift of God, not a result of works, so that no one may boast."*

Those words are simple but yet profound. Paul wants to make it absolutely clear that there is nothing that you and I can do to merit eternal life. It is a gift that must be received through faith. While these truths are agreed on by those of the household of faith, many of us do not often stop and reflect on what that means for our everyday lives. Did you know that you are accepted and deeply loved by God? This love and acceptance in Christ makes us heirs of all things in the heavenly places.*

Many believers never meditate on the fact that they are loved and accepted by God. Their neglect or lack of understanding drives them to despair when life gets tough. My prayer for you is that you will come to know your standing in Christ. Let us seek the Lord as we reflect on this month's meditations.

*Ephesians 2:8-9, Ephesians 1:12, 22

# WE ARE CHOSEN

Even as He chose us in Him before the foundation of the world,
that we should be holy and blameless before him.
Ephesians 1:4

## WHAT DOES IT MEAN TO BE CHOSEN BY GOD?

There are three things to consider regarding our election. First, there is nothing in and of ourselves that have merited the privilege of election. We are chosen unconditionally through His free and sovereign grace. This gives us no reason to boast, but rather to place all of our confidence in the merit of Christ alone.

Secondly, God chose us before the foundation of the world. Our salvation is not based on faltering opinions, but is rather etched in the granite of eternity. The Lord has decreed it, and therefore our redemption is forever sealed.

Finally, He has chosen us to be without fault before His throne of grace. Christians are justified, because Christ has assumed the guilt and the punishment of their sins. Dear friend, do you ever pause to reflect on God's electing love for you? Let us not fear that old time doctrine of election, but rather rejoice in the grace that has set us free.

———————————◇———————————

*Father, You have chosen us to be a people who are holy and blameless before You. Help me to fully comprehend the blessings of Your unconditional election. I pray these things in Jesus' name. Amen.*

# WE ARE ADOPTED

He predestined us for adoption as sons through Jesus Christ,
according to the purpose of His will.
Ephesians 1:5

## WHAT DOES IT MEAN TO BE ADOPTED?

Biblically speaking, being adopted means that we now belong to the family of God. This further implies that we are heirs of eternal life. We are no longer strangers or enemies of God, but rather we are His sons and daughters through faith.

The saints, who are adopted, enjoy all the privileges of being heirs with Christ. These privileges have been granted to us freely through the eternal counsels and foreknowledge of God.* On these grounds, we can rest in the fact that His purposes concerning us shall not fail.

In Christ, all the saints possess a loving Father, Who gives His children good and perfect gifts.*

Dear Christian, do you doubt the goodness of God? Consider your adoption this day. The God, Who did not spare His Son,* is now your loving heavenly Father.

---

*Father, we are no longer strangers, but rather Your sons and daughters. Help me to rest assured in Your faithful and loving promises.*

*I pray these things in Jesus' name. Amen.*

*Acts 2:23, James 1:17, Romans 8:28

# WE ARE ACCEPTED

To the praise of His glorious grace,
with which he has blessed us in the Beloved.
Ephesians 1:6

## WHAT DOES IT MEAN TO BE ACCEPTED IN CHRIST?

Being accepted in Christ means that we are embraced by the Father.

Notice that this acceptance finds its condition in the Person of Jesus. The Christian is now united to Him by faith, and therefore receives grace instead of wrath. Prior to grace I thought that salvation was a prize that I could obtain. It isn't until grace reveals the depravity of my heart that I come to realize the hopelessness of my condition. When I come to this realization, I finally understand what Paul has been teaching us all along. Salvation is not a prize to be earned, but rather a gift to be received.

And the grace of our Lord was exceedingly abundant, with faith and love which are in Christ Jesus.* For He made Him who knew no sin to be sin for us, that we might become the righteousness of God in Him.*

Dear friend, have you considered where you would be without grace? Let us not strive to earn God's blessing, but rather rest in the grace He so freely gives.

———————◆———————

*Father, You have given me salvation as a free gift. Help me to cease from my dead works so that I can enter into Your rest.*

*I pray these things in Jesus' name. Amen.*

*1 Timothy 1:14, 2 Corinthians 5:21

# WE ARE REDEEMED

In him we have redemption through his blood …
Ephesians 1:7

## WHERE DO I FIND REDEMPTION FROM THE SLAVERY OF SIN AND DEATH?

I find my redemption in the Person and work of Jesus Christ.

Here in the text, Paul wants us to understand that the benefits of our redemption are found in our union with Christ. The saints are united to Him by faith, and in Him they find redemption "through his blood."

Peter tells us, in his epistle, knowing that you were not redeemed with corruptible things, like silver or gold, from your aimless conduct received by tradition from your fathers, but with the precious blood of Christ, as of a lamb without blemish and without spot.* The Christian has been set free from the power of sin and death, and now they find forgiveness instead of judgment.

Dear Christian, have you reckoned yourself to be free from the power of sin? Let us be a people who walk in the freedom we now have in Christ. If God so loved us, we also ought to love one another.*

---

*Father, I am no longer a slave to sin, but rather an heir with Christ. Help me to walk in the liberty of my newfound freedom.*

*I pray these things in Jesus' name. Amen.*

*1 Peter 1:18-19, 1 John 4:11

# WE ARE FORGIVEN

... the forgiveness of our trespasses, according to the riches of his grace.
Ephesians 1:7

## WHY DO WE, AS SAINTS, NEED FORGIVENESS?

The question of forgiveness is an important one, but it is sadly one that is largely neglected in our day.

Evangelicals tend to focus on how they were saved, but they rarely reflect on why they were saved. Accordingly, if we are going to understand the depths of God's love for us, then we must also understand the extent to which we were saved.

The truth of the matter is that we have broken God's Law, and have therefore committed sin against an infinitely righteous Judge.

As a result of the evidence that has been revealed against us, we were sentenced to an eternity of wrath. This judgment leaves the sinner without any hope of meriting eternal life. Once we understand how hopeless our condition is before God, then we are able to appreciate more fully the forgiveness that has been offered to us in Christ.

King David understood and appreciated his forgiveness when he wrote, "Against you, you only, have I sinned and done what is evil in your sight, so that You may be justified in Your words and blameless in Your judgment."*

Dear friend, do you understand the depths from which you were saved? Let us be those who reflect, not only on how God saves us, but also on the extent to which we were saved.

————◇————

*Father, I am a sinner of the most wretched kind, but instead of judgment You showed me mercy. Help me to reflect more fully on the forgiveness I now have in Christ.*

*I pray these things in Jesus' name. Amen.*

*Psalm 51:4

# WE ARE MYSTERIOUS

Making known to us the mystery of his will,
according to His purpose which He set forth in Christ.
Ephesians 1:9

## WHAT IS THE GREAT MYSTERY OF THE SAINTS?

There are three things within this text that we should understand. First, this great mystery has been revealed to us by God. He is both the Concealer and Revealer of knowledge. Secondly, this great mystery is revealed to us at the appointed time. The Old Testament saints worshiped the One True God, but they operated with a limited understanding of the Gospel.

In the fullness of times, the Lord has revealed the glorious plan of redemption to His saints. All believers throughout the ages are the benefactors of this revelation.

Finally, God has revealed this mystery through the Person of Jesus Christ. The saints possess all wisdom and knowledge through their union with Him. In Him, both Jewish and Gentile believers are united together. There no longer remains a middle wall of separation,* but rather a unity of love and joy. In light of this truth, let us love one another as Christ has loved us.

---

*Father, You have put all things under subjection to Your Son.* Help Your saints to worship Him in both unity and love.*

*I pray these things in Jesus' name. Amen.*

*Ephesians 2:14, Ephesians 1:22

# WE ARE HEIRS

In Him we have obtained an inheritance, having been predestined
according to the purpose of Him who works all things
according to the counsel of His will.
Ephesians 1:11

## HOW WOULD YOU LIKE TO COME INTO AN INHERITANCE?

Many of us would like to receive a large inheritance, but there are many
challenges that may arise in acquiring a large estate. There may be estate
taxes owed on the property, or growing conflict amongst the heirs. In
addition to the financial and relational strains that come from an inheritance, there is also the grief that accompanies the loss of a loved one.

Ultimately, there is nothing in this life that brings true and lasting peace.

As for the rich in this present age, do not to be haughty, nor set your
hopes on the uncertainty of riches, but on God, who richly provides us
with everything to enjoy.*

It is important not to place our hope in the things of this world, but
rather to place our hope in the joys of possessing eternal life. Those, who
have trusted in Christ, have been given an inheritance that is incorruptible and undefiled.* While we endure hardships in this life, we long for
the day when we will enter into the joy of the Lord.

In light of this eternal truth, let us reflect more fully on the true riches
that we now possess in Christ.

———————————◆———————————

*Father, there is nothing more certain than the promise of eternal life. Help
me not to lose heart in the disappointments of life, but rather to rest my hope
fully on the expectations of glory.*

*I pray these things in Jesus' name. Amen.*

*1 Timothy 6:17, 1 Peter 1:4

# WE ARE SEALED

In Him you also, when you heard the word of truth, the gospel of your salvation, and believed in Him, were sealed with the promised Holy Spirit.
Ephesians 1:13

## HOW CERTAIN IS THE PROMISE OF ETERNAL LIFE?

Absolutely. The promise of eternal life is absolutely certain since it is fixed in the eternal counsels of God.

Here in the text above, the Apostle Paul reminds us of the surety of our hope. He wants us to come to grips with the certainty of our calling. We, who have been made alive through faith, have been sealed with the promised Holy Spirit, who is the guarantee of our inheritance until we acquire possession of it, to the praise of His glory.*

But God, being rich in mercy, because of the great love with which He loved us, even when we were dead in our trespasses, made us alive together with Christ.*

The Holy Spirit is likened to a down payment. God has secured our redemption through the sacrifice of His Son, and has given us a down payment as a sign and seal of His covenant. Therefore we have, in Christ, the assurance of a future rest.

Have you come to rest in the sure promises of salvation? May we look to the God of our Lord Jesus Christ, the Father of glory, to give us the Spirit of wisdom and of revelation in the knowledge of Him.*

---

*Father, all things have been given to Your Son, and I am a co-heir with Him. Help me not to place my confidence in any human merit, but to rest in the finished work of Christ Jesus.*

*I pray these things in Jesus' name. Amen.*

*Ephesians 1:14, 2:4-5, 1:17

# WE ARE CONQUERORS

And he put all things under his feet and
gave him as head over all things to the church.
Ephesians 1:22

## WHO HAS BEEN GIVEN ALL AUTHORITY OVER THE CHURCH?

Paul tells us that it is Christ Who is the head over all things to the Church.*
By virtue of His death and resurrection, God has given all things to Jesus.
The Father has even put the enemies of Christ under His feet. Yet the
knowledge of His reign also carries with it implications for all the saints.

We, who are joint-heirs with Christ, have been made to reign with Him,
provided we suffer with Him in order that we may also be glorified with
Him.* Therefore, we can rest assured in the victory we now have in Him.

While we suffer much in this present age there is coming a day when we
will enter into glory. The saying is trustworthy, for if we have died with
Him, we will also live with Him; if we endure, we will also reign with
Him.* In light of this truth, let us not lose heart over our present trials,
but rather rejoice in the hope of eternity.

———————◇———————

*Father, You have given us all things in Christ. Help me to have a deeper
understanding of the hope of my calling.*

*I pray these things in Jesus' name. Amen.*

* Ephesians 1:22, Romans 8:17, 2 Timothy 2:11-12

# WE ARE ALIVE

Even when we were dead in our trespasses, made us alive together
with Christ—by grace you have been saved.
Ephesians 2:5

## WHAT DOES IT MEAN TO BE RAISED WITH CHRIST?

Those, who have been raised with Christ, have been set free from their
former corruptions and sins.

Here in the text, Paul is reminding us of the depths from which we have
been saved. The Christian was dead in trespasses and sins, in which we
once walked, following the course of this world, following the prince of
the power of the air, the spirit that is now at work in the sons of disobedience.* We had no desire for the things of God, and we were without
hope in this world.*

Yet we were not left in our sins, but delivered through an act of Divine
grace.

The old hymn writer says it best when he writes, "Twas grace that taught
my heart to fear, and grace my fears relieved; How precious did that grace
appear the hour I first believed!" [7]

Thus the Christian remains a debtor to the kindness of God. Where
would we be without the Gospel of Christ? Let us, who have been delivered from our former sins, sing the praises of our King.

---

*Father, where would I be without Your grace? Thank You, for the gift of eter-
nal life, and help me to share the grace of God with others.*

*I pray these things in Jesus' name. Amen.*

*Ephesians 2:1-2, Ephesians 2:12

# WE ARE SEATED WITH CHRIST

And raised up with Him and seated us with Him in the
heavenly places in Christ Jesus.
Ephesians 2:6

## HOW CAN WE FATHOM THE GRACE OF GOD?

In the first few verses of Ephesians, chapter two, Paul the Apostle lays down the foundation for grace. He says that we were children of wrath,* and that we were those who were dead in our trespasses.* Yet in spite of our once fallen condition, God was moved to great compassion for us. He not only had compassion on us, but He also made us heirs of all things.* We are no longer enemies of God, but rather those who enjoy the blessings of His fellowship.

We were raised with Christ, so we should seek those things which are above, where Christ is, sitting at the right hand of God. Set your mind on things above, not on things on the earth.*

Why then do we seek the approval of others? We, who are born again, have the approval of the Most High God! In light of this eternal truth, let us not place our identity in the approval of man, but rather rejoice in the fact that we are now accepted in the Beloved.*

———————◆———————

*Father, You have made me to reign with Christ. Help me not to place my identity in my career or in my appearance, but rather in the standing of Your blessed Son.*

*I pray these things in Jesus' name. Amen.*

*Ephesians 2:3, Ephesians 2:1, Hebrews 1:2, Colossians 3:1-2, Ephesians 1:6

# WE HAVE A GIFT

For by grace you have been saved through faith.
And this is not your own doing; it is the gift of God.
Ephesians 2:8

## IS THERE ANY ROOM FOR BOASTING?

As a saint, you must know this. If there is one thing that the Apostle Paul is clear about it is that salvation is a free gift. It cannot be earned through our works.

This concept of grace is a difficult concept for our society to grasp. We are a people who are used to working for our dreams and desires. Yet the problem we face is rooted in a much deeper issue. Man seeks to elevate himself whenever possible. This self-aggrandizement stems out of the sinful matters of the heart. Sinful flesh will always try to rob from God the glory due His name.

The salvation of sinners leaves no room for boasting. We have been justified freely by His grace through the redemption that is in Christ Jesus.* We are the recipients of grace, so then, it does not depend on man's desire or effort, but on God's mercy.* In light of this eternal truth, let us give all glory and honor to the One Who has secured our redemption.

---

*Father, salvation is a gift, it's all grace. Help me to preach a Gospel that gives all glory to You.*

*I pray these things in Jesus' name. Amen.*

*Romans 3:24, Romans 9:16

# WE ARE THE MASTERPIECE OF GOD

For we are his workmanship, created in Christ Jesus for good works,
which God prepared beforehand, that we should walk in them.

Ephesians 2:10

## WHAT IS YOUR FAVORITE WORK OF ART?

When we look at a masterful piece of art, it is impossible not to admire its intricate detail and design. Here in the text, the Apostle Paul likens Christians to a work of art. He refers to us as God's workmanship, or as the original Greek text puts it, His poema, from where we get our English word, "poem" or "poetry." You and I are a masterpiece made by God Himself.

In the work of salvation, God has taken lowly sinners from the depths of their depravity, and has made them into a masterpiece of grace. His marvelous work of redemption even makes the angels in heaven marvel.*

Yet there is more. We are also saved unto good works. There is a working out of what the Lord has already worked within us. So we are to put on the new self, created to be like God in true righteousness and holiness.* Thus in the doing of His will we are His poetry in motion.

Dear friend, we are God's poem, His workmanship, and He wants to express Himself in us. Let our conduct be honorable, that when they speak against you as evildoers, they may, by your good works which they observe, glorify God.*

---

*Father, we are to live continually in Your grace. Help us not to rely on the arm of the flesh,* but to rest daily in the works which You have prepared for us beforehand.*

*I pray these things in Jesus' name. Amen.*

*1 Peter 1:12, Ephesians 4:24, 1 Peter 2:12, 2 Chronicles 32:8

# WE ARE SAVED UNTO GOOD WORKS

Created in Christ Jesus for good works.
Ephesians 2:10

## HOW CAN YOU PLEASE GOD?

Many people dedicate themselves to various good works. They think that they will earn God's acceptance through their own merit. In an effort to please God, they separate themselves from worldly pleasures, and they afflict on themselves all sorts of evils. By the same token, in our attempts to earn favor with God, how can we know if we have done enough things to please Him? The truth of the matter is that man could never do enough works to please God.

The prophet Isaiah tells us we are all like an unclean thing, and all our good works are like filthy rags.* They are not accepted by God, because the evidence of our sin has already been revealed. The Bible tells us to be discreet, chaste, good, obedient, that the word of God may not be blasphemed. To be sober-minded, in all things showing yourself to be a pattern of good works; in doctrine showing integrity, reverence, incorruptibility, sound speech that cannot be condemned, having nothing evil to say of you.*

Are you living each moment of your life by faith? Let us live the only life that can be pleasing to God—a life lived out by faith.

———————◦———————

*Father, I do not have to labor in my own strength. Thank You, for sending Your Son to finish the work of salvation. Help me to simply walk in obedience to Your Word.*

*I pray these things in Jesus' name. Amen.*

*Isaiah 64:6, Titus 2:5-8

# WE ARE FRIENDS OF GOD

But now in Christ Jesus you who once were far off have been brought near by the blood of Christ.

Ephesians 2:13

## DID YOU KNOW THAT THE SAINTS ARE FRIENDS OF GOD?

Paul is writing to let the saints at Ephesus know what blessings they have in Christ. Here in the text, he wants them to understand that they now have communion with the Most High God.

We, the saints, have great reason to rejoice because we are no longer aliens and strangers from the covenants of promise, having no hope and without God in the world.* The Gospel has removed our separation from Him, and has given us direct access to the throne of grace. Let us then with confidence draw near to the throne of grace, that we may receive mercy and find grace to help in time of need.*

In like manner, all the saints enjoy the benefits of their friendship with God. We possess all His covenant promises through faith. Dear friend, do you long for communion with your Creator? Let us be those who are unified together for the purpose of enjoying the Lord in worship.

---

*Father, Your blessings to me are greater than I can count. Give me the grace to yearn more and more for a deeper communion with You.*

*I pray these things in Jesus' name. Amen.*

*Ephesians 2:12, Hebrews 4:16

# WE ARE RECONCILED

And might reconcile us both to God in one body through the cross,
thereby killing the hostility.
Ephesians 2:16

## WHAT DOES IT MEAN TO BE RECONCILED TO GOD?

In Christ, God reconciled the world to Himself, not counting our trespasses against us, and entrusting to us the message of reconciliation.*

Many people walk around with the agonies of unresolved conflict. Their conflicts eat away at their joy and peace, as they remain in their broken relationships. In such a way, the Christian was once at enmity with God.* The Apostle Paul says that we were enemies that remained under His Divine wrath. Yet instead of judgment, we now enjoy peaceful communion with our heavenly Father. This newfound peace also trickles down into our unity with other believers. There is a holistic effect that takes place in the life of God's people through the Gospel. As a result, we are one new man* in Christ.

In light of this truth let the saints enjoy, not only our fellowship with God, but also our fellowship with one another. Let us be ambassadors for Christ, to implore others, on behalf of Christ, to be reconciled to God.*

———————————

*Father, You are no longer our enemy. We now have peace with You through the death of Your Son. Help us to spread the message of reconciliation to others.*

*I pray these things in Jesus' name. Amen.*

*2 Corinthians 5:19, Romans 8:7, Ephesians 2:15, 2 Corinthians 5:20

# WE ARE CITIZENS

So then you are no longer strangers and aliens, but you are fellow
citizens with the saints and members of the household of God.

Ephesians 2:19

## HAVE YOU EVER HAD TO GAIN CITIZENSHIP INTO ANOTHER COUNTRY?

If so, then you have probably experienced just how difficult that process can be. Fortunately for believers, they do not have to wait years
to become citizens of God's Kingdom. They are granted access into the
heavenly country by faith.

For our citizenship is in heaven, from which we also eagerly wait for the
Savior, the Lord Jesus Christ, who will transform our lowly body that it
may be conformed to His glorious body, according to the working by
which He is able even to subdue all things to Himself.*

We, who were once strangers, have been made heirs to the covenant
promises of God. Instead of foreigners we are now citizens who dwell
together in unity. Do you possess a love for the saints? Let us be a people
whose love for one another is evident to all.

———————◆———————

*Father, we can now rejoice in the fact that we are heavenly citizens of Your
kingdom. Help us to love one another, and to dwell together in unity.*

*I pray these things in Jesus' name. Amen.*

*Philippians 3:20-21

# WE ARE LOVED

And to know the love of Christ that surpasses knowledge that
you may be filled with all the fullness of God.
Ephesians 3:19

## ARE YOU SEARCHING FOR LOVE IN ALL THE WRONG PLACES?

Millions of people live their lives without a sense of belonging or love.
They try to fill the void in their hearts with trivial pursuits, but it only
leaves them in despair.

Here in the text, Paul wants us to experience the kind of love that will
satisfy our deepest longing. This is a love that is given to us in the Person
of Jesus Christ. The Apostle's prayer is that we will gain a greater understanding of God's love—a love that surpasses all human knowledge.

There is no finite mind that can truly grasp the boundless goodness of
God, and yet this love was put on display for us on the Cross. In a demonstration of infinite perfection, Jesus Christ died to save sinners. He
willingly and humbly exchanged His life for the benefit of His enemies.

Do you want to know where you can find true love? Then reflect on the
sacrifice of Christ. He is a Savior Who loves us unconditionally.

———————◆———————

*Father, Your love for us is stronger than the grave.\* Help me to comprehend
with all the saints Your love which surpasses all knowledge.\**

*I pray these things in Jesus' name. Amen.*

\*Song of Solomon 8:6, Ephesians 3:18

# WE ARE GIFTED

But grace was given to each one of us according to the
measure of Christ's gift.

Ephesians 4:7

## WHAT IS THE MEASURE OF CHRIST'S GIFT?

I submit to you that infinite goodness cannot be weighed out or measured on a scale. The Apostle Paul wants us to understand the greatness of Christ's gift.

We serve a God Who is the Giver of every good and perfect gift.* This gift not only offers us the forgiveness of our sins, but it also offers us a life of abundant joy. One of the many joys we experience as Christians is the joy of serving the body of Christ. All of us, who have received eternal life, have been blessed with unique abilities and spiritual gifts. These gifts enable us to serve one another in love.

In this is love, not that we loved God, but that He loved us and sent His Son to be the propitiation for our sins. Beloved, if God so loved us, we also ought to love one another.*

Dear friend, are you using your God-given gifts for the benefit of the saints? If not, then prayerfully consider the ways in which you can serve in your local church.

———————◆———————

*Father, Your grace abounds toward Your people. Help me not to get puffed up in my spiritual gifts, but rather to serve one another in love.*

*I pray these things in Jesus' name. Amen.*

*James 1:17, 1 John 4:10-11

# WE ARE EQUIPPED

To equip the saints for the work of ministry,
for building up the body of Christ.
Ephesians 4:12

## HOW DOES GOD EQUIP HIS SAINTS?

God equips His people through the ministry of the local church. Throughout the centuries, the Lord has raised up many for the calling of the ministry. There were apostles who saw the risen Christ. They were sent throughout the ancient world to spread the gospel of peace. Paul also talks about prophets who were gifted in exhorting, edifying, and comforting God's people. Their purpose was to communicate the things that were revealed for our instruction.

The saints still benefit greatly from the prophetic gift of evangelists and pastors who minister daily to the needs of others. Ultimately, these gifts are provided for our growth in grace until we all come to the unity of the faith and of the knowledge of the Son of God, to maturity, to the measure of the stature of the fullness of Christ*

Are you part of a church that faithfully equips the saints? I encourage you to find out where you can be equipped for the work of the ministry.

———————◇———————

*Father, You have given some to be apostles, some to be prophets, and some to be evangelists and pastors.* Thank You for giving us faithful men who equip the saints. Help me to submit myself under the authority of those who faithfully watch over our souls.*

*I pray these things in Jesus' name. Amen.*

*Ephesians 4:13, Ephesians 4:11

# WE ARE LIGHT

For at one time you were darkness, but now you are light in the Lord.
Walk as children of light.
Ephesians 5:8

## CAN YOU IMAGINE A WORLD WITHOUT LIGHT?

The existence of human life could not be sustained without light. God has made the sun to keep the earth warm, and to help preserve our planet's ecosystem. The natural light also keeps mankind from stumbling around in the darkness.

In like manner, the Apostle Paul uses light as a means of illustration. God's Word brings light into the darkness of a sinful world. It reveals the wickedness of mankind, and it shows us the way to eternal life. Therefore, Paul wants us to understand our position in Christ. Since the saints are children of the light,* we ought to conduct ourselves in a manner that is worthy of our calling.*

Dear friend, do you bear the light of Christ's testimony in a fallen world? Let us be those who live in such a way that others will see our good works, and glorify our Father in heaven.*

———— ◆ ————

*Father, Your children no longer walk in darkness. You have made us to be those who shine the light of Your testimony in a dark and fallen world. Help me to walk worthy of my calling so that others will come to know You.*

*I pray these things in Jesus' name. Amen.*

*Ephesians 5:8, Ephesians 4:1, Matthew 5:16

# WE ARE ARMED

Put on the whole armor of God, that you may be able to
stand against the schemes of the devil.
Ephesians 6:11

## WOULD YOU GO INTO BATTLE WITHOUT THE PROPER WEAPONS?

The Romans were known for their skill in making war. Their soldiers were well-trained and well-prepared for battle. It is through the armor of these skilled fighters, that Paul makes his illustration. He wants Christians to know that they also face a fierce battle. Yet their battle is not a physical war with spears and shields, but rather a spiritual war that is fought against the devil.

If the saints are going to be prepared for the attacks of their adversary, then they will have to put on the armor of God. Paul's point in this text is simple—God has given us the means of grace necessary to be victorious over sin, the flesh, and the devil. For this reason, it will be well with us if we use the means He has provided for our growth in grace. Therefore take up the whole armor of God, that you may be able to withstand in the evil day, and having done all, to stand firm.*

Dear friend, are you prepared for the spiritual battle at hand? Let us be those who find ourselves well-trained and well-prepared for the attack of our adversary.

---

*Father, You have given us the means necessary for the battle at hand. Give me the grace to be ready for the warfare against the devil.*

*I pray these things in Jesus' name. Amen.*


*Ephesians 6:13

# WE ARE HOLY

He has now reconciled in His body of flesh by His death,
in order to present you holy...
Colossians 1:22

## WHAT DOES IT MEAN TO BE HOLY?

When dealing with the holiness of God, there are a few things to consider. First, we understand that He is qualitatively different and distinct from His creation. He is the Creator, and we are the creature. There is no being that can be compared to Him. Secondly, God's holiness also points to His perfectly righteous character. It is this second aspect of God's holiness that Paul is referring to in our text.

God's people, who fell short of His righteous requirements, are now presented holy and blameless though the death of Jesus Christ. Our Father in heaven no longer views us in our filthy garments of sin, but rather in the pure righteousness of His Son. Thus, we are no longer under His Divine wrath, but the saints have now received forgiveness for our trespasses.

In light of this eternal truth, let us not allow our past sins to condemn us, but rather hold fast to the promises of God in the Gospel. Just as He chose us in Him before the foundation of the world, that we should be holy and without blame before Him in love.*

---

*Father, the accuser of the brethren* continuously hurls accusations against Your beloved, but You have completely removed our sins from us. Give me the grace to remain in the hope of the Gospel without wavering or doubting.*

*I pray these things in Jesus' name. Amen.*

*Ephesians 1:4, Revelation 12:10

# WE ARE BLAMELESS

… and blameless and above reproach before Him.
Colossians 1:22

## HOW CAN GOD DECLARE US BLAMELESS BEFORE HIM?

Paul addresses that important question by referring back to the Gospel. The fact of the matter is that we were guilty of breaking God's holy Law, and consequently found ourselves under His Divine wrath.

Thus, it is only through Jesus Christ that we stand blameless before the Father.

He has reconciled us back to God through His death on the Cross. On account of this, we need to sanctify ourselves, having cleansed ourselves by the washing of water with the Word, and to present ourselves to Jesus as a glorious church, without stain or wrinkle or any such blemish, but holy and blameless.*

The saints are blameless before God, if indeed we continue in the faith, stable and steadfast, not shifting from the hope of the gospel that we heard, which has been proclaimed in all creation under heaven.*

---

*Father, thank you for making us blameless and above reproach. Help me to be diligent to be found by You in peace, without spot and blameless;* in the faith, in hope of the Gospel.*

*I pray these things in Jesus' name. Amen.*

*Ephesians 5:26-27, Colossians 1:23, 2 Peter 3:14

# WE ARE ROOTED

Rooted and built up in Him and established in the faith ...
Colossians 2:7

## WHAT DOES IT MEAN TO BE ROOTED IN CHRIST?

Paul wanted the believers at Colossae to understand the foundation of their faith. False heresy abounded in their day, and he therefore instructed them to remain in the doctrines of Christ. Paul's point is simply this: Jesus Christ is the head of the Church, and thus the saints will find nourishment and strength in Him. Why then were the Colossians deceived through strange doctrines?

Many centuries have been removed, but not much has changed. There are many false teachers who feast amongst the flock of God, and it is important for us to remain steadfast in the teaching of the apostles. Beware lest anyone cheat you through philosophy and empty deceit, according to the tradition of men, according to the basic principles of the world, and not according to Christ.*

In light of this truth, let us be those who are not tossed to and fro by every wind of doctrine,* but rather those who have their roots firmly planted in Christ.

---

*Father, there are so many false teachings that circulate amongst Your flock. Give me the grace to remain rooted in the teachings of Christ.*

*I pray these things in Jesus' name. Amen.*

*Colossians 2:8, Ephesians 4:14

# WE ARE BUILT UP

*… and built up in him and established in the faith, just as you were taught, abounding in thanksgiving.*

Colossians 2:7

## HOW ARE THE SAINTS BUILT UP IN CHRIST?

Our growth in grace will be built up if we hold fast to the teachings of Christ.

There were gnostic philosophers who presented a threat to the Colossian believers. Many were troubling them with their false teaching, but Paul likens their doctrine to empty deceit.* His point is simply this: if the saints at Colossae were going to mature, and be built up, then they would need to remain rooted in the doctrines of Christ. Jesus has been given all authority over the saints, and therefore, we are to guard His teachings very closely.

Dear friend, do you find nourishment in the Word of God? It is only as you feed on the Word of God that your soul will be strengthened and built up. For the word of God is living and powerful, and sharper than any two-edged sword, piercing even to the division of soul and spirit, and of joints and marrow, and is a discerner of the thoughts and intents of the heart.* In light of this eternal truth, let us study and hold fast to the wonderful truths of Scripture.

---

*Father, we are built up and established in Jesus Christ. He is the head over all things even the Church. Give me the grace not to deviate from His teachings, but rather to remain rooted in His Word.*

*I pray these things in Jesus' name. Amen.*

*Colossians 2:8, Hebrews 4:12, Ephesians 1:22

# WE HAVE A LIVING HOPE

Blessed be the God and Father of our Lord Jesus Christ! According to His great mercy He has caused us to be born again to a living hope through the resurrection of Jesus Christ from the dead.

1 Peter 1:3

## WHAT IF THE RESURRECTION OF JESUS CHRIST NEVER HAPPENED?

Scripture teaches us that if the resurrection never happened, then we would be a people without hope. Fortunately for the saints, Jesus no longer remains in the grave. He has been raised, and therefore He has begotten us again to a living hope.

Here in the text, Peter wants us to understand the certainty of our hope. We have a hope which is as steadfast as the promises of God. We have an inheritance that is imperishable, undefiled, and unfading, kept in heaven for us.*

For this reason, the Christian has great reason to rejoice. Amidst the uncertainties and difficulties of life, the saints possess a living hope. In light of this eternal truth, let us rest our minds more fully on the glory which awaits us in eternity.

---

*Father, You have not left us without hope, but rather You have given us an inheritance that is incorruptible. Give me the grace to rest fully in the future glory that awaits me.*

*I pray these things in Jesus' name. Amen.*

*1 Peter 1:4

# WE ARE KEPT

Who by God's power are being guarded through faith for a salvation
ready to be revealed in the last time.

1 Peter 1:5

## HAVE YOU EVER MISPLACED A VALUABLE POSSESSION?

If so, then you understand just how stressful it is. I remember losing my
wallet, and it took me a day to actually find it. You can only imagine
the relief I felt when I discovered it to be on the floor of my vehicle.
Fortunately for the believer, our salvation cannot be lost.

Here in the text, the Apostle Peter wants us to understand salvation is a
complete work of grace. The same God, Who raised Jesus from the dead,
is the same God Who has begotten us again to a living hope.* Therefore
the saint can rest assured that He is faithful to guard our souls.

Dear friend, have you ceased from your own works to serve the living
God? If so, then never lose sight of Christ, but rather continue to trust
Him daily for the preservation of your soul. For everyone who has this
hope in Him purifies himself, just as He is pure.*

---

*Father, You have predestined us, You have called us, You have justified us,
and You guard us. Help me to understand the great truths of the grace You
offer to me in the Gospel.*

*I pray these things in Jesus' name. Amen.*

*1 Peter 1:3, Romans 8:11, 1 John 3:3

# WE HAVE A PRECIOUS FAITH

So that the tested genuineness of your faith—more precious than gold that perishes though it is tested by fire—may be found to result in praise and glory and honor at the revelation of Jesus Christ.

1 Peter 1:7

## WHAT IS THE SAINT'S PERSPECTIVE IN TRIALS?

Peter has been communicating to us the hope of our salvation. In order to better illustrate our newfound hope, he relates our faith to gold.

Gold is one of the most precious metals on the face of the earth. It possesses great value to those who find it. However, our faith is more precious than gold, because it will endure the demands of time. The saints possess a gift of immeasurable greatness that keeps them anchored and rooted in storms. Thus we do not lose hope in our present afflictions, but rather look to a day when we will enter into the fullness of joy.*

The saints have been given exceedingly great and precious promises, that through these we may be partakers of the divine nature, having escaped the corruption that is in the world through lust.* In light of this eternal truth, let us reflect more fully on the surety of our precious faith.

———————◆———————

*Father, life is so uncertain. Give me the grace to rest more fully on the testing of the genuineness of my faith, to be found in praise and glory and honor for Jesus Christ.*

*I pray these things in Jesus' name. Amen.*

* Psalm 16:11, 2 Peter 1:4

# WE ARE A MARVEL

It was revealed to them that they were serving not themselves but you,
in the things that have now been announced to you through those who
preached the good news to you by the Holy Spirit sent from heaven,
things into which angels long to look.

1 Peter 1:12

## DID YOU KNOW THAT THE ANGELS IN HEAVEN MARVEL AT THE WORK OF REDEMPTION?

In a day where many look to strange signs and wonders, the greatest marvel is the salvation of sinners. In what ways are the saints a marvel? There are many ways, but one of the most miraculous ways is the recovery of our souls.

No mind can comprehend the wisdom of God. Even the angelic hosts of heaven would not have conceived such a marvelous redemption. Man, who was utterly lost, deserved the judgment of God. Our predicament caused a great dilemma, because Divine justice had to be met.

Thus it was only in the wisdom of God that a remedy could be provided for our souls. Mercy and truth have met together; righteousness and peace have kissed. Righteousness will go before Him, and shall make His footsteps our pathway.*

How often have you been amazed by the work of God in a sinner's heart? Let us join the angels in their marvel of the great work that God has done for the saints in the Person of Jesus Christ.

◆——————◇——————◆

*Father, where would we be without Your mercy and truth? Help us to rejoice in the work that You are doing in the lives of the saints.*

*I pray these things in Jesus' name. Amen.*

# OCTOBER
## WHAT IS WORSHIP?

Many view worship as the time of singing before the sermon. Others view worship as the entire order of a Sunday morning service. Worship encompasses a much broader spectrum.

The first mention of the word "worship" is found in Genesis 22:5, where it says, "Then Abraham said to his young men, 'Stay here with the donkey; I and the boy will go over there and worship and come again to you.'"

The word "worship" literally means "to bow down." And it refers to the bowing down of my will to God. You can sing praises with your arms raised, but you may be resisting God in your heart. Here Abraham decided to bow down his will to God. "I will worship and we will come back to you." [8] This was in obedience to God's command to Abraham to sacrifice his only son, Issac.* In Abraham's obedience to God, he worshiped Him.

The essence of worship really boils down to the work that God has done within His children. In other words, worship should simply be the outflow of the redemptive reality within our hearts. We, who are in Christ, worship God with our entire lives. There should be a desire within us to engage Him in our homes, at our offices, in our neighborhoods, and also in our churches.

My prayer is that these reflections will help you shed light on the biblical foundation of worship. Therefore, let us go to the Scriptures seeking a deeper understanding of our communion with God.


Genesis 22:2-18

# OUR PURPOSE

And this is eternal life, that they know You the only true God,
and Jesus Christ whom You have sent.
John 17:3

## WHAT IS OUR PURPOSE IN LIFE?

Our purpose in life is to know the one true God. Here in the text, Jesus sums up eternal life. Eternal life is not merely knowing God intellectually, but also knowing Him through experience. We are invited to experience His goodness first hand. Yet how can sinful man ever enjoy communion with a holy God?

The Scriptures tell us that He is of purer eyes than to behold evil.* Fortunately for us, God has made a way for us to have fellowship with Him. In our passage above we are given a glimpse into the heart of the Father. He gave us His Son to be the sacrifice for our sins. God revealed this in the very first book of the Bible to Abraham. And Abraham said, "My son, God will provide Himself a lamb for a burnt offering."* Now, as a result of Christ's obedience to the Father, the saints enjoy the blessing of His communion.

Have we really come to understand eternal life in the only true God and Jesus Christ? Let's better acquaint ourselves with Jesus, and experience the joy of eternal life.

───────◆───────

*Father, You have made a way for me to enjoy Your fellowship. Help me to acknowledge Your Son as the only way to truly enjoy eternal life.*

*I pray these things in Jesus' name. Amen.*

*Habakkuk 1:13, Genesis 22:8

# OUR COMMUNITY

Not neglecting to meet together, as is the habit of some, but encouraging one another, and all the more as you see the Day drawing near.

Hebrews 10:25

## ARE YOU PART OF A LOCAL CHURCH?

The author of Hebrews is writing to a persecuted set of believers. There were many who were tempted to draw back, and depart from the faith. Thus, the writer expresses the importance of holding fast to their Christian confession. One of the ways that they were encouraged to hold fast to Christ was to stay connected with the local church.

It is within the context of the local church that worshipers of Jesus Christ could be encouraged and strengthened in their faith.

Many centuries have been removed, but the same holds true for every worshiper in this present age. Worship is not merely a solo act, but one to be enjoyed within community. No Christian is as vulnerable to sin, as one who isolates themselves from fellowship.

Jesus said, "For where two or three are gathered together in My name, I am there in the midst of them."*

In light of this eternal truth, let us not seek to isolate ourselves from others, but rather seek to cultivate a habit of worshiping together in community.

———————◇———————

*Father, You have called me to be part of a local church. Help me not to forsake the assembling of ourselves together, but rather to encourage one another daily.*

*I pray these things in Jesus' name. Amen.*

*Matthew 18:20

# THE MINISTRY OF THE WORD

So shall My word be that goes out from My mouth; it shall not return
to Me empty, but it shall succeed in the thing for which I sent it.

Isaiah 55:11

## WILL GOD'S WORD EVER FAIL?

Here in the text, Yahweh declares to Isaiah the power of His Word. The
word of the Lord shall not fail, but it will accomplish all that God pleases.
We can find refuge in this steadfast promise made to God's people.

And then Isaiah declares, "For you shall go out with joy, and be led out
with peace; the mountains and the hills shall break forth into singing
before you, and all the trees of the field shall clap their hands. Instead of
the thorn shall come up the cypress tree, and instead of the brier shall
come up the myrtle tree; and it shall be to the Lord for a name, for an
everlasting sign that shall not be cut off."*

Thousands of years have passed since Isaiah's prophecy, but the Church
still needs the Word of God for strength and encouragement. It is through
the ministry of His Holy Word, that the saints have joy, peace, and can
break forth with singing with all creation. As we worship in His Word,
we are being conformed more into the image of Christ.

How then can the Church's efforts be blessed without the Scriptures? If we
are to be a healthy Church, then we need to be a Church that is instructed
in the testimonies of the Lord. In light of this eternal truth, let us be a
people who worship together under the public proclamation of the Word.

* * *

*Father, Your Word is powerful and sharper than any two-edged sword.* Help
us to submit ourselves under the authority of men who faithfully preach the
Word of God in an act of worship.*

*I pray these things in Jesus' name. Amen.*

*Isaiah 55:12-13, Hebrews 4:12

293

# WORSHIPING THROUGH BAPTISM

Can anyone withhold water for baptizing these people,
who have received the Holy Spirit just as we have?
Acts 10:47

## WHAT IS THE PURPOSE OF BAPTISM?

Baptism is a public proclamation that a person now belongs to Jesus Christ. It played a large role in the First Century Church.

Here in the text, the Apostle Peter had just preached the Gospel to many in the city of Caesarea, and while Peter was still speaking these words, the Holy Spirit fell upon all those who heard the word.* Then Peter commanded them to be baptized in the name of the Lord.* Their public profession was the outward manifestation of an inward reality.

Many centuries have been removed since baptism became an ordinance, but its importance within our worship is still relevant for us today. We, who are grafted into the covenant promises, have a sure sign and seal from God. It is through baptism that we recognize our old man to be buried with Christ, and our new man to be raised with Him* in newness of life.*

For as many of you as were baptized into Christ have put on Christ.* Therefore, let us not neglect the command to be baptized, but rather let us worship the Lord through this precious means of grace.

———————◦———————

*Father, You have given us various means of grace for the benefit of our souls. Help me not to neglect them, but rather to utilize them for my growth in grace.*

*I pray these things in Jesus' name. Amen.*

*Acts 10:44, 48, Colossians 2:12, Romans 6:4, Galatians 3:27

# WORSHIPING THROUGH COMMUNION

And he took bread, and when he had given thanks, he broke it and gave it to them, saying, "This is my body, which is given for you. Do this in remembrance of me." And likewise the cup after they had eaten, saying, "This cup that is poured out for you is the new covenant in my blood."
Luke 22:19-20

## WHAT IS THE PURPOSE OF COMMUNION?

Communion, much like baptism, is a sign and seal of God's covenant to His people. In the partaking of the Lord's Table, we are remembering His sacrifice on behalf of sinners. It was on the Cross that Jesus's body was broken on behalf of His people, and it was through the shedding of His blood that our everlasting covenant with God is secured.

The cup of blessing which we bless, is it not the communion of the blood of Christ? The bread which we break, is it not the communion of the body of Christ? For we, though many, are one bread and one body; for we all partake of that one bread.*

Now, as we enjoy the ordinance of communion, we find strength and nourishment for our souls. God has invited all the saints to feast with Him, but we are also warned not to partake of Christ's body and blood in an unworthy manner.*

Dear friend, are you cautious in approaching the Lord's Table? Let us, as the covenant community of faith, examine our hearts and find refreshment through the partaking of communion.

---

*Father, You have given Your Church the blessing of communion. Help me not to approach Your table in an unworthy manner, but rather to approach Your table through faith.*

*I pray these things in Jesus' name. Amen.*

*1 Corinthians 16:16-18, 1 Corinthians 11:27

# WORSHIPING THROUGH PUBLIC PRAYER

If my people who are called by my name humble themselves, and pray and seek my face and turn from their wicked ways, then I will hear from heaven and will forgive their sin and heal their land.

2 Chronicles 7:14

## DO YOU BELONG TO A CHURCH THAT EMPHASIZES CORPORATE PRAYER?

Here in the text, we are given instructions on how to be effective in prayer. There is something glorious about a people who pray and worship the Lord together. Our God loves it when His people offer up their petitions to Him.

First, we must be a people who humble ourselves before God. Grace is not found with the proud, but with those who are contrite. If we are to approach the Lord in prayer, then we must first acknowledge our place before Him. Secondly, we must be diligent in offering up our petitions. The Apostle James tells us that the effective and fervent prayers of the righteous avail much.* God gives justice to His elect, who cry to Him day and night. He will not delay long over them. Jesus says, "I tell you, He will give justice to them speedily."* Finally, we must repent and turn from our sins. If the Church humbly acknowledges their sins and turns away from them, then they have assurance that God hears them.

This eternal truth should cause us to worship the Lord, not only in our private prayer closets, but also within the community of faith.

———————◆———————

*Father, we are a people called by Your name. Help us to be a Church that worships You in prayer, both in our private lives, but also in our local congregations.*

*I pray these things in Jesus' name. Amen.*

*James 5:16, Luke 18:7-8

# WORSHIPING THROUGH PREACHING

And how are they to preach unless they are sent? As it is written,
"How beautiful are the feet of those who preach the good news!"

Romans 10:15

## HOW DOES A PERSON COME TO FAITH IN CHRIST?

Paul the Apostle provides us the answer to that question in the tenth chapter of Romans. It is upon hearing the Word of God that the Holy Spirit illuminates the unconverted mind.

His point is simply this: the Gospel is the only means whereby the seeds of faith are planted and cultivated. Yet if the keys to the kingdom lie in the message of the Cross, why then do many churches use other means to seek out the salvation of sinners? That question should burn in the hearts of every pastoral staff across the world.

Jeremiah the prophet said if he couldn't mention the Lord, or speak any more in His name, his heart would be on fire, and he became weary holding it in.*

If the Church is going to be an effective witness for Jesus Christ, then she must stay faithful to the preaching of the Gospel. We need to be a people who do not employ the use of worldly means or church growth methods, but rather a people who worship and seek to remain faithful to the stewardship of the Gospel.

---

*Father, You have delivered to us a message of chief importance. Help me to share in the passion of Paul who stated, "Woe is me if I do not preach the Gospel."**

*I pray these things in Jesus' name. Amen.*

*Jeremiah 20:9, 1 Corinthians 9:16

# WORSHIPING IN REVERENCE

And one called to another and said: "Holy, holy, holy is the Lord of hosts; the whole earth is full of His glory."

Isaiah 6:3

## DO YOU WORSHIP THE LORD IN REVERENCE?

Take note of the heavenly manner in which the angels worship God. First they worship His glorious character. If we are to approach or regard God, then we must understand that He is holy. There is no one like Him Who knows the end from the beginning, and the beginning from the end.*

Secondly, the angels acknowledge His glorious works. They declare that the whole earth is full of His glory. In nature, we observe the imprint of the invisible and immortal God. Creation testifies to His glory in all of its intricate detail.

One day the saints will worship, "Great and marvelous are Your works, Lord God Almighty! Just and true are Your ways, O King of the saints! Who shall not fear You, O Lord, and glorify Your name? For You alone are holy. For all nations shall come and worship before You, for Your judgments have been manifested."*

In this way, it is important for us to acknowledge our place before Him. He is the Potter and we are the clay.* If we are to worship Him, then we must understand that He possesses every claim over our lives. In light of this eternal truth, let us ascribe all honor and glory to Him Who sits on the throne.*

———————◈———————

*Father, You are a holy God Who is veiled in mystery. Help me to worship You in the beauty of holiness.*

*I pray these things in Jesus' name. Amen.*

*Isaiah 46:10, Revelation 15:3-4, Isaiah 64:8, Revelation 5:13, Psalm 96:9

# WORSHIPING IN HONOR

Ascribe to the Lord the glory due his name;
worship the Lord in the splendor of holiness.
Psalm 29:2

## IN WHAT WAYS DO YOU HONOR GOD?

There are many practical ways in which we can honor the Lord. King David exhorts us here to acknowledge the glory of God, which is due His name.

God has power over all creation. The voice of the Lord is powerful; the voice of the Lord is full of majesty.* The voice of the Lord divides the flames of fire. The voice of the Lord shakes the wilderness.* His sovereignty extends to every circumstance under heaven. Even the flood, in Noah's day, served His divine purposes. For as in those days before the flood, people were eating and drinking, marrying and giving in marriage, until the day that Noah entered the ark, and they did not understand until the flood came and took them all away; so will the coming of the Son of Man be.*

It would be well with the people of God if they would always worship and give glory to Him. His works give us plenty of reason to worship and honor His name. Have you stopped to reflect on the glorious works of Yahweh? Let us not lose that sense of wonder, but rather worship the Lord and give Him the honor due His name.

---

*Father, all things come from Your loving hand. Even the trials we face have a special blessing for Your children. Deliver me from the error of self-importance, and help me to worship the glory and honor of Your name.*

*I pray these things in Jesus' name. Amen.*

*Psalm 29:4, 7-8, 2 Peter 3:6-7, Matthew 24:38-39

# WORSHIPING THROUGH PRAISE

Addressing one another in psalms and hymns and spiritual songs, singing and making melody to the Lord with your heart.

Ephesians 5:19

## WHAT ARE SPIRITUAL SONGS AND HYMNS?

Here in the text, please note Paul's progression of thought. In the prior verses of this chapter he provided us with a series of negative commands. Have no fellowship with the unfruitful works of darkness, but rather expose them.* Do not be unwise, but understand what the will of the Lord is.* Do not be drunk with wine, in which is dissipation—then he focuses on some positive commands, be filled with the Holy Spirit, speaking in psalms and hymns, singing to the Lord, giving thanks always, and submitting to one another in the fear of God.*

This describes the godly disposition of those who are filled with the Holy Spirit and worship through praise.

One of the primary characteristics of the godly man or woman is that their lips are filled with the praises of God. They have filled their hearts with the glorious melodies of heaven. Thus, they have many reasons to echo His praises.

Dear friend, has the Lord rewritten your story? If so, then you have much reason to rejoice. Let us be a people whose lips sing the praises of our worthy King.

◆————◆————◆

*Father, You have given Your people many reasons to praise You, even apart from those reasons, are worthy of our praise. Help me to be filled with the Holy Spirit, and give me many songs to sing unto You.*

*I pray these things in Jesus' name. Amen.*

*Ephesians 5:11, 17, 18-21

# WORSHIPING IN SPIRIT AND IN TRUTH

God is spirit, and those who worship him must worship in spirit and truth.
John 4:24

## WHAT IS THE ESSENCE OF TRUE WORSHIP?

In ancient times, people associated the worship of a deity with a temple. Jerusalem was the place where many people would travel to offer t heir worship to the one true God. However, Jesus communicates to us a radical new way of worship. He communicates this new way of worship to us by appealing to two things.

First, He appeals to God's nature. God is not confined to a temple made with hands—even heaven, the highest heaven, cannot contain Him, much less a temple*—but rather God dwells in the midst of His people. Secondly, He appeals to God's worshipers. The saints are people who are likened to living stones—rejected indeed by men, but chosen by God and precious, being built up a spiritual house, a holy priesthood, to offer up spiritual sacrifices acceptable to God through Jesus Christ.* We, who are in Christ, are the holy temple being built up in our most precious faith.* Like so, those who seek to worship the Lord must have His Spirit dwelling inside of them.

Dear friend, does God's Spirit dwell inside of you? Let us be a people who worship together in both spirit and truth.

———— ◇ ————

*Father, You have made the Church Your dwelling place. Help me to worship You in spirit and truth.*

*I pray these things in Jesus' name. Amen.*

*2 Chronicles 6:18, 1 Peter 2:4-5, John 4:24

# WORSHIPING WITH THE MIND

Do your best to present yourself to God as one approved, a worker who has no need to be ashamed, rightly handling the word of truth.

2 Timothy 2:15

## DID YOU KNOW THAT YOU CAN WORSHIP GOD WITH YOUR MIND?

Here in this portion of the Scripture, Paul exhorts Timothy to remain true to the teachings of the Apostles. There were many who were mishandling the doctrines of Christ, leading the people in ungodliness.* They had strayed concerning the truth, upsetting the faith of some,* and there were foolish, ignorant controversies, leading to quarrels.* Therefore, Timothy was instructed to be diligent in his study of the Word. False teachers have always sought to sway the sheep away from the truth. Thus, it is the duty of believers to understand how to accurately handle the Scriptures.

Notice also, that our motives for studying should be for the edification of others. Faithful students and servants of God's Word are able to warn others of the dangers of false teaching. Yet our exhortations should be handled with the utmost care and love, being gentle to all, able to teach, patient, in humility.*

There are many who seem to be on a quest for right doctrine at the expense of love, but the Lord has shown us a more excellent way.* In light of this truth let us be worshipers who seek to understand the Scriptures for the edification and service of others.

———————◆———————

*Father, if I am to worship You with my mind, then I must also hide Your Word within my heart. Give me the grace to be a compassionate preacher of righteousness.* *

*I pray these things in Jesus' name. Amen.*

*2 Timothy 2:16, 18, 23, 24-25, 1 Corinthians 12:31, 2 Peter 2:5

# WORSHIPING THROUGH CHARITY

If among you, one of your brothers should become poor, in any of your towns within your land that the Lord your God is giving you, you shall not harden your heart or shut your hand against your poor brother.

Deuteronomy 15:7

## DO YOU REGARD THE POOR?

Throughout the Scriptures, we see God's heart for the poor.

Here in the text, Moses is providing instructions for the Sabbatical year. The children of Israel were to forgive the debts of their brethren. The clearing of debts was supposed to happen at the end of every seven years. It was the accustomed practice that slaves, who owed a debt, were to be set free. Once freed, many of these slaves were poor and had nothing to eat. Therefore the Lord commands slave masters to set their slaves free with the necessities that would be sufficient for their needs. These masters were to give liberally and with joy.

Ultimately this text points us to the fact that we were debtors who were given the free gift of the Gospel. If we have freely received, then how much more ought we to freely give?* Paul said to the Corinthians, "He who sows sparingly will also reap sparingly, and he who sows bountifully will also reap bountifully. So let each one give as he purposes in his heart, not grudgingly or of necessity; for God loves a cheerful giver.*

In light of this eternal truth let us worship God by freely giving to others, not only the necessities for their bodies, but also the Gospel message for their souls.

———————◈———————

*Father, I have freely received Your gracious gift of eternal life. Help me to cultivate Your generous disposition towards others.*

*I pray these things in Jesus' name. Amen.*

*Matthew 10:8, 2 Corinthians 9:6-7

303

# WORSHIPING THROUGH OUR SERVICE

*Even as the Son of Man came not to be served but to serve,*
*and to give His life a ransom for many.*
Matthew 20:28

## DO YOU HAVE A SERVANT'S HEART?

Here in the text, Jesus is responding to a mother's request on behalf of her sons. She asked the Lord if her sons could sit on His throne with Him. His response to her is telling, "You do not know what you are asking. Are you able to drink the cup that I am to drink?"* In their misguided zeal for greatness, they completely missed the mark. They supposed that true greatness meant a prominent position in the kingdom, but our Lord reminded them that true greatness comes at a cost.

Jesus said, "Whoever would be great among you must be your servant, and whoever would be first among you must be your slave, even as the Son of Man came not to be served but to serve, and to give His life as a ransom for many."*

Many of us want a great kingdom without paying a great cost, although our Lord reminds us that the road to greatness is marked out by a life of humble service. If we are going to be great in the kingdom, then we must be servants of all. Have you found yourself seeking a path to greatness? If so then imitate the humility of Christ in your service to other people.

＊━━━━━━━━━◆━━━━━━━━━＊

*Father, You have given me a road map to greatness. Help me not to seek great things for myself, but rather to worship You and be a servant of all.*

*I pray these things in Jesus' name. Amen.*

*Matthew 20:22, 26-28

# WORSHIPING WITH A PURE HEART

Religion that is pure and undefiled before God, the Father,
is this: to visit orphans and widows in their affliction,
and to keep oneself unstained from the world.

James 1:27

## THE SIMPLEST THINGS IN LIFE ARE OFTEN THE MOST PROFOUND

We have a tendency to complicate things, but true religion boils down to the very practical. Here, the Apostle James sums up the essence of pure and undefiled religion: those who are worshipers of God have a heart for the afflicted.

It is by faith alone that we inherit the promise of eternal life, but it is through faith that we obey God in the daily grind of life. True worshipers desire to serve those in need, and to guard themselves from the stains of worldliness. If our worship is not birthed out of a pure heart for God, then it will only reveal itself to be blind hypocrisy. Whoever has this world's goods, and sees his brother in need, and shuts up his heart from him, how does the love of God abide in him?*

What is the state of your heart this day? Let us be a people who worship the Lord through a godly sincerity that is evident to all.

---

*Father, You desire mercy and not sacrifice.\* Help me to worship You through the practice of pure and undefiled religion.*

*I pray these things in Jesus' name. Amen.*


*Hosea 6:6, 1 John 3:17

# WORSHIPING WITH OUR THOUGHTS

His delight is in the law of the Lord,
and on His law he meditates day and night.
Psalm 1:2

## DO YOU WORSHIP GOD WITH YOUR THOUGHTS?

The Psalmist has marked out for us the path of blessing. He notes two key things about worshipers whom God has blessed. First, they delight in the Law of the Lord. It is their aim not to merely know God's ways, but also to love God's ways. The truth brings joy and refreshment to their souls. For instance, they love to be instructed by His testimonies. Secondly, their delight causes them to meditate day and night in God's Word. Meditating on His Word keeps them fruitful in all seasons of life.

In like manner, the saints have been given great and precious promises* which are found in the Holy Scriptures. If we dwell on those things that are lovely, then we will find a remedy for those sins that easily ensnare us. Finally, beloved, whatever is true, whatever is honorable, whatever is just, whatever is pure, whatever is lovely, whatever is commendable, if there is any excellence, if there is anything worthy of praise, think about these things.*

Do you delight in the Law of the Lord? Let us be those who delight and set our minds on the things that are from above.*

---

*Father, Your Word keeps me grounded and anchored in Christ. Help me to be constantly delighting in Your ways.*

*I pray these things in Jesus' name. Amen.*

*2 Peter 1:4, Philippians 4:8, Colossians 3:2

# WORSHIPING WITH MY SPEECH

Let your speech always be gracious, seasoned with salt, so that you may know how you ought to answer each person.

Colossians 4:6

## DO YOU WORSHIP GOD WITH YOUR SPEECH?

The Scriptures continually point out the importance of guarding our tongues. The person who has learned to control their speech has mastered a wonderful virtue. Here, Paul is communicating the importance for a worshiper of God to use gracious speech in a broken and fallen world. If we are to answer any objections that are raised to the Gospel, then we need to be those who answer our critics in a spirit of love and grace. When we only concern ourselves with the importance of winning the argument, we often lose the opportunity to make a meaningful impact in the lives of unbelievers.

Therefore, let no corrupt word proceed out of your mouth, but what is good for necessary edification, that it may impart grace to the hearers.* It is equally important for the Christian to master both the knowledge of Scripture and the law of kindness.*

Do you have the law of kindness on your tongue? Let us be those who use our speech effectively for the sake of the Gospel.

———◦———

*Father, the tongue is a small instrument, but it often causes a great measure of harm.* Help me to be ready to give a gracious and wise answer to everyone that asks of us.*

*I pray these things in Jesus' name. Amen.*

*Ephesians 4:29, Proverbs 31:26, James 3:5

# WORSHIPING IN UNITY

Behold, how good and pleasant it is when brothers dwell in unity.

Psalm 133:1

## HOW DO WE WORSHIP THE LORD IN UNITY?

The Psalmist reflects on the pleasantries of unity by highlighting two important illustrations. In verse 2, he says, "It is like the precious oil on the head, running down on the beard of Aaron, running down on the collar of his robes!"* It was the custom of the law to anoint the head of the priest with oil. The anointing of oil was for the purpose of authenticating their ministries before God and man.

In verse 3, he says, "It is like the dew of Hermon, which falls on the mountains of Zion!"* Many commentators have differed in their interpretation, but ultimately we see a picture of fruitfulness. When dew descends upon the face of a mountain it preserves and nourishes its vegetation.

The main idea of the Psalm is simply this: When God's people dwell together in unity, their witness to an unbelieving world is authenticated. A Church that is unified has the blessing of the Lord in her midst, and therefore, she remains fruitful in all her labors.

In light of this eternal truth, let us seek to worship the Lord together in the bond of unity and peace.

---

*Father, You have united Your Church together in Christ. Help me to serve others, and dwell together in unity.*

*I pray these things in Jesus' name. Amen.*

*Psalm 133:2, 3

# WORSHIPING WITH BOLDNESS

But if not, be it known to you, O king, that we will not serve your gods
or worship the golden image that you have set up.

Daniel 3:18

## ARE YOU BOLD IN YOUR WORSHIP OF GOD?

It was no small thing for Shadrach, Meshach, and Abednego to defy the king of Babylon. They were instructed to bow down before his golden image, but they would not deny the Lord their God. These faithful young men thought it better to bare the reproach of their Creator than to enjoy the fading comforts of a season.

Their worship to God influenced the king to declare, "Blessed be the God of Shadrach, Meshach, and Abednego, who trusted in God and yielded up their bodies rather than serve and worship any god except their own God."*

Their willingness to suffer for the sake of Christ still speaks to us in this present age. Many centuries have passed since the fall of Babylon, but there are many who remain bold in their witness for the Gospel. In a world that grows hostile towards God, there is a need for worshipers who are willing to be God's martyrs. Let us therefore stand in the world's fiery furnace with a willingness to suffer reproach for the sake of the kingdom.

---

*Father, You have promised Your people that they would be persecuted for Your sake. Help me not to shrink back in fear, but rather to press on for the sake of Christ.*

*I pray these things in Jesus' name. Amen.*

*Daniel 3:28

# WORSHIPING IN LOVE

This is my commandment, that you love one another as I have loved you.
John 15:12

## DO YOU LOVE YOUR BROTHERS AND SISTERS IN CHRIST?

There is no greater mark of a Christian than one who loves their fellow believers. Here in the text, Jesus is communicating the importance of abiding in Him.

I am the vine; you are the branches. Whoever abides in Me and I in him, he it is that bears much fruit, for apart from Me you can do nothing.*

He likens Himself as the vine, and His followers as the branches. Those, who have been united to Christ by faith, have His love within them. This is a not a love that proceeds from the natural man, but rather a Divine love which has been granted to us from above. If we have His love within us, then it will manifest itself in Christ-like love for worshipers of God.

Dear friend, do you view others through the lens of unconditional love or do you tend to be more critical-hearted of your brethren? Let us be those who demonstrate God's unmerited favor to those around us.

———————

*Father, You have commanded us to love one another. Help me to demonstrate Your unconditional love to others.*

*I pray these things in Jesus' name. Amen.*

*John 15:5

# WORSHIPING IN HOLINESS

For God has not called us to impurity, but in holiness.
1 Thessalonians 4:7

## WHAT IS YOUR CALLING IN CHRIST?

God calls you and me to an entirely different quality of life. We are not to live as those who are enslaved by their sinful lusts, but rather as those who have been set free from their former sins.

Here in the text, the Apostle Paul warns the Thessalonian worshipers of God to abstain from sexual immorality. He says, "For this is the will of God, your sanctification: that you abstain from sexual immorality."*

Paul urges the saints to abstain from sexual sin in two ways. First he reminds them of their sanctification. We, who are in Christ, have been set apart for good works.* In fact, it is God's will that we be conformed more into the image of His Son. Secondly, Paul warns them of the judgment that awaits the unconverted when he said, "The Lord is an avenger in all these things, as we told you beforehand and solemnly warned you."*

What about you dear friend? Is your heart sensitive towards the will of God? Let us be those who walk worthy of our profession of faith.

---

*Father, You have called us not to walk in the ways of the world, but rather to walk worthy of our calling. Examine me, O Lord, and prove me; try my mind and my heart* to be pleasing in Your sight.*

*I pray these things in Jesus' name. Amen.*

*1 Thessalonians 4:3, Ephesians 2:10, 1 Thessalonians 4:6, Psalm 26:2

# WORSHIPING IN WISDOM

Look carefully then how you walk, not as unwise but as wise.

Ephesians 5:15

## WHAT DOES IT MEAN TO WALK IN WISDOM?

The Apostle Paul explains how we can walk wisely in this world by highlighting God's character. Namely, Christians are exhorted to be imitators of God, as beloved children. And walk in love, as Christ also has loved us and given Himself for us, an offering and a sacrifice to God for a sweet-smelling aroma.*

Those who walk in the ways of Christ put to death their sinful passions and lusts. They are living for a greater purpose and mission. Instead of building a fading empire on the earth, they are building an enduring legacy of love. Prior to our faith in Christ, we were living for our own selfish desires. Now that we are born again, our goal is to glorify God, and to advance His kingdom.

Dear worshiper of God, what are you living for here on earth? Let us be those who make wise use of our time in this life through our humble service to our King.

---

*Father, You have given us a greater purpose than merely living for ourselves. Help me to use my time wisely to advance Your kingdom.*

*I pray these things in Jesus' name. Amen.*

*Ephesians 5:1-2

# WORSHIPING IN HUMILITY

Likewise, you who are younger, be subject to the elders. Clothe yourselves, all of you, with humility toward one another, for God opposes the proud but gives grace to the humble.

1 Peter 5:5

## WHAT DOES HUMILITY LOOK LIKE IN ACTION?

The Apostle Peter puts forth the principle of humility: meekness under pressure.

If we are to suffer persecution, then let us reflect the lowliness of our Lord Jesus Christ. It is not that we suffer for the sake of the Gospel, but that we suffer well. After applying the principle of humility to suffering, Peter now seeks to apply that same principle to our conduct within the Church. He communicates to us the importance of humility by offering up both a command and a promise.

Those, who are under the watchful care of elders, must submit themselves under their authority. The Lord has placed shepherds over the Church for our benefit. Therefore, it is to our benefit that we submit to their leadership. If we clothe ourselves with humility, then Peter promises that we will enjoy the grace of God. Humble yourselves, therefore, under the mighty hand of God so that at the proper time He may exalt you.*

In light of this truth let us submit ourselves under the authority of faithful shepherds who care for our souls.

———————•———◦———•———————

*Father, You have entrusted faithful men to watch over our souls. Help me to walk in humility, and to subject myself under the care of faithful men.*

*I pray these things in Jesus' name. Amen.*

*1 Peter 5:6

# WORSHIPING THROUGH REST

So then, there remains a Sabbath rest for the people of God, for whoever has entered God's rest has also rested from his works as God did from His.
Hebrews 4:9-10

## WHAT DOES IT MEAN TO ENTER INTO THE REST OF GOD?

The writer to the Hebrews has been communicating the importance of faith to his Jewish listeners by bringing to mind the example of Moses. Those who murmured and complained against Moses in the wilderness failed to enter into the Promised Land.

Hebrews 4:8, 11 reads, "Do not harden your hearts as in the rebellion, on the day of testing in the wilderness, where your fathers put me to the test... and I swore in my wrath, 'They shall not enter my rest.'" Their unbelief caused them to wonder in the wilderness for forty years. There's a reason the author draws a parallel between rest and faith. It is by faith that we enter into the rest of God.

Jesus has finished the work of our redemption, and has passed into the heavens. His priesthood is an everlasting priesthood that is built on incorruptible promises. In light of this eternal truth, He can be trusted to save our souls. Dear worshiper of God, rest from your works and put your trust in the finished work of Christ.

———◆———

*Father, You have given Your people rest. Help me to lay aside my doubts and unbelief, and look to Your Son for the saving of my soul.*

*I pray these things in Jesus' name. Amen.*

# WORSHIPING WITH OUR LIVES

I appeal to you therefore, brothers, by the mercies of God, to present your bodies as a living sacrifice, holy and acceptable to God, which is your spiritual worship.

Romans 12:1

## HOW CAN WE OFFER ACCEPTABLE WORSHIP TO GOD?

Our worship should be offered up to God in faith. The Apostle Paul points out that in light of everything that God has done for us through the Gospel, it is only reasonable that we worship Him whole-heartedly.

How can we worship with our lives? The Scripture instructs, "Do not be conformed to this world, but be transformed by the renewal of your mind, that by testing you may discern what is the will of God, what is good and acceptable and perfect."*

Our worship to Him should simply be a response to the work that He has accomplished within us. The worshipers of God have been washed from their sins, and regenerated by the Holy Spirit. Thus, the worship of the one true God has become the sole aim of our lives.

So then, my friends, because of God's great mercy to us I appeal to you, offer yourselves as a living sacrifice to God, dedicated to His service and pleasing to Him. This is the true worship that we should offer.

———————◦———————

*Father, You do not delight in sacrifice of bulls and goats,* but rather through the obedience of faith. Help me to present myself to You as a living sacrifice.*

*I pray these things in Jesus' name. Amen.*

*Romans 12:2, Psalm 51:16

# WORSHIPING THROUGH PRAYER

Praying at all times in the Spirit, with all prayer and supplication. To that end keep alert with all perseverance, making supplication for all the saints.

Ephesians 6:18

## DO YOU PRAY WITHOUT CEASING?

In Ephesians 6:10-18, Paul has been showing us how to engage in the spiritual battle at hand. We are to put on the full armor of God so that we can withstand the wicked schemes of the devil. Now as he approaches the end of his discourse on spiritual warfare, it is only fitting that he emphasizes the importance of prayer.

A Christian who will not kneel before the Lord will not be able to withstand the spiritual forces of evil.

As true worshipers of God, we are to be in constant prayer both for ourselves and for others. Rejoice always, pray without ceasing, and in everything give thanks; for this is the will of God in Christ Jesus for us.* Fortunately for us we have a Comforter, the Holy Spirit, Who knows exactly what we need. If we rely on His wisdom and strength, then we can rest assured that our prayers will be fruitful.

In light of this eternal truth let us be a people who worship God through the continual habit of prayer.

—————————◆—————————

*Father, thank You for the privilege of prayer. Help me not to neglect this important grace, but rather utilize it for the benefit of my soul.*

*I pray these things in Jesus' name. Amen.*

*1 Thessalonians 5:16-18

# WORSHIPING THROUGH FAITH

By faith Enoch was taken up so that he should not see death, and he was not found, because God had taken him. Now before he was taken he was commended as having pleased God.

Hebrews 11:5

## WHAT KIND OF LEGACY WILL YOU LEAVE BEHIND?

Enoch left an enduring legacy of faith. It is written of him that "he pleased God." Let wisdom teach us that the means by which we please the Lord is through a life of faith. It is by grace through faith* that the everlasting doors of salvation are opened unto us.* In his foolishness, man boasts in his own merits, but the wise glory only in the Cross of Christ.*

God is pleased when we put our faith and trust in Him. It would seem to me that the opposite then would also be true. God is displeased when we don't trust Him, when we doubt His promises, and when we live in fear and anxiety. We are continually exhorted in the Scriptures to trust in the Lord. It pleases God when we take Him at His Word.

Dear friend, let us learn from the example of Enoch. Though Scripture does not speak much of him, it reveals enough for our instruction. Let us therefore not lose heart in the grind of everyday life, but rather live every moment by faith. [9]

———————————◆———————————

*Father, let it be said of me that I lived a life of faith in Your Son. Help me not to get weighed down with the monotony of life, but rather to seize every moment for Your glory.*

*I pray these things in Jesus' name. Amen.*

*Ephesians 2:8, Psalm 24:7, Philippians 3:18

317

# WORSHIPING GOD ALONE

But they who wait for the Lord shall renew their strength; they shall mount up with wings like eagles; they shall run and not be weary; they shall walk and not faint.

Isaiah 40:31

## WHO IS LIKE OUR GOD?

The children of Israel had forsaken the Lord for the worship of idols. In their foolishness, they worshiped and served the creature rather than the Creator.* Thus, Isaiah pleads with them to forsake their idols and turn to the true and living God. He exhorts them by pointing out the foolishness of idols, and then by reminding them of Yahweh's marvelous works by saying, "He gives power to the faint, and to him who has no might He increases strength."*

His point to the people is simply that deliverance is only found in the one true God. Why then would anyone look to any other source for salvation? It is fitting that Isaiah's name means "the Lord is Salvation." He was a prophet who always pointed others to the one true God.

Dear friend, do you worship God alone or do you have competing interests? Let us be those who do not long after strange idols, but rather worship the One Who has power over the nations.

---

*Father, there is no one like You. You are the only wise God Who saves His people from their sins.* Give me the grace to abstain from idols so that I can worship You with singleness of heart.**

*I pray these things in Jesus' name. Amen.*

*Romans 1:25, Isaiah 40:29. Matthew 1:21, Jeremiah 32:39

# WORSHIPING THROUGH OBEDIENCE

Has the Lord as great delight in burnt offerings and sacrifices, as in obeying the voice of the Lord? Behold, to obey is better than sacrifice, and to listen than the fat of rams.

1 Samuel 15:22

## WHAT DOES THE LORD REQUIRE OF US?

He requires that we trust Him by faith, but the fruit of that faith is obedience.

In this portion of Scripture, the Lord's request to King Saul was very simple: "Now go and strike Amalek and devote to destruction all that they have."* He was not to spare men, women, children, or cattle, but rather to wipe out everything. Yet instead of obeying the Lord's voice, he chose to spare the king, some spoils and cattle.

Soonafter, when the prophet Samuel confronted Saul, he justified his actions: "But the people took of the spoil, sheep, and oxen, the best of the things devoted to destruction, to sacrifice to the Lord your God in Gilgal."* It is tragic when disobedience disguises itself in the form of religion, but nevertheless we can learn from the error of Saul. Let wisdom teach us that it is not for man to choose his own mode of worship.

If we are going to worship the Lord, then it must be on His terms alone. In light of this truth, let us look to God's Word alone for the prescribed manner of worship—obedience.

*Father, You do not delight in sacrifices, but rather in a heart that is fully given over to Your purposes. Help me to avoid the tragic error of Saul, and worship You in spirit and truth.**

*I pray these things in Jesus' name. Amen.*

*1 Samuel 15:3, 1 Samuel 15:21, Psalm 51:16, John 4:24

# WORSHIPING IN HOPE

All the nations you have made shall come and worship before you,
O Lord, and shall glorify Your name.
Psalm 86:9

## WHAT IS THE HOPE OF GOD'S WORSHIPERS?

King David is in the midst of a crisis. He cries out, "O God, insolent men have risen up against me; a band of ruthless men seeks my life, and they do not set you before them."* Thus Psalm 86 is a prayer that is birthed out of anguish. David's soul is greatly vexed, but he does not lose hope. Instead he calls to mind God's marvelous character.

All the nations you have made shall come and worship before you, O Lord, and shall glorify your name. For you are great and do wondrous things; you alone are God. Teach me your way, O Lord, that I may walk in your truth; unite my heart to fear your name.* This gives the King great comfort in the midst of his turmoil, because he understands that God is in control.

In like manner the saints also have great reason to hope. The Lord has made them victorious over sin and death. Our final victory gives us great consolation in the midst of life's storms. Therefore, let us not live as those who have no hope,* but rather rest assured in the future deliverance that awaits us.

---

*Father, You have given the Kingdoms of this world to Your Son. Help me not to be discouraged in my present trials, but rather rest fully in the hope that awaits me in glory.*

*I pray these things in Jesus' name. Amen.*

*Psalm 86:14, 9-11, 1 Thessalonians 4:13

# WORSHIPING IN JOY

Serve the Lord with gladness! Come into his presence with singing!
Psalm 100:2

## DO YOU SERVE THE LORD WITH GLADNESS?

There are many reasons why we can be joyful, but one of the primary reasons that the psalmist appeals to us in this portion of Scripture is God's steadfast love.

For the Lord is good; His steadfast love endures forever, and His faithfulness to all generations.*

The saints possess a great Shepherd Who watches over their souls. His blessings towards them are more than they can count. Therefore why would we not rejoice, and sing of the goodness of the Lord? He has loved us with an everlasting love.* We, who were deserving of judgment, have received kindness and mercy.

Dear worshiper of God, have the circumstances of life depleted your joy in Christ? If so, then recall to mind the wonderful ways in which God has loved you. He is a gracious master Who is worthy to receive our praise and adoration.

---

*Father, You are a good and gracious God. Help me to cultivate an attitude of joy, and a habit of praise.*

*I pray these things in Jesus' name. Amen.*

*Psalm 100:5, Jeremiah 31:3

# NOVEMBER
## WHO IS WISDOM?

What is the difference between godly wisdom and worldly wisdom? The primary difference is that godly wisdom makes a person wise unto salvation.* There are many people who have discovered the pinnacles of success through the means of worldly wisdom, but they still find themselves without hope.

Jesus asked the question, "What do you benefit if you gain the whole world but lose your own soul? Is anything worth more than your soul?"* If we are going to have eternal life, then we must possess a wisdom that is from above. We need to set our minds on things that are above, not on things that are on earth.*

If you find a person who possesses godly wisdom, then I will show you a person who hates every false way.* Those who possess godly wisdom exercise spiritual discernment in all things. They have the ability to navigate skillfully throughout life's toughest decisions.

My prayer for you, as we reflect on the Proverbs this month, is that you will come to value godly wisdom more than the riches of this world.

*2 Timothy 3:15, Matthew 16:26, Colossians 3:2, Psalm 119:104

# WISDOM UNDERSTANDS

To know wisdom and instruction, to understand words of insight.
Proverbs 1:2

## WHAT IS THE PURPOSE OF WISDOM?

The issues of life are filled with many complexities. There are ethical matters, social conflicts, difficult decisions, and financial pressures that we encounter on a day-to-day basis. So, the purpose of wisdom and instruction is to gain understanding. Wisdom is the best means for the best ends.

King Solomon spoke 3,000 proverbs, and his songs were 1,005.* As we begin our journey to find wisdom, he wants us to take the truths of Scripture and apply them to our everyday circumstances. It takes a great deal of skill to navigate wisely through the mundane details of life, but fortunately for us, we have the wisdom of God written down for our instruction.

Thus, in the book of Proverbs, we have wisdom for kings, wisdom for parents, wisdom for children, wisdom for husbands and wives and wisdom for employers and employees. If we will humbly seek the Lord, then we will be rewarded with that excellent knowledge that is from above.

———————⟡———————

*Father, life can be overwhelming at times. Give me the wisdom I need to navigate my circumstances with godly instruction and understanding.*

*I pray these things in Jesus' name. Amen.*

*1 Kings 4:32

# WISDOM RECEIVES INSTRUCTION

To receive instruction in wise dealings,
in righteousness, justice, and equity.
Proverbs 1:3

## WHERE DO WE GET WISDOM?

In order to know wisdom, I must be willing to receive instruction.

King Solomon, one of the richest men who ever lived, said, "I looked on all the works that my hands had done and on the labor in which I had toiled; and indeed all was vanity and grasping for the wind. There was no profit under the sun. Then I turned myself to consider wisdom and madness and folly."*

The Book of Proverbs tells us that a person can go only one of two ways: the way of wisdom or the way of folly—foolishness. Here in the text, Solomon wants us to know he was a man that did it his way. And that way led to emptiness. On the other hand, sound instruction teaches a person how to live righteously in a dark and sinful world. The fool disregards instruction to the peril of his own soul, but the wise will receive instruction and possess an incorruptible inheritance that endures the test of time. Ultimately, when we listen to advice and accept instruction, we will gain wisdom in the future.*

---

*Father, there are only one of two paths that I can tread: disregarding instruction or receiving instruction. Please keep me on the true path of wisdom that leads to instruction.*

*I pray these things in Jesus' name. Amen.*

*Ecclesiastes 2:11-12, Proverbs 19:20

# WISDOM IS PRUDENT

To give prudence to the simple, knowledge and discretion to the youth.
Proverbs 1:4

## WHAT IS PRUDENCE?

Prudence differs from wisdom in this, that prudence implies more caution and reserve than wisdom, or is exercised more in foreseeing and avoiding evil, than in devising and executing that which is good. It is sometimes mere caution or circumspection.[10]

Those who exercise prudence carefully weigh out the potential consequences of their actions.

Here in the text, King Solomon is writing to young people, hoping they understand the importance of exercising prudence in all things. Paul wrote to Timothy, a young man, "Beloved, flee also youthful lusts; but pursue righteousness, faith, love, peace with those who call on the Lord out of a pure heart.* If young people are going to be spared from the devastating consequences of sin, then they will need prudence to be their guide.

In like manner, all of us need knowledge and discretion as we navigate through the difficult circumstances of life. This is not a knowledge that can come through might or power, but rather a knowledge that is given to us from the Holy Spirit.*

Therefore, God extends His invitation for wisdom to even the simple-minded, or those with a child-like faith. If we will ask God for prudence, then He will graciously grant to us the knowledge and discretion that we need.

---

*Father, there are real dangers and unintended consequences that come with making foolish choices. Give me the grace that I need to exercise prudence in all manners of life.*

*I pray these things in Jesus' name. Amen.*

*2 Timothy 2:22, Zechariah 4:12

# WISDOM GUIDES

Let the wise hear and increase in learning,
and the one who understands obtain guidance.
Proverbs 1:5

## WHAT IS THE MARK OF WISDOM?

The mark of wisdom is the ability to discern truth from error. Those who are wise lend a willing ear to godly instruction and are guided by it.

The Hebrew word for "guidance" plainly means "steerings," like a steer-ing wheel in a car. This suggests moving one's life in the right direction. Here in the text, Solomon wants us to know that wisdom is accompanied by understanding and guidance. If we are instructed by his wise teachings, then we will find ourselves far from the path of the wicked. Yet how can we attain to such knowledge of God?

Scripture tells us, "Where there is no counsel, the people fall; but in the multitude of counselors there is safety.* For by wise counsel you will wage your own war, and in a multitude of counselors there is safety.*

People, in their natural and fallen state, cannot grasp the things that are spiritually discerned. Thus, if we are going to become wise unto salva-tion, then we are going to need a wisdom that is given to us by Divine grace. We find that in God's Word and in the multitude of God's people.

Are you learning and being guided by God at your church? Have you sur-rounded yourself with a multitude of godly people? Let us seek the Lord for His grace to learn and be steered by the Scriptures and His people.

---

*Father, it is not in a person to direct their own steps.* You are the only One Who gives wisdom to the wise and understanding to the simple.* Grant me the grace to be steered by Your guidance.*

*I pray these things in Jesus' name. Amen.*

*Proverbs 11:14, Proverbs 24:6, Jeremiah 10:23, Psalm 119:130

# WISDOM FEARS THE LORD

The fear of the Lord is the beginning of knowledge;
fools despise wisdom and instruction.

Proverbs 1:7

## WHAT DOES IT MEAN TO FEAR THE LORD?

We fear the Lord by showing Him the proper reverence due His name.

When opening up the Scriptures, we have to ask ourselves a very important question: Do we take God's instruction seriously? Those who take God seriously tremble at His Word. Jesus said, "For the gate is narrow and the way is hard that leads to life, and those who find it are few."* This is the only safe way to travel for God's people.

In today's opening text, Solomon illustrates the importance of fearing the Lord by drawing a contrast between the wise and the foolish. The fool who disobeys God's Word will reap the devastating consequences of sin, but the wise person who obeys God's Word will reap the benefits of everlasting life.

The Psalmist said, "The fear of the Lord is the beginning of wisdom; a good understanding have all those who do His commandments. His praise endures forever."*

Dear friend, has grace made your heart tender to fear God's Word? Let us be a people who walk in humble obedience to Him by faith.

---

*Father, You have the words to eternal life.\* Give me the grace this day to be one who trembles at Your Word.*

*I pray these things in Jesus' name. Amen.*

*Matthew 7:14, Psalm 111:10, John 6:68

# WISDOM IS VALUED

Hear, my son, your father's instruction, and forsake not your mother's
teaching, for they are a graceful garland for your head
and pendants for your neck.

Proverbs 1:8-9

## WHAT IS THE VALUE OF GODLY WISDOM?

Here in the text we find a father who admonishes his son. His father's
admonition is to keep the instructions of his parents, but this command
is also wed to a wonderful promise. If his son will keep himself in the
ways of wisdom, then it will serve him as a faithful companion throughout his lifetime.

The Apostle Paul tells us, "Children, obey your parents in the Lord, for
this is right. Honor your father and mother" (this is the first commandment with a promise), that it may go well with you and that you may live
long in the land."*

In like manner, the wisdom of God is a faithful guide to the upright.
Those who heed righteous instruction will find themselves preserved
from the devastating consequences of sin. They have made the Lord their
trust, and therefore, look forward to an eternal resting place of peace.

Dear friend, have you come to value God's wisdom as a graceful garland
for your head and pendants for your neck? Let us be a people who treasure godly wisdom far beyond worldly riches.

◆————————◆————————◆

*Father, You have given us Your Word for our instruction. Help me to value
Your wisdom beyond any earthly treasure or jewel.*

*I pray these things in Jesus' name. Amen.*

*Ephesians 6:1-3

328

# THE PATH OF WISDOM

My son, if sinners entice you, do not consent.
Proverbs 1:10

## HOW CAN I PRESERVE MY WAYS FROM EVIL?

I can preserve my ways from evil by submitting myself to the wisdom of Christ.

Today's text warns us against the enticements of sin. Wisdom teaches us not to cast our lot with the deeds of evildoers. However, if we are going to keep our ways pure before God, then we need to understand how to discern the devices of the enemy.

Solomon tells us that the wicked join forces together. If they say, "Come with us,* do not walk in the way with them; hold back your foot from their paths, for their feet run to evil, and they make haste to shed blood.* Such are the ways of everyone who is greedy for unjust gain; it takes away the life of its possessors.*

The wicked prey on the simple-minded and the weak. There is no regard for God's Law before their eyes, but rather they actively recruit others to join them in their folly. For this reason, we are warned not to consent to their allurements nor walk in their ways. Though they join forces together against the Lord of hosts, they will reap the consequences of their folly.

In light of this eternal truth, let us heed the words of Solomon so that our feet will not be entangled in the snares of death.

---

*Father, it is so important to listen to Your wisdom. Help me not to be enticed by the fading pleasures of sin, but rather to live my life by faith in Your Son. I pray these things in Jesus' name. Amen.*

*Proverbs 1:11, 15-16, 19

# WISDOM CRIES OUT

Wisdom cries aloud in the street, in the markets she raises her voice; at
the head of the noisy streets she cries out; at the entrance
of the city gates she speaks.
Proverbs 1:20-21

## HAVE YOU ANSWERED THE CALL OF WISDOM?

The wisdom of God is not far from any of us, but rather makes its appeal
to us daily. Its cry reaches out to the ends of the earth.

If there are any who lack wisdom then they are invited to drink of its wells.
Yet many will not accept the gracious invitation of wisdom nor answer
to its beckon call. In their folly they have rejected heavenly instruction to
the peril of their souls.

Jesus cried out, "If anyone thirsts, let him come to Me and drink. He
who believes in Me, as the Scripture has said, out of his heart will flow
rivers of living water." But this He spoke concerning the Spirit, whom
those believing in Him would receive."*

If you desire wisdom, then hear the words of Jesus and Solomon. Listen
to the gracious call of wisdom, and be filled with the Holy Spirit who
offers rivers of living water. Resist the hollow cries of folly, and submit
yourself to the wisdom of the Cross. Those, who are ruled by Christ, find
in Him a well of living water for their souls.

This eternal truth beckons us to seek the Lord daily for the gracious gift
of an outpouring of His wisdom.

———— ◆ ————

*Father, wisdom cries out to the ends of the earth.* Please give me your Holy
Spirit to receive Your heavenly wisdom.*

*I pray these things in Jesus' name. Amen.*

*John 7:37-39, Acts 1:8

# DO NOT DISREGARD WISDOM

Therefore they shall eat the fruit of their way,
and have their fill of their own devices.
Proverbs 1:31

## THERE ARE CONSEQUENCES TO DISREGARDING WISDOM

In the verses before our opening text, Solomon warns, "Because they hated knowledge and did not choose the fear of the Lord, would have none of my counsel and despised all my reproof,* they shall eat the fruit of their own way."

One of the greatest tragedies in life is when God gives you over to your own lustful desires. When the conscience is seared, the sinner finds himself in a very vicarious position. The Apostle Paul tells us that those who disregard God's Word are storing up for themselves treasures of wrath for the day of wrath.* Their willful persistence in sin has cost them their families, their reputations, and ultimately their souls.

To those who find it easier and easier to persist in their disobedience, there is hope. Their only requirement is to entreat the Lord that He may grant repentance in time of need. Though their sins be as red as scarlet, they shall be white as snow.*

---

*Father, it is a dangerous thing when we disregard wisdom. Help me to be one who hears and does Your Word.*

*I pray these things in Jesus' name. Amen.*

*Proverbs 1:29-30, Romans 2:5, Isaiah 1:18

# THE SAFETY OF WISDOM

But whoever listens to me will dwell secure and will be at ease,
without dread of disaster.

Proverbs 1:33

## FRIEND, WOULD YOU LIKE TO DWELL IN SAFETY?

You are admonished, then, to listen to the words of Solomon.

The safety that I speak about is not a safety from trials, but rather a safety from the consequences of sin. The person who listens to godly wisdom has experienced peace with God through the death of His Son.* Yet it is only as I submit myself to the lordship of Jesus Christ that I will reap the rewards of eternal life.

Who shall separate us from the love of Christ? Shall tribulation, or distress, or persecution, or famine, or nakedness, or peril, or sword? For I am persuaded that neither death nor life, nor angels nor principalities nor powers, nor things present nor things to come, shall be able to separate us from the love of God which is in Christ Jesus our Lord.*

In light of this eternal truth, let us who have received Christ by faith, dwell in safety from the judgment that awaits the wicked.

———————◆———————

*Father, there is no greater joy than possessing eternal life. Help me to resist the folly of people so that I may dwell in safety from the snares of the enemy. I pray these things in Jesus' name. Amen.*

*Romans 5:10, Romans 8:35, 38-39

# WISDOM KNOWS GOD

Then you will understand the fear of the Lord
and find the knowledge of God.

Proverbs 2:5

## FRIEND, DO YOU LACK KNOWLEDGE?

Our text today offers us a wonderful promise. The wisdom of God is not far off from us, but rather is made readily available to all who ask of Him. But we must approach God in faith if we expect to hear from Him.

Solomon instructs us to treasure God's commandments, incline our hearts to His understanding, and to seek God's wisdom like silver—like a hidden treasure.* Only then will we find the knowledge of God.

The Apostle James exhorts us to offer up our petitions to the Lord without wavering or doubting.* Those, who waver at the promises of God through unbelief, cannot expect to uncover the long lost treasures of wisdom and knowledge. If we are to find the knowledge of God, we must approach Him with all boldness and confidence.

Friend, do you rest assured in the faithful promises of God? Let us not doubt His goodness, but rather seek Him diligently, like hidden treasure, for the knowledge of God.

---

*Father, You are very generous in Your gifts to Your children. Help me to seek You for the wisdom that I need without wavering or doubting.*

*I pray these things in Jesus' name. Amen.*

*Proverbs 2:1-4, James 1:6

# WISDOM WALKS RIGHTEOUSLY

So you will walk in the way of the good and keep to the paths of the
righteous. For the upright will dwell in the land, and
the blameless will remain in it.
Proverbs 2:20-21

## HOW CAN WE KNOW IF WE ARE WALKING IN THE WAY OF WISDOM?

If we submit ourselves to God's Word, then there is no surer mark of faith
than the fruit of those who walk in His Law.

In the prior verses to our text, Solomon warns his son about the dangers
of the adulterous woman. If he will listen to his father's instruction, then
he will find himself delivered from her enticements. For her house leads
down to death, and her paths to the dead. None who go to her return,
nor do they regain the paths of life.* If we don't heed this counsel, the
Scripture cautions, "The wicked will be cut off from the earth, and the
unfaithful will be uprooted from it.*

The path of righteousness is not merely an outward conformity to rules,
but rather an inward desire to please the Lord. All those, who have been
redeemed by the blood of Christ, delight in His testimonies. Godly wisdom has taught them the value of living righteously in this sinful and fallen
world. As a result, they are preserved from the devastating effects of sin.

Dear friend, do you find yourself on the path of wisdom? Let us be those
who delight in wise godly instruction from our elders and walk in the
ways of the Lord.

---

*Father, sin lies at the door,* and it desires to have me. Give me wisdom to
abstain from every evil lust, and to embrace the way of the Cross.*

*I pray these things in Jesus' name. Amen.*

*Proverbs 2:18-19, 22, Genesis 4:7

# WISDOM INHABITS THE LAND

For the upright will inhabit the land,
and those with integrity will remain in it.
Proverbs 2:21

## HOW DO YOU INHABIT LAND?

Our text today provides a command and a promise. Solomon tells us if we are upright and have integrity, then we will find our feet preserved from the enticements of sin and inhabit the land and remain in it.

Furthermore, God's Word tells us to trust in the Lord, and do good and we will dwell in the land, and feed on His faithfulness. On the contrary, evildoers shall be cut off. Only those who wait on the Lord shall inherit the earth. So, our instruction is to depart from evil, and do good so that we will dwell forevermore.*

The life of the believer is fraught with various trials and temptations. Yet in all things we have the blessing of fellowship with God. Throughout the sum of Scripture we are led to one inescapable conclusion—the Lord shall be victorious over sin and the devil.

All those, who have submitted themselves to the wisdom of the Cross, will share in the final victory to come. In light of this eternal truth, let us submit our ways to Him Who is able to keep us from stumbling.*

---

*Father, You alone are able to keep us upright and give us integrity to inhabit and remain at peace with You. Give me the grace to die to my own ways and to submit myself to Your wisdom.*

*I pray these things in Jesus' name. Amen.*

*Psalm 37:3, 9, 27, Jude 24

# WISDOM IS A STEADFAST LOVE

Let not steadfast love and faithfulness forsake you; bind them around your neck; write them on the tablet of your heart.

Proverbs 3:3

## WHAT ARE THE CHARACTERISTICS OF WISDOM?

Those who are wise possess the love of God. They do not claim any rights to themselves, but rather exemplify a peaceful and quiet disposition.

In the New Testament, the Apostle James understands the value of godly wisdom. He writes that wisdom from above is first pure, then peaceable, gentle, open to reason, full of mercy and good fruits, impartial and sincere.* Paul wrote, "A servant of the Lord must not quarrel but be gentle to all, able to teach, patient."* Those, who have been trained by wisdom, carry it with them in all seasons of life. Clearly, they are an epistle of Christ, written not with ink but by the Spirit of the living God, not on tablets of stone but on tablets of flesh, that is, on their hearts.*

If we hope to know wisdom, then we must also internalize it. We must store the treasures of a steadfast love and faithfulness on the tablets of our hearts. Dear friend, have you experienced growth in the areas of love and faithfulness? Let us be those who wear the wisdom of God like a beautiful garment around our necks.

---

*Father, You are the source of all wisdom and knowledge. Help me to exemplify Your wisdom in the everyday grind of life.*

*I pray these things in Jesus' name. Amen.*

*James 3:17, 2 Timothy 2:24, 2 Corinthians 3:3

# WISDOM TRUSTS WHOLEHEARTEDLY

Trust in the Lord with all your heart, and do not lean on your own
understanding. In all your ways acknowledge Him,
and He will make straight your paths.
Proverbs 3:5-6

## DO YOU TAKE GOD AT HIS WORD?

In times of great trial, you are going to wrestle with the question of God's
faithfulness.

Without a doubt, Solomon emphasizes the totality of trusting in the
Lord. In verse five, we are exhorted to trust Him "with all" our hearts.
Next in verse six, we are instructed to acknowledge Him in "all our ways."
Our faith must be a whole-hearted endeavor. If we are going to trust the
Lord, then we must place the entirety of our lives into His hands.

While this may be true, this is often an art form that can only be learned
through the crucible of experience. There are many seasons of difficult
and perplexing circumstances, but it is in these storms where we have to
train our eyes to focus on the unseen.

Solomon continues, "Be not wise in your own eyes; fear the Lord, and
turn away from evil. It will be healing to your flesh and refreshment to
your bones."*

Will we trust God by faith or will we conform our ways to the world? Let
us not be wise in our own eyes or misled by the wisdom of the world,
but rather place "all" of our trust in the invincible God.

———————◇———————

*Father, Your ways are higher than my ways. In every season of life give me the
grace to walk by faith and not by sight.* *

*I pray these things in Jesus' name. Amen.*

*Proverbs 3:7-8, 2 Corinthians 5:7

# WISDOM HONORS GOD

Honor the Lord with your wealth and with the first fruits of all your
produce; then your barns will be filled with plenty,
and your vats will be bursting with wine.

Proverbs 3:9-10

## DO YOU HONOR THE LORD WITH YOUR WEALTH?

King Solomon reminds us that it is important to put the Lord first in
everything. Of course, his command to honor God does not come without a faithful promise. If God's children will give unto the Lord the best
of their produce, then He will richly provide for their needs. The overarching principle is simply that if we honor God then He will honor us.
He will not leave us nor forsake us, but rather promises to be everything
to us.

Furthermore, it is foolish to store up treasures for ourselves here on earth.
The riches of this life are fading, but the promises of God are everlasting.
The author of Hebrews tells us, "Keep your life free from love of money,
and be content with what you have, for he has said, 'I will never leave
you nor forsake you.' So we can confidently say, 'The Lord is my helper;
I will not fear.'"*

This eternal truth teaches us the importance of honoring Him, not only
with our wealth, but also with our lives as well.

———◆———◆———◆———

*Father, the cattle on a thousand hills are Yours.* You have promised to provide for those Who trust You. Give me the grace to invest my wealth for the
furtherance of Your Kingdom.*

*I pray these things in Jesus' name. Amen.*

*Hebrews 13:5-6, Psalm 50:10

# WISDOM IS CONFIDENT

Do not be afraid of sudden terror or of the ruin of the wicked,
when it comes, for the Lord will be your confidence
and will keep your foot from being caught."
Proverbs 3:25-26

## WHAT IS THE BENEFIT OF WALKING IN WISDOM?

The Lord will be your advocate.

Today's text reminds us that the way of the wicked is ruin. Evildoers constantly live in fear because they know that the consequences of their actions will eventually catch up to them.

At the same time, the righteous dwell safely in the arms of their God. They do not need to worry about the sudden calamity that falls on the wicked, because they have made the Lord their trust.* The Lord is their light and their salvation and they shall have no fear. The Lord is their strength in life and they shall not be afraid.* He is an ever-present Protector of His people, and He will keep their feet from being caught.

What a great relief to know it is better to have the Lord on our side than to join forces with the wicked. His presence alone is worth infinitely more than an innumerable host of angels. In light of this truth let us not live in despair, but rather place our confidence in our great Jehovah.

---

*Father, You alone are the All Sufficient Protector of Your people. Help me not to join forces with the wicked, but rather to place all my confidence in Your strength.*

*I pray these things in Jesus' name. Amen.*

*Psalm 40:4, Psalm 27:1

# WISDOM IS PEACE

Do not envy a man of violence and do not choose any of his ways,
for the devious person is an abomination to the Lord,
but the upright are in His confidence.
Proverbs 3:31-32

## DO YOUR DESIRES LINE UP WITH GOD'S WILL?

We live in a society that wears confrontation like a badge of honor. Contrarily, Solomon reminds us that it is folly to be envious of those who are given over to violence, lest you learn his ways and set a snare for your soul.* Those who are violent are under the just condemnation of God. Though they prosper in the present moment, they are abominable in His eyes.

Rather, let us be instructed by the wisdom that is from above.* Let us speak evil of no one, but be peaceable, gentle, showing all humility to everyone. For we ourselves were also once foolish, disobedient, deceived, serving various lusts and pleasures, hateful and hating one another. But when the kindness and the love of God our Savior toward us appeared, He saved us, through the washing of regeneration and renewing of the Holy Spirit.

Those who have been taught of God possess a sweet and tender disposition towards others.* They have learned that it is better to live in peace than to lash out in anger. Dear friend, would you like to exemplify the life of Christ? If so then do not envy the wicked,* but rather learn from our Lord's meek and lowly spirit.

------◆------

*Father, we live in a culture of rage. Help me not to envy those who are given over to violence, but rather to submit myself to Your peaceable wisdom.*

*I pray these things in Jesus' name. Amen.*

*Proverbs 22:25, James 3:17, Titus 2:3-5, Proverbs 24:19

# WISDOM REMEMBERS

Get wisdom! Get understanding! Do not forget, nor turn away
from the words of my mouth.

Proverbs 4:5

## DO YOU STORE GOD'S WISDOM IN YOUR HEART?

Emphatically, Solomon makes it clear that it is not merely enough to
know wisdom on an intellectual level. We must also be those who store
His truths in our hearts. Those, who possess godly wisdom, walk in its
ways. They are not forgetful hearers, but rather doers of God's Word.
Wisdom has taught them that it is a dangerous practice to turn a deaf ear
to His testimonies.

In like manner, the Apostle James warns us that if anyone is a hearer of
the word and not a doer, he is like a man who looks intently at his natural
face in a mirror. For he looks at himself and goes away and at once forgets
what he was like. But he who looks into the perfect law of liberty and
continues in it, and is not a forgetful hearer but a doer of the work, this
one will be blessed in what he does.*

Dear friend, are you a doer of God's Word? Let us be those who not only
gain wisdom, but also those who keep it.

---

*Father, it is a dangerous practice to forget the things which You have taught
us. Help me to not only hear Your words, but also keep Your words.*

*I pray these things in Jesus' name. Amen.*

*James 1:23-25

# WISDOM IS YOUR GUARD

*Do not forsake her, and she will keep you;*
*love her, and she will guard you.*
Proverbs 4:6

## FRIEND, WHO IS GUARDING YOU?

Do not forsake wisdom because it will preserve you from the crooked ways of evil.

The book of Proverbs makes it clear that we can only take one of two possible paths. We are either on the path of wisdom or we are on the path of folly. Those who are on the path of folly will not receive God's wisdom. They scoff at the true way, because they suppose the Cross to be foolishness. Those who are wise, however, have learned to embrace the wisdom of Christ. They have submitted to His ways, and have been given the promise to dwell in safety from the wrath of God.

God's Word promises, "When wisdom enters your heart, and knowledge is pleasant to your soul, discretion will preserve you; understanding will keep you, to deliver you from the way of evil, from the man who speaks perverse things, from those who leave the paths of uprightness to walk in the ways of darkness.*

What about you dear friend? Do you cling to the testimonies of Yahweh? Let us be those who long after wisdom more than the treasures of this world.

*Father, You bring to nothing the wisdom of man. Help me to submit myself to Your wisdom.*

*I pray these things in Jesus' name. Amen.*

*Proverbs 2:10-13

# WISDOM'S HEART

Keep your heart with all vigilance, for from it flow the springs of life.
Proverbs 4:23

## WHAT DOES IT MEAN TO KEEP OUR HEARTS WITH VIGILANCE?

The Scriptures deal extensively with the matters of the heart.

In the book of Jeremiah it reads, "The heart is deceitful above all things, and desperately sick; who can understand it? 'I the Lord search the heart and test the mind, to give every man according to his ways, according to the fruit of his deeds.'" And the psalmist declared, "Search me, O God, and know my heart! Try me and know my thoughts!"

It's essential, Solomon advises, to guard our hearts because it is from the heart that the issues of life spring. It has often been said that a man is outwardly what he is inwardly. The heart is the seat of the emotions and desires, and thus, we are to guard it like a precious jewel. For this reason Jesus said to all His disciples, "Blessed are the pure in heart, for they shall see God."*

Dear friend, have you been tending to the matters of your heart? Let us not neglect the care of our souls, but rather let us be vigilant in keeping a pure heart.

---

*Father, all sin is birthed out of a corrupt heart. Give me the grace to keep myself pure and in Your love always.*

*I pray these things in Jesus' name. Amen.*

*Jeremiah 17:9-10, Psalm 139:23, Matthew 5:8

# WISDOM SPEAKS KINDNESS

Put away from you crooked speech, and put devious talk far from you.
Proverbs 4:24

## IS YOUR SPEECH SEASONED WITH SALT?*

The way that we use our tongue is a reflection of what is in our heart. Jesus said, "What comes out of the mouth proceeds from the heart, and this defiles a person."*

Folly deceives us to think that it is best to simply speak whatever is on our mind, but wisdom demonstrates the importance of weighing our words carefully. Every action has a consequence. A person who has been instructed by wisdom will cautiously consider the potential consequences of their words before they speak. This is definitely an art form that can only be mastered as we are trained by wisdom and conformed more into the image of Christ. As we grow in grace, our tongues become an instrument of edification.

Dearly beloved, are your words a reflection of the glory of God? Let our speech always be gracious, seasoned with salt, so that we may know how we ought to answer each person.* Let us put away anger, wrath, malice, slander, and obscene talk. Let us not lie to one another, seeing that we have put off the old self with its practices and have put on the new self, which is being renewed in knowledge after the image of our Creator.*

---

*Father, the tongue is a little instrument that can cause catastrophic damage. Give me the wisdom I need to weigh out our words before I speak. Help me to have the law of kindness always upon my lips.* *

*I pray these things in Jesus' name. Amen.*

*Matthew 15:18, Colossians 4:6, Colossians 3:8-10, Proverbs 31:26,

# WISDOM LOOKS DIRECTLY FORWARD

Let your eyes look directly forward, and your gaze be straight before you.
Proverbs 4:25

## DO YOU FOCUS ON THE TASK AT HAND?

Why do you think Solomon encourages us to look directly forward? He knows that if we flirt with the allurements of evil, or entertain the suggestions of sin, we tend to fall headlong into iniquity. Thus wisdom teaches us that all sin, both small and great, wages war on our souls.

Solomon warns us not to even entertain the temptations of sin. There are enticements that approach the Christian from all angles and from all sides. In short, if we are going to be victorious over the devil, then we must stay focused on our task at hand.

Jesus said, "If your right eye causes you to sin, pluck it out and cast it from you; for it is more profitable for you that one of your members perish, than for your whole body to be cast into hell."*

Dear friend, have you gone to any length necessary to have mastery over your lusts? Let us not make provision for our flesh, but rather be diligent to root out every evil through the power of the Holy Spirit.

---

*Father, there are many temptations which seek our harm. Give me wisdom to turn away my eyes from looking at worthless things, and revive me in Your way.* *

*I pray these things in Jesus' name. Amen.*

*Matthew 5:29, Psalm 119:37

# WISDOM PONDERS THE PATH

Ponder the path of your feet; then all your ways will be sure.
Proverbs 4:26

## DO YOU PONDER THE PATH OF YOUR FEET?

I remember the first time that I went rock climbing. I had never been on the face of a mountain before and the experience terrified me. You better believe that I was very strategic in the placement of my feet.

In reflecting upon my rock climbing experience, I see a parallel with the proverb above. Solomon wants us to be aware of the subtle nature of evil. There are temptations that wage war on our souls. Thus, we are warned to consider carefully our course of direction.

Those who are foolish do not think about the potential consequences of their actions, but those who are wise consider their steps before they proceed. If we find ourselves reaping the consequences of our sin then it is already too late. See then that we walk circumspectly, not as fools but as wise, redeeming the time, because the days are evil.* Let us think about our ways, and turn our feet to His testimonies.*

In light of this eternal truth, let us exercise caution in all the ways we go.

◆———————◆———————◆

*Father, You have taught me to walk circumspectly. Help me to exercise prudence in all my ways to Your everlasting glory.*

*I pray these things in Jesus' name. Amen.*

*Ephesians 5:15-16, Psalm 119:59

# WISDOM IS FIDELITY

For the lips of a forbidden woman drip honey, and her speech is smoother than oil, but in the end she is bitter as wormwood, sharp as a two-edged sword.
Proverbs 5:3-4

## ARE YOU EASILY FLATTERED?

If so, then you are warned to be on guard against the enticing speech of an immoral woman!

Here in the text, Solomon's exhortation is given to us by means of contrast. First, he describes the flattery of the adulterer's speech, and then he describes the bitter consequences of her advancements. This forbidden, or strange, woman uses sweet and enticing speech to draw in her victims. Her appeal in the moment masks the consequences of eternity. The sweet taste of her empty words goes down to the very soul with bitterness.

Listen to me, Solomon says, Keep your way far from her, and do not go near the door of her house,* for a man's ways are before the eyes of the Lord, and he ponders all his paths.* He shall die for lack of instruction, and in the greatness of his folly he shall go astray.*

How many marriages, ministries, and reputations have been ruined as a result of flattery? Dear friend, if you want to be spared from the devastating consequences of adultery, then listen to the words of Solomon. Do not entertain the temptations of a strange woman or man, but rather enjoy the blessings of your own marriage.

---

*Father, the love of a spouse is sweet. You have ordained the marriage bed and called it good.* Give me the grace not to be allured by the suggestions of an adulterer, but rather to treasure the spouse of my youth.*

*I pray these things in Jesus' name. Amen.*

*Proverbs 5:8, 21, 23, Hebrews 13:4

# WISDOM IS MODEST

Her feet go down to death; her steps follow the path to Sheol; she does not ponder the path of life; her ways wander, and she does not know it.

Proverbs 5:5-6

## WHAT IS AN IMMORAL WOMAN?

Friend, would you like to be more on guard against the immoral woman? If so, then let's consider her ways. Note that she does not ponder the path of life. The seductress lives only for the moment. She does not concern herself with the matters of eternity. Instead, her motivations are fueled by her passions. In folly, she has bought into the lie that it is best to do whatever makes her happy, but she lacks understanding.

Solomon tells us, "For her house leads down to death, and her paths to the dead; none who go to her return, nor do they regain the paths of life.* Her house is the way to hell, descending to the chambers of death.*

Here wisdom warns us that her ways lead to death. She may occupy your pleasure for a moment, but you will reap the devastating effects of her passion. In short, mark well her steps and keep yourself far from her reach. If you will be instructed by the words of wisdom, then your life will be preserved from her snares.

---

*Father, we live in a very sensual culture. Give me the grace to be on guard against the seductress who flaunts and flatters to get my attention.*

*I pray these things in Jesus' name. Amen.*

*Proverbs 2:18-19, Proverbs 7:27

# WISDOM KEEPS AWAY FROM SIN

Keep your way far from her and do not go near the door of her house.

Proverbs 5:8

## DO YOU KEEP YOUR FEET FAR FROM THE ADULTEROUS WOMAN?

Once again, King Solomon offers us a little more bit of advice about the adulterous woman. He instructs us to keep our way far from the temptress, and not to go near the door of her house. The fool tempts fate by flirting with her allurements, but the wise guard all their ways from her snares.

"I find more bitter than death, King Solomon said, "from the woman whose heart is snares and nets, whose hands are fetters. He who pleases God shall escape from her, but the sinner shall be trapped by her."*

Wisdom has taught us that it is better to resist the passing pleasures of a season than to reap the consequences of everlasting judgment. Ultimately Solomon's instructions come with good intentions. Even Jesus said, "For whoever is ashamed of Me and My words in this adulterous and sinful generation, of him the Son of Man also will be ashamed when He comes in the glory of His Father with the holy angels."* If we will hear these words of wisdom, then we will reap the benefits of everlasting life. In light of this eternal truth, let us not be weighed down with various lusts of this world, but rather experience the freedom we have in Christ.

---

*Father, the dangers of adultery are all around us. There are devious things that sinners, in times past, did not have at their fingertips. Give me the grace I need to guard against these temptations and be pleasing in Your sight.*

*I pray these things in Jesus' name. Amen.*

*Ecclesiastes 7:28, Mark 8:38

# WISDOM IS FAITHFUL

Drink water from your own cistern, flowing water from your own well.

Proverbs 5:15

## DO YOU DRINK WATER FROM YOUR OWN CISTERN?

Here in the text, we are encouraged to enjoy the blessings of the marriage bed. In the prior verses, Solomon referred to the seductress as "the forbidden woman."*

Then the king proceeds to characterize the love of a spouse as a blessing by writing, Let your fountain be blessed, and rejoice in the wife of your youth, a lovely deer, a graceful doe. Let her breasts fill you at all times with delight; be intoxicated always in her love.*

There is a sexual intimacy that is both ordained and blessed by God above. Though the act of adultery brings forth judgment, the intimacy of marriage brings forth great joy. The point of Solomon's poetic discourse is simply that God has gifted us the enjoyment of sex for marriage, and that it is an intimacy to be shared with no one else.

And then Solomon says, "Why should springs be scattered abroad like streams of water in the streets?"* Indeed, sexual desires should be controlled and channeled in one's marriage, not wasted. Let us be those who guard the sanctity of our marriages to the glory of God.

---

*Father, You have ordained marriage both for Your glory and our joy. Give us the grace not to cheapen our marriages through the forbidden act of adultery. I pray these things in Jesus' name. Amen.*

*Proverbs 5:3, 18-19, Proverbs 5:16

# WISDOM WATCHES

For a man's ways are before the eyes of the Lord,
and he ponders all his paths.
Proverbs 5:21

## WHY SHOULD A PERSON PONDER THEIR STEPS?

We should ponder our steps because the Lord ponders our steps as well. All sin is committed in the sight of God, Who is the revealer of secrets.* Those, who have been trained by wisdom, understand that there is no sin that is hidden from God's sight.

The eyes of the Lord are in every place, keeping watch on the evil and the good.* For the eyes of the Lord run to and fro throughout the whole earth, to show Himself strong on behalf of those whose heart is loyal to Him.*

Of course, God's omniscience should serve as a motivation for us to guard ourselves against the enticements of evil. Solomon, here in today's text, wants us to understand that every act is weighed in the balances* and will eventually be brought into judgment. Thus, it is wise to reflect on the infallible truth that God is always watching.

Dear friend, do you ponder your steps? Let us be those who live every moment in light of eternity.

・――――――◇――――――・

*Father, there is no deed or thing hidden from Your sight. Help me to live every moment with the understanding that You are always watching.*

*I pray these things in Jesus' name. Amen.*

*Daniel 2:47, Proverbs 15:3, 2 Chronicles 16:9, Daniel 5:27

# WISDOM LISTENS

The iniquities of the wicked ensnare him, and he is held fast
in the cords of his sin. He dies for lack of discipline,
and because of his great folly he is led astray.
Proverbs 5:22-23

## WHAT IS THE DESTINY OF THE WICKED?

The final outcome of the wicked is summed up for us here in three ways.

First, the wicked are enslaved by their sin. Solomon uses the imagery of a wicked sinner being bound by cords. The king wants us to understand that there is no freedom in turning a deaf ear to godly wisdom.

Secondly, the wicked are on a path that leads to death. Solomon tells us that the wicked lack discipline. They have obtained no mastery over their sinful lusts.

Finally, the wicked have been led astray because of their great folly. Evil people do not regard the instruction of the Lord and they perish for lack of knowledge.

Listen and live! Hear the words of Solomon! For the commandment is a lamp and the teaching a light, and the reproofs of discipline are the way of life.* If you will answer the call to wisdom, then your feet will be kept from devastating consequences of evil. This eternal truth should awaken us to be those who are swift to hear, and swift to obey God's Word.

---

*Father, there is no real freedom in sin, but only judgment. Grant me the grace I need to answer the call of wisdom.*

*I pray these things in Jesus' name. Amen.*

*Proverbs 6:23

# DECEMBER

## WHY DO WE NEED WISDOM?

As we finish out the year, let's continue our reflections on the book of Proverbs. There is so much to glean from the rich words of Solomon. He has shown us the way of righteousness, and it would be foolish for us to turn away from it now.

James said, "If any of you lacks wisdom, let him ask God, who gives generously to all without reproach, and it will be given him that you may be perfect and complete, lacking in nothing.*

My desire is that we won't see a list of do's and don'ts, but rather the redemptive work of Christ on our behalf. There is no one who can sub-mit to the ways of wisdom, without first being subdued by it. Therefore, let us hear the conclusion of the whole matter to fear God and to keep His commandments, for this is man's all. For God will bring every work into judgment, including every secret thing, whether good or evil.*

My prayer is that you will see the glory of God as we linger a bit longer in the book of Proverbs. Let us seek the Lord for His illumination so we may comprehend the great truths of wisdom.

*James 1:5, 4, Ecclesiastes 12:13

# TO DISCERN DEBT

My son, if you have put up security for your neighbor, have given your pledge for a stranger, if you are snared in the words of your mouth, caught in the words of your mouth, then do this, my son, and save yourself.

Proverbs 6:1-3

## ARE YOU CAUGHT IN THE WORDS OF YOUR MOUTH?

Why do we need wisdom? To warn us against the folly of putting ourselves on the hook for someone else's debt. Those who make themselves a surety for the debt of another may find themselves ensnared by the words of their mouth. If we are bound to pay the debt of another, then Solomon offers us some valuable advice.

In the following verses he implores us to plead urgently with our neighbor and to give our eyes no sleep and our eyelids no slumber, but to save ourselves like a gazelle from the hand of the hunter, like a bird from the hand of the fowler.* In other words, don't rest until the debt is satisfied. Only fools suppose that a promise is made to be broken, but the wise place a heavy urgency on the importance of keeping their word. Wisdom has taught them that it is better not to pledge at all, rather than to pledge and fall short on their commitment.

Dear friend, have you weighed out the costs before making yourself a surety for others? Let wisdom teach us from being caught in the words of our mouth.

———————◆———————

*Father, You have kept Your covenant promises to Your children by giving us Your beloved Son. He made Himself a surety for us by baring our sins on the Cross. Give me the grace to keep myself from the folly of making rash promises. I pray these things in Jesus' name. Amen.*

*Proverbs 6:3-5

# TO DETECT LAZINESS

A little sleep, a little slumber, a little folding of the hands to rest, and poverty will come upon you like a robber, and want like an armed man.

Proverbs 6:10-11

## ARE YOU A PERSON PRONE TO LAZINESS?

Why do we need wisdom? To instruct us to be diligent in all matters of life, and that includes watching out for idleness. The sin of laziness brings many to poverty and ruin.

Take note of the illustration that Solomon uses to describe poverty. He likens poverty to an armed robber. The fool, who will not dedicate themselves to their craft, will be robbed of many blessings from God. In like manner, the person who is diligent in their work must also be diligent with their soul. It has often been said that the road to hell is paved with good intentions. It does little to no good to prosper in your business, if you do not tend to your soul. For what does it profit a man to gain the whole world but lose his own soul?*

Folly coaxes us that we have plenty of time to deal with the matters of eternity, but wisdom teaches us the importance of spiritual diligence for today. In light of this eternal truth, let us be diligent to die to sloth, and to prepare ourselves for the coming of the Lord.

———————◇———————

*Father, You have taught us the virtue of diligence. Give us the grace to abstain from the sin of idleness, and to be diligent in making our calling and election sure.* *

*I pray these things in Jesus' name. Amen.*

*Mark 8:36, 2 Peter 1:10

# TO EXPLAIN HAUGHTINESS

There are six things that the Lord hates, seven that are an abomination to him: haughty eyes.

Proverbs 6:16-17

## DO YOU HAVE HAUGHTY EYES?

Why do we need wisdom? To teach us what the Lord hates. For the next few days, we are going to study what is an abomination to God. Today, wisdom teaches us the folly of pride.

In the prophecies of Isaiah, we see the apex of pride in the example of Lucifer. He was the most beautiful of all angelic hosts. The Lord had given him a high position of authority in heaven, but in his pride he was not content with his lot. Instead he wanted to exalt himself above the Most High. Thus he was removed from his office, and banished from the fellowship of the Lord.

Isaiah records for us, "You are fallen from heaven, O Lucifer, son of the morning! You are cut down to the ground, for you have said in your heart, 'I will exalt my throne above the stars of God; I will be like the Most High.' Yet you shall be brought down to the lowest depths of the Pit."*

This eternal truth of wisdom teaches us that the Gospel is made effectual in the soul that is humble. It was Christ Who modeled the ultimate example of humility—even to the point of death on the Cross.* It is imperative in the Christian faith to avoid the snares of a proud look with haughty eyes and humble ourselves before our Maker.

---

*Father, You hate a proud look. It was pride that led to Lucifer's undoing. Please give me the grace to walk in the humility of Christ.*

*I pray these things in Jesus' name. Amen.*

*Isaiah 14:12-15, Philippians 2:8

# TO SPOT LYING

There are six things that the Lord hates,
seven that are an abomination to him ... a lying tongue.
Proverbs 6:16-17

## WHAT VALUE DO YOU PLACE ON TELLING THE TRUTH?

Wisdom warns against the dangers of deception. It was through a lie that Satan deceived Eve, when he said, "Has God indeed said, 'You shall not eat of every tree of the garden'? For God knows that in the day you eat of it your eyes will be opened, and you will be like God, knowing good and evil.'"* Lucifer lied and tempted Eve with the same lure that brought about his own downfall: pride, "to be like God."

Satan deceived Eve into thinking that the Lord did not have her best interests in mind. In her folly, Eve believed the lie of the devil, and thus, plunged the human race headlong into sin.

Throughout the ages there have been many lies that have ruined families, reputations, and livelihoods. Yet the most damaging lies are the ones that are aimed at perverting the Gospel. How many false religious movements have been birthed out of a small perversion of the truth? Satan has bound many well-intentioned souls on the road to hell. We must be on guard, therefore, against the destructive lies of our adversary. Folly deceives us into thinking that there are many ways to heaven, but wisdom teaches us that the gate is narrow and the way is hard that leads to life, and those who find it are few.* In light of this truth let us put away a lying tongue, and delight ourselves in God's eternal truth.

---

*Father, You delight in the truth. Give me the grace to tell the truth and abstain from every false way.\**

*I pray these things in Jesus' name. Amen.*

*Genesis 3:1, 5, Matthew 7:14, Psalm 119:104

357

# TO NOTE INJUSTICE

There are six things that the Lord hates, seven that are an
abomination to him ... hands that shed innocent blood.
Proverbs 6:16-17

## DO YOU HATE THE SHEDDING OF INNOCENT BLOOD?

Wisdom warns against those that shed innocent blood, and have little to
no regard for the value of human life. They do not esteem the justice of
God, but rather delight in preying on the weak.

Murder is a gross sin for two reasons. First it is an act that is contrary to
the character of God. He is a just God, Who hates the perversion of His
justice. Secondly, it seeks to usurp His holy authority. The Lord is the giver
and taker of life, and thus the fate of all humanity lies in His hands alone.
Ultimately we know that all sins are birthed out of a corrupt heart. Those
who hate their brethren are likened to murderers in the eyes of the Lord.

Jesus said, "Everyone who is angry with his brother will be liable to
judg-ment."* This sounds harsh, but the truth is, sin starts in our
hearts and the actions follow. Anyone who hates a brother or sister is
a murderer, and you know that no murderer has eternal life residing
in him.* By looking at the heart, Jesus has let us know that we are all
guilty. It isn't just "those people." We all need help.

Dear friend, let us not harbor anger in our hearts. Let us be quick to
forgive, because out of the heart proceeds all types of evil.

———————◦———————

*Father, all sin is birthed out of the corrupt condition of our hearts. Search me,
oh God, to see if there is any wicked way within me.*

*I pray these things in Jesus' name. Amen.*

*Matthew 5:21, 1 John 3:15, Psalm 139:23-24

# TO PRESERVE OUR HEARTS

"There are six things that the Lord hates, seven that are an abomination to him … a heart that devises wicked plans.
Proverbs 6:16, 18

## WHAT IS THE CONDITION OF YOUR HEART?

Wisdom teaches that the wicked schemes of a person are devised out of his heart. Was it not Cain, who, through jealousy and anger within his heart, plotted to kill his brother Abel?* The Bible tells us that ultimately Cain went out from the presence of the Lord.* Was it not greed that led Judas to the betrayal of our Lord? In folly he plotted against the King of glory for thirty pieces of silver.*

Time would fail me to speak of the wicked plots that were devised by Laban,* Balaam,* and Haman.* We know that their evil deeds were exposed, and that the wrath of God fell on them for their corruption. They have forsaken the right way and gone astray, who loved the wages of unrighteousness; but they were rebuked for their iniquity. Their plans are wells without water, clouds carried by a storm, for whom is reserved the blackness of darkness forever.*

Let us learn the importance of setting right our conduct before the Lord. It is certainly better to have favor with the Lord than to be despised in His eyes.

---

*Father, true wisdom gives itself for the benefit of others. Give me the grace to keep my feet far from the wicked schemes of man, and help me to walk uprightly in this dark and sinful world.*

*I pray these things in Jesus' name. Amen.*

*Genesis 4:5-6, 17, Matthew 26:15, Genesis 29:25, Numbers 31, Esther 3:5, 2 Peter 2:15-17

# TO PERCEIVE EVIL

There are six things that the Lord hates, seven that are an
abomination to him … feet that makes haste to run to evil.
Proverbs 6:16, 18

## DO YOUR FEET RUN TO EVIL?

Why do we need wisdom? To give us discernment in a society that calls
good evil and evil good.* Solomon warns us to listen to his words. Those,
whose feet run to evil, are an abomination to the Lord.

Notice how evildoers' feet not only run to evil—they make haste to
run to evil. They take great delight in lawlessness. Folly has deceived
them to think that it is honorable to live in their shameful lusts, but
wisdom warns us not to partake in their sinful deeds.

The Prophet Isaiah writes, "Their feet run to evil, and make haste to shed
innocent blood; their thoughts are thoughts of iniquity; wasting and
destruction are in their paths. The way of peace they have not known, and
there is no justice in their ways; they have made themselves crooked paths;
whoever takes that way shall not know peace."* Those, who are wise, live
in such a way as to please the Lord. They have learned that it is better to
suffer reproach for the sake of Christ, than to join forces with the wicked.

Has wisdom taught you to hate every false way? Let us be those who
not only hate wicked schemes, and have nothing to do with the fruitless
deeds of darkness, but rather expose them.*

*Father, the wicked join forces against You, but their doom is sure. Give me the
grace to keep my feet far from their ways.*

*I pray these things in Jesus' name. Amen.*

*Isaiah 5:20, 59:7-8, Ephesians 5:11

# TO SPEAK TRUTH

There are six things that the Lord hates, seven that are an abomination to him …a false witness who breathes out lies.
Proverbs 6:16, 19

## ARE YOU A FAITHFUL WITNESS?

Why do we need wisdom? To understand what it means to have a lying tongue. Solomon warns us about the perils of being a false witness. Back in ancient times, a false witness sought to testify against the life of another person. With this in mind, their false testimony was forbidden by the Law of Moses.

We need wisdom to instruct us to simply speak the truth about someone. It is folly to slander the character of another person. For wisdom teaches that a man who bears false witness against his neighbor is like a club, a sword, and a sharp arrow.* Therefore, put away lying, and let each one of us speak truth with each other, for we are all members of one body, the Church.* We live in a day where men are accused of infidelity, and often convicted in court without a fair trial. A false witness ruins a person's reputation, and brings all kinds of evil on the accused.

In light of this eternal truth, let us be a people who are instructed in the ways of wisdom to speak truth, justice and peace. Those, who remain faithful in their witness, will be a proper reflection of Christ.

———◆———◆———◆———

*Father, it is shameful to bear false witness against the innocent. Give me the grace to speak the truth, and to guard the reputation of others.*

*I pray these things in Jesus' name. Amen.*

*Proverbs 25:18, Ephesians 4:25, Zechariah 8:16

# TO LEARN UNITY

There are six things that the Lord hates, seven that are an abomination
to him ...and one who sows discord among brothers.
Proverbs 6:16, 19

## DO YOU DWELL WITH OTHERS IN UNITY?

Why do we need wisdom? To teach us unity. There are always going to
be those who live in constant conflict with others. They view their divisive spirit as a badge of honor. Even today, we see many conflicts rising
through the use of social media. How many of us have been embattled
in a heated Facebook debate with others? Wisdom warns that a perverse
man sows strife, and a whisperer separates the best of friends. A violent
man entices his neighbor, and leads him in a way that is not good.*

Yet Christ has shown us a better way.

The Christian can uphold their convictions in a spirit of unity and peace.
This does not mean that we will never have enemies, but rather that we
strive to maintain the unity of peace even with our adversaries. Folly
deceives us into thinking that it is honorable to be divisive, but wisdom
teaches us that it is better to live in harmony with others. Let us avoid
foolish and ignorant disputes, knowing that they generate strife,* and be a
Church that is united for the sake of the Gospel. This is a sight to behold.

In light of this eternal truth, let wisdom instruct us to walk in a manner
that is gentle to all, able to teach, patient, and in humility,* pleasing to
the Lord.

*Father, You hate those who sow discord among the brethren. Please give me
the grace to maintain a unity of peace with my brothers and sisters in Christ.
I pray these things in Jesus' name. Amen.*

*Proverbs 16:28-29, 2 Timothy 2:23, 24

# TO RECOGNIZE ADULTERY

Whoever commits adultery with a woman lacks understanding;
he who does so destroys his own soul.
Proverbs 6:32

## DO YOU LACK UNDERSTANDING?

Why do we need wisdom? To teach us common sense. Adultery is a sin that has destroyed many families and reputations. Thus, Solomon wants his son to understand by comparing an adulterer to a thief in the previous verse. The thief, who steals food, will have to pay back what he has stolen. Yet how can an adulterer repay what he owes? The man who commits adultery not only sins against himself, but he also sins against God and others. For the ancient Israelites, marital fidelity was a mark of one's fidelity to God.

Solomon warns, "An adulterer will get wounds and dishonor, and his disgrace will not be wiped away."* Likewise, the Apostle Paul pleaded, "Flee from sexual immorality. Every other sin a person commits is outside the body, but the sexually immoral person sins against his own body. Do you not know that your body is a temple of the Holy Spirit within you, whom you have from God? You are not your own, for you were bought with a price. So glorify God in your body."*

Let wisdom teach us the importance of guarding our virtue, marriages and our reputations.

◆———————◇———————◆

*Father, adultery is a sin that causes devastating consequences. Help me to be on guard against the adulterous person who uses flattery to gain advantage over me.*

*I pray these things in Jesus' name. Amen.*

*Proverbs 6:33, 1 Corinthians 6:18-20

# TO DWELL WITH PRUDENCE

I wisdom dwell with prudence, and I find knowledge and discretion.
Proverbs 8:12

## WHO IS WISDOM'S COMPANION?

Why do we need wisdom? To illuminate that the one, who exercises great wisdom, has also mastered the art of prudence.

There are many commentators that view the book of Proverbs as an instruction manual for kings. The historical accounts of Solomon liken him to the wisest of all rulers. He used a great deal of prudence and discretion to rule righteously in the fear of the Lord. Yet Solomon does not only explore the importance of wisdom in diplomatic situations, but he also sees wisdom and prudence pertaining to the creation of the worlds. Solomon tells us when God marked out the foundations of the earth, wisdom was beside Him as a master craftsman; and wisdom was daily His delight, rejoicing always before Him.*

The Lord's marvelous works exemplify His infinite wisdom. With wisdom, dwells prudence and one will find knowledge and discretion. Hear Solomon's instruction and be wise, and do not disdain it. Blessed is the man who listens, watches and waits. For whoever finds wisdom, obtains favor from the Lord; but he who sins against Him wrongs his own soul. All those who hate wisdom love death.* In light of this eternal truth, let us seek the Lord daily for that heavenly wisdom which is from above.

———————◦———————

*Father, Your wisdom is adorned in prudence, knowledge, and discretion. Give me ears to receive Your heavenly instructions.*

*I pray these things in Jesus' name. Amen.*

*Proverbs 8:29-30, 33-36

# TO HATE EVIL

The fear of the Lord is hatred of evil. Pride and arrogance and the way of evil and perverted speech I hate.

Proverbs 8:13

## WHAT IS THE FEAR OF THE LORD?

Why do we need wisdom? To show us how to fear the Lord. Solomon earlier had said that to fear the Lord is the beginning of knowledge,* but here in the text he expounds upon that principle.

How can we fear the Lord? We can fear the Lord by hating pride, arrogance, perverted speech, and any other evil way. Folly seeks to promote and advance itself, but wisdom teaches us to walk in the humility of Christ. Those, who are wise, seek to build others up through their actions and words. On the other hand, the world seeks to exploit others for its own selfish ambitions.

Dear friend, would you like to possess the favor of God? If so, then listen to the words of Solomon. Hate evil and love God. God loves those who love Him, and those who seek wisdom diligently will find her. Riches, honor, and righteousness are with wisdom. Its fruit is better than gold and choice silver.* There is much joy and assurance that comes from having fellowship with the Most High.

In light of this eternal truth, let us hate pride, arrogance, evil and perverted speech. In them is death,* but in wisdom one finds all godly riches.

---

*Father, it is a fearful thing to fall into Your hands. Give me the grace to adorn myself in the humility of Christ.*

*I pray these things in Jesus' name. Amen.*

*Proverbs 1:7, 8:17-19, 36

# TO ATTAIN A GODLY LEGACY

The memory of the righteous is a blessing,
but the name of the wicked will rot.
Proverbs 10:7

## HOW WOULD YOU LIKE TO BE REMEMBERED?

Why do we need wisdom? For our legacy. We live in a society that only concerns itself with the here and now, but the wise store up for themselves an enduring and godly legacy.

In today's text there is a contrast that is painted between the righteous and the wicked. Those, who are righteous, possess the treasures of a good name. The Lord has prepared for them an eternal resting place, and they shall not be moved. Scripture tells us that a good name is to be chosen rather than great riches* and that a good reputation is more valuable than costly perfume. The day we die is better than the day we are born.* We should rejoice because our names are written in the Book of Life in heaven.

Contrarily, wisdom teaches that the name of the wicked will rot. Evildoers have made this life their inheritance, but it will soon perish. Their name, though honored among sinners, will be tarnished in shame.

Dear friend, have you thought about your legacy? Let us be those who build an enduring legacy with the righteous so that our memory will be a blessing to others.

---

*Father, it is wise to consider my life in light of eternity. Please give me the grace to cultivate a blessed legacy through faith.*

*I pray these things in Jesus' name. Amen.*

*Proverbs 22:1, Ecclesiastes 7:1, Luke 10:20

# TO GUARD OUR LIPS

When words are many, transgression is not lacking,
but whoever restrains his lips is prudent.
Proverbs 10:19

## ARE YOU A PERSON OF FEW WORDS?

Wisdom warns us to guard our words carefully. There are all sorts of evil that can be prevented if we learn to exercise prudence in our speech.

The Apostle James offers us words of wisdom in his epistle when addressing the tongue. He said the tongue is a fire, a world of unrighteousness. The tongue is set among our members, staining the whole body, setting on fire the entire course of life, and set on fire by hell.* How many wars and rumors of wars* have been started by unwise words? Even a fool is counted wise when he holds his peace; when he shuts his lips, he is considered perceptive.* So then, a person who has knowledge spares his words, and a person of understanding is of a calm spirit.*

Therefore wisdom teaches us to think carefully before we speak. In doing so we not only prevent the harm of others, but we also preserve ourselves from sin. Dear friend, do you carefully weigh out your words? Let us be people who think carefully before we speak.

---

*Father, it is wise to exercise prudence in my speech. Please give me the grace to speak with the law of kindness on my tongue.\**

*I pray these things in Jesus' name. Amen.*

*James 3:6, Matthew 24:6, Proverbs 17:28, 27, Proverbs 31:26

# TO TEACH INTEGRITY

The integrity of the upright guides them,
but the crookedness of the treacherous destroys them.
Proverbs 11:3

## DO YOU VALUE INTEGRITY?

Why do we need wisdom? To teach us about integrity.

Here we are instructed by wisdom to walk uprightly before God and man. In the immediate context, Solomon is dealing with the affairs of business. He warns us against the use of a false balance, and then he proceeds to deal with the topic of wealth. The point he is trying to make is simply this: we are to conduct ourselves with integrity before God since we will give an account of our actions before Him.

Wisdom instructs that the righteousness of the blameless keeps his way straight, but the wicked falls by his own wickedness. The righteousness of the upright will be delivered, but the treacherous are taken captive by their lust.*

Therefore, it is wise to live moment by moment in light of the judgment to come. We live in a world that uses the ends to justify the means, but that is a great folly. Wisdom teaches us that it is better to have favor with God than to have favor with man. If we submit to Christ in this life, then we will reign with Him for all eternity.

In light of this eternal truth, the way of integrity is to let righteousness and justice guide all of our affairs.

---

*Father, what is esteemed by man is highly despised in Your eyes. Give me the grace to conduct all of my affairs with the integrity that is from above.*

*I pray these things in Jesus' name. Amen.*

*Proverbs 11:5-6

# TO CAPTURE SOULS

The fruit of the righteous is a tree of life,
and whoever captures souls is wise.
Proverbs 11:30

## DOES YOUR SPEECH BUILD OTHERS UP OR TEAR OTHERS DOWN?

Wisdom instructs us how to be wise in our conversations to capture souls. Solomon has been warning us against the dangers of perverse speech, and now he shifts his focus to the blessings of wise speech.

It is a beautiful thing to hear a tongue that proclaims the Gospel, but take note of the illustration above. The righteous are likened to a tree of life. The person who is wise will use their words to go to great lengths to snatch others from the fires of hell. They store up everlasting fruits of righteousness. The Apostle Paul said, I have made myself a servant to all, that I might win the more.* The Apostle James confirmed, "Let him know that he who turns a sinner from the error of his way will save a soul from death and cover a multitude of sins.*

Do you use your conversations for the glory of God? Let us be those who share the great news of salvation with others to shine like the brightness of heaven, and turn many to righteousness.*

❖———————◆———————❖

*Father, it is wise to use our speech for the edification of others. Give me the grace not to tear others down with my words, but rather to build them up to bring them to You.*

*I pray these things in Jesus' name. Amen.*

*1 Corinthians 9:19, James 5:20, Daniel 12:3

# TO FIND WISE TEACHERS

The teaching of the wise is a fountain of life,
that one may turn away from the snares of death.
Proverbs 13:14

## WHO ARE YOUR TEACHERS?

Why do we need wisdom? To find wise teachers!

Here in the text we are instructed to learn from wise teachers. It is through wisdom that our souls are preserved from death. You see, this is not a wisdom that is attained through flesh and blood, but rather a wisdom that finds its source in the very nature of God. For by this, your days will be multiplied, and years of life will be added to you.*

King Solomon likens those who teach godly wisdom to a fountain of life. The mouth of the righteous is a well of life.* They teach that the fear of the Lord is a fountain of life, to turn one away from the snares of death.* Those who hear their instruction will dwell safely from the devastating consequences of sin.

Dear friend, would you like to be directed to the fountain of life? If so, then listen to the words of Solomon. Those, who submit themselves to the wisdom of the Cross, will find their feet placed on solid ground. Though they are overtaken by many sorrows they will experience the assurance of eternal life. In light of this eternal truth, let us find faithful teachers who will instruct us in godly wisdom.

---

*Father, we dwell safely from sin through the wisdom of the Cross. Help me to receive Your wisdom with meekness and humility.*

*I pray these things in Jesus' name. Amen.*

*Proverbs 9:11, 10:11, 14:27

# TO DIRECT OUR STEPS

There is a way that seems right to a man,
but its end is the way of death.
Proverbs 14:12

## DO YOU WALK BY FAITH OR BY SIGHT?

Why do we need wisdom? To show us which way to go.

There are a few implications that we can draw from the text above. First, man is a finite creature with limited knowledge. If he makes his decisions based on what he sees then he is only operating with a limited assessment of things. Secondly, God is an infinite being Who possesses perfect and complete knowledge. He can see those things which finite man cannot see.

Fortunately for us, He makes His wisdom readily available to those who seek Him. Folly deludes us into thinking that we can do whatever seems right in our own eyes, but wisdom teaches us that it is better for the Lord to direct our steps. In His perfect wisdom, He can see to it that our feet do not slide into danger.

Jesus said, "I am the way, the truth, and the life."* We can't trust our own feelings, but we can trust Jesus Christ. He has been down the path that we're on and knows where it leads. Follow Him. In light of this truth, let us be those who do not trust in worldly wisdom, but rather those who put our trust in the Lord.

---

*Father, it is not in a man to direct his own steps. Help me not to be led by the desire of my eyes, but rather rely moment by moment on Your perfect wisdom. I pray these things in Jesus' name. Amen.*

*John 14:6

# TO TRUST IN THE LORD

The backslider in heart will be filled with the fruit of his ways,
and a good man will be filled with the fruit of his ways.
Proverbs 14:14

## ARE YOU DOING THINGS YOUR WAY OR GOD'S WAY?

Wisdom teaches us not to depart from the ways of the Lord. Those who turn a deaf ear to instruction will reap what they sow. They will keep the company of fear, because they would not heed the wisdom of God. For if, after they have escaped the pollutions of the world through the knowledge of the Lord and Savior Jesus Christ, they are again entangled in them and overcome, the latter end is worse for them than the beginning.*

For he who sows to his flesh will of the flesh reap corruption, but he who sows to the Spirit will of the Spirit reap everlasting life. Therefore, let us not grow weary while doing good, for in due season we shall reap if we do not lose heart.*

With this in mind, the righteous will experience the peace of knowing that they have made the Lord their trust. While their journey is met with various troubles, they look forward to a day when every tear will be wiped from their eyes.* Wisdom has taught them that it is better to trust in the Lord than to be filled with the fruit of their own ways.

Dear friend, let us not lean on the wisdom of man, but rather commit all our ways into the hands of Divine sovereignty.

✦————————◆————————✦

*Father, sin seeks to separate us from Your loving instruction. Give me the grace not to lean on my own understanding, but rather to let You be my Shepherd. I pray these things in Jesus' name. Amen.*

*2 Peter 2:20, Galatians 6:8-10, Revelation 21:4

# TO KNOW TRANQUILITY

A tranquil heart gives life to the flesh, but envy makes the bones rot.
Proverbs 14:30

## FRIEND, WOULD YOU LIKE TO EXPERIENCE JOY IN YOUR LIFE?

Then pay close attention to Wisdom. There is a cancer that is far more deadly to the soul than any other pain or sickness. This cancer is the sin of envy. It is a harmful poison that eats away at your joy, and manifests itself in many evils. Envy causes us to focus more on what other people have rather than focusing on the many blessings that God has already given to us. Those who are envious of others commit a great folly, and cause great harm to their souls.

The Scriptures tell us if you have bitter envy and self-seeking in your hearts, do not boast and lie against the truth. This wisdom does not descend from above, but is earthly, sensual, demonic. For where envy and self-seeking exist, confusion and every evil thing are there.*

Therefore, if you would like to experience joy, then listen to wisdom. Be thankful for the many ways in which the Lord has blessed you. Let not your soul envy the exaltation of others, but rather be happy for them. Folly tricks us to resent those who have been blessed, but wisdom teaches us to rejoice with those who rejoice.*

Dear friend, do not be weighed down with bitter envy. Let wisdom teach you to rejoice in the Lord, and be happy for others.

———————◇———————

*Father, envy is a deadly poison that eats away my joy. Give me the wisdom that rejoices with others.*

*I pray these things in Jesus' name. Amen.*

*James 3:14-15, Romans 12:15

# TO LIVE IN HARMONY

Better is a dry morsel with quiet than a house full of feasting with strife.
Proverbs 17:1

## DO YOU VALUE A PEACEFUL HOME?

Why do we need wisdom? To show us how to live in one accord.

There are many things that money can buy, but it cannot buy a happy home. Harmony in the home is worth infinitely more than a lifetime of wealth. How many people have forfeited the blessings of a happy household for the fleeting pleasures of money?

As God's chosen ones, holy and beloved, have compassionate hearts, kindness, humility, meekness, and patience, bearing with one another and, if one has a complaint against another, forgive each other, as the Lord has forgiven you. And above all, put on love, which binds everything together in perfect harmony.*

So if you would like a peaceful house, then listen to the words of Wisdom. Folly lies to us that material goods will make us happy, but wisdom teaches us that it is better to make your family a priority over wealth. The Lord has ordained the family structure for our benefit, and it would be well with us to cultivate a godly home. In light of this eternal truth let, our homes be a reflection of praise and worship in every season of life.

———————◆———————

*Father, it is wise to tend to the spiritual needs of our families. Give me the grace to prioritize the things that will bring me lasting peace.*

*I pray these things in Jesus' name. Amen.*

*Colossians 3:12-14

# TO BE SLOW TO ANGER

A hot-tempered man stirs up strife,
but he who is slow to anger quiets contention.
Proverbs 15:18

## FRIEND, WOULD YOU LIKE TO AVOID MANY EVILS?

Wisdom teaches to keep ourselves from the hot-tempered person. Anger is a vice that causes many calamities. It has led to the destruction of civilizations, and has brought many souls to ruin. We are warned, therefore, against its divisive ways. If we let wisdom rule our emotions then we will preserve ourselves from many troubles. For the end of a thing is better than its beginning; the patient in spirit is better than the proud in spirit. So, do not hasten in your spirit to be angry, for anger rests in the bosom of fools.*

The Apostle James, in dealing with the topic of anger, has this to say: "Let every person be quick to hear, slow to speak, slow to anger, for the anger of man does not produce the righteousness of God."* The person who can rule their passions can prevent the dangers of war.

Dear friend, have you learned how to control your temper? Let us be people whose emotions have been subdued by the lordship of Jesus Christ.

———————◆———————

*Father, the sin of anger has led to the ruin of many souls. Give me the grace I need to have mastery over my passions.*

*I pray these things in Jesus' name. Amen.*

*Ecclesiastes 7:8-9, James 1:19

# TO SURRENDER MY PLAN FOR HIS

The plans of the heart belong to man,
but the answer of the tongue is from the Lord.
Proverbs 16:1

## WHO ESTABLISHES THE WAYS OF MAN?

Wisdom teaches us that even the designs of men are in the hands of the Lord. A man's heart plans his way, but the Lord directs his steps.* Even the king's heart is in the hand of the Lord, like the rivers of water; God turns it wherever He wishes.* By His word, kings are established over nations, and empires are brought to nothing. All things, whether good or evil, serve God's ultimate purposes.

Let wisdom teach us to cast all our care upon Him, for He cares for us.* In doing so, our souls will be preserved from many anxieties. If we submit all our ways to Him then He will show us the path of life, for it is God who works in you both to will and to do for His good pleasure.*

In light of this eternal truth, let us not waste our lives away in fear, but rather remain at rest in the loving providence of God.

---

*Father, our hearts devise many plans, but You have the final word. Give me the grace to trust that all Your ways are best.*

*I pray these things in Jesus' name. Amen.*

*Proverbs 16:9, 21:1, 1 Peter 5:7, Philippians 2:13

# TO EXAMINE OUR HEARTS

All the ways of a man are pure in his own eyes, but the Lord weighs the spirit.
Proverbs 16:2

## WHO IS THE PERFECT DISCERNER OF HEARTS?

Why do we need wisdom? We need wisdom, because the Lord discerns our motives with perfect accuracy and precision.

Here in the text, Solomon wants us to understand the frailties of man. On the surface our motives may appear to be fine, but underneath the surface are all kinds of evils. We are reminded that all actions, which appear to be pure, are tested in the beakers of Divine wisdom. God's Word tells us our hearts are deceitful, and desperately sick and no one can understand it. But the Lord searches the heart and test the mind, to give every man according to his ways, according to the fruit of his deeds.*

In light of God's perfect knowledge, we would do well to examine all our ways before Him. King David, in dealing with the topic of the Lord's omniscience, offers up a wonderful prayer. He prayed the following: "Search me, O God, and know my heart! Try me and know my thoughts! And see if there be any wicked way in me, and lead me in the way everlasting!"* It would be well with all the saints if we prayed like David.

Let us be those who bring all thoughts and deeds before the scrutiny of God's examination.

———————◆———————

*Father, we are constantly being deceived by the deceptions of sin. Give me the grace to bring all of my motives before You in self-examination.*

*I pray these things in Jesus' name. Amen.*

*Jeremiah 17:9-10, Psalm 139:23-24

# TO COMMIT TO GOD'S WAYS

Commit your work to the Lord, and your plans will be established.
Proverbs 16:3

## HAVE YOU SUBMITTED YOURSELF TO THE WAYS OF THE LORD?

If not, then you can anticipate a lot of heartache and frustration. There is no work that can prosper unless the Lord blesses it. wisdom teaches us that we are to commit all our ways to Him. When we put our trust in Him, we can expect true rest for our souls. We are not striving nor experiencing inner turmoil, because wisdom has taught us to submit to God's will.

When we commit our ways to the Lord, and trust also in Him, He shall bring it to pass.* Cast your burden on the Lord, and He shall sustain you; He shall never permit the righteous to be moved.* Yes, cast all your care upon God, for He cares for you.* The soul who commits themselves into His care will be at peace. They have learned that it is folly to kick against the plans of the Lord.

Have you submitted yourself to the wisdom of the Cross? Dearly beloved, consider well these faithful words: "Commit your work to the Lord, and your plans will be established."

---

*Father, it is hard for us to kick against the goads, to resist Your leading.* Preserve me from the stubbornness of my own ways, and help me to commit all things into Your loving hands.*

*I pray these things in Jesus' name. Amen.*

*Psalm 37:5, Psalm 55:22, 1 Peter 5:7

# TO REST IN GOD

The heart of a man plans his way, but the Lord directs his steps.
Proverbs 16:9

## CAN THE PURPOSES OF GOD BE FRUSTRATED?

The question of God's sovereignty often comes to the surface when we face great difficulties. Wisdom teaches us to comprehend His sovereignty when He has not directed us in a way that we expect. But in these difficult times, we can take solace in this wonderful text above. All things come from the hand of the Lord. Our hearts may store up many dreams and desires, but it is the Lord Who makes our ways to prosper.

There are many plans in a man's heart, nevertheless the Lord's counsel—that will stand.* So also, the steps of a good man are ordered by the Lord, and He delights in his way.* Indeed God has spoken it; He will also bring it to pass. He has purposed it; He will also do it.*

Dear soul, if you could grasp God's sovereignty, then you would find much peace for your heart. Unfortunately, there are many who have not seen the hand of sovereignty in their circumstances. They have experienced years of unfulfilled dreams and hopes, and their hearts are filled with the bitter wormwood of disappointment. In light of this truth, we must learn that whatever God wills is safest and best for us. He has established our steps, not for evil, but for our joy. Let us put all fears to rest, and give thanks for the lot that has been placed in our laps.

---

*Father, Your lot falls to us in pleasant places.\* Give me the eyes of faith to trust that Your ways are higher and better than mine.*

*I pray these things in Jesus' name. Amen.*

*Proverbs 19:21, Psalm 37:23, Isaiah 46:11, Psalm 16:6

# TO WALK JUSTLY

He who justifies the wicked and he who condemns the righteous are both alike an abomination to the Lord.

Proverbs 17:15

## WHAT DOES THE LORD REQUIRE OF US?

Wisdom teaches that the Lord requires us to be just. God delights in absolute and perfect justice. It is a great evil when the guilty are pardoned and the innocent are condemned. Thus, it is important for leaders to rule justly in the sight of God and man. Those, who pervert justice, will give an account to the Just Judge of the earth. Yet if God judges rightly, then how can we escape His judgment?

The evidence of our sins has been brought before Him, and we stand convicted of transgressing His holy law. Where is our pardon? All of our works are as filthy rags before Him.* Ah! Look no further than to the wisdom of God. Jesus Christ, the Holy and Just One, has suffered the wrath of God for the unjust. The sinless Lamb has satisfied the just requirements of the Law in our stead, and now we can experience the forgiveness for our sins.

So what does the Lord require? He has told us what is good; and the Lord requires of us to do justice, and to love kindness, and to walk humbly with our God.* Therefore be merciful, just as your Father also is merciful.* In this moment, marvel at the grace and mercy of God in the Gospel. Let us reflect on the perfect wisdom of the Lord in the salvation of sinners.

———◦———

*Father, the wisdom of the Cross brings to nothing the wisdom of man. In Your perfect wisdom, You used the unjust to bring about the salvation of sinners. Give me the grace to be just, to love kindness, and to walk humbly with my God.*

*I pray these things in Jesus' name. Amen.*

*Isaiah 64:6, Micah 6:8, Luke 6:36

# TO KEEP PEACE

The beginning of strife is like letting out water,
so quit before the quarrel breaks out.
Proverbs 17:14

## DEAR FRIEND, HOW CAN YOU STOP A QUARREL?

Why do we need wisdom? To teach us that the most effective way of stopping a quarrel is to prevent it from happening. Those who are wise weigh out all the potential consequences of their actions. They understand how quickly a little dispute can turn into a big conflict.

Note well the illustration in the proverb above. Once a faucet is turned on, the water has already flowed out, and there is no point of return. In such a way, those who encourage quarrels cause great harm to themselves and to others.

The Apostle Paul teaches, "If it is possible, as much as depends on you, live peaceably with all men. If your enemy is hungry, feed him; if he is thirsty, give him a drink; do not be overcome by evil, but overcome evil with good."* Aspire to lead a quiet life, to mind your own business, and to work with your own hands, that you may walk properly toward those who are outside, and that you may lack nothing.*

Therefore, let wisdom teach us the value of keeping the unity of peace. Those who strive for peace among the brethren preserve their souls from sin. Do you strive for peace with others? Let us do everything we can to prevent a quarrel before it starts.

---

*Father, it is so important to maintain the unity of peace. Give me the grace to abstain from a divisive spirit.*

*I pray these things in Jesus' name. Amen.*

*Romans 12:18, 20-21, 1 Thessalonians 4:11-12

# TO CHOOSE TRUE FRIENDS

Faithful are the wounds of a friend; profuse are the kisses of an enemy.
Proverbs 27:6

## DO YOU SURROUND YOURSELF WITH "YES-MEN?"

Here wisdom reveals to us the marks of a true friend. A true friend will not always tell you what you want to hear, but they will tell you what you need to hear. King Solomon likens the words of a friend to "faithful wounds." It is not always pleasant to hear a rebuke, but it is vital in making one wise unto salvation.* A faithful friend may cause a little pain temporarily, but their words will yield the peaceable fruit of righteousness to those who are trained by them.* Jesus said, "As many as I love, I rebuke and chasten."*

The same cannot be said for deceptive words. The words of an enemy are sweet to the taste, but they go down to the soul with much bitterness. Solomon likens those, who will not be honest with you, to an enemy. Though their kisses are pleasant to the flesh, they offer no eternal benefits for the soul.

Do you pick your friends wisely? If not then consider the words of Solomon, and surround yourself with faithful friends.

———◆———◇———◆———

*Father, it is much easier to surround ourselves with people who flatter us, but we need faithful friends in our lives. Give me the grace to surround myself with people who care deeply about my soul.*

*I pray these things in Jesus' name. Amen.*

* 2 Timothy 3:15, Hebrews 12:11, Revelation 3:19

# TO CHOOSE A GODLY SPOUSE

An excellent wife who can find? She is far more precious than jewels.
The heart of her husband trusts in her, and he will have no lack of gain.
Proverbs 31:10-11

## WHO CAN FIND AN EXCELLENT WIFE?

Much of the Proverbs is devoted to warning us against the dangers of the immoral woman, but King Lemuel wants us to recognize the marks of a virtuous woman. Those who are wise can discern the difference between the two.

Notice that the King likens the excellent wife to a precious jewel. Her value exceeds the value of gold or silver. She is a crown for her husband's head, and a banner of faithfulness over his ways. He does not have to fear that her heart is not with him, because her godly character brings him much peace. Those men who possess her are blessed in all their ways. For husbands, likewise, dwell with them with understanding, giving honor to the wife, as to the weaker vessel, and as being heirs together of the grace of life, that your prayers may not be hindered.* For the eyes of the Lord are on the righteous, and His ears are open to their prayers.*

In a day and age where the culture looks for outward beauty, let us seek a spouse who possesses an inward beauty and righteousness that is from above.

---

*Father, who can find a virtuous wife? Her faithfulness is like a precious crown on her husband's head. Grant us the grace not to see as man sees, but rather look beyond the beautiful exterior to a person's heart.*

*I pray these things in Jesus' name. Amen.*

*1 Peter 3:7, 12

# TO DISCERN BEAUTY

Charm is deceitful, and beauty is vain,
but a woman who fears the Lord is to be praised.
Proverbs 31:30

## DO YOU LOOK BEYOND THE OUTWARD EXTERIOR?

Wisdom teaches us that outward beauty is only skin deep. The outward beauty of a person will only last for a short amount of time. It is wise to look beyond the surface and consider the matters of the heart.

Do you desire a person who fears the Lord?

Here we are told that a woman who fears the Lord is to be praised. There are many, who married out of lust, but live, in constant regret. They failed to look beyond the surface and are now reaping the consequences of their folly. If we are going to walk wisely in this evil age, then we will need to focus on matters of eternity.

Do you have wedding plans on the horizon? Make sure your potential spouse fears the Lord. Look for the incorruptible beauty of a gentle and quiet spirit, which is very precious in the sight of God.* Remember that beauty does not last, but a godly spouse will build with you an enduring legacy.

———————◉———————

*Father, we live in a culture of lust. Give me the wisdom to look beyond the surface, and consider the matters of a person's heart.*

*I pray these things in Jesus' name. Amen.*

*1 Peter 3:4

# NOTES

January 1
1. Batstone, Bill, "A Shelter, Lord To Every Generation", Psalms Alive!, (Maranatha Music, 1971)

January 18
2. A.W. Tozer, *Knowledge of the Holy*, p. 69, (HarperOne, 2009).

The Month of March
3. J.I. Packer, *Knowing God*, p. 69, (InterVarsity Press, 1993).

March 13
4. The 1689 *Baptist Confession of Faith*, Chapter 1, paragraph 1.

May 4
5. A.W. Pink, *An Exposition of The Sermon on the Mount*, page 23.

June 4
6. C.S. Lewis, *The Weight of Glory*, p. 26 (HarperOne, 2001).

September 10
7. "Amazing Grace", by John Newton, 1779

The Month of October
8. Chuck Smith, The Word for Today Bible, p. 30 (The Word For Today, 2012)

October 27
9. ibid, p. 1592

November 3
10. Webster's American Dictionary of the English Language, 1828.

Made in the USA
Monee, IL
29 February 2020